Soul Journey

from Lincoln to Lindbergh

Revealing the Mysteries of Karma and Rebirth

Richard Salva

"And if ye will receive it, this is Elias, which was for to come. He that hath ears to hear, let him hear."
—Matt. 11:14-15

Crystar Press
San Jose, California

Cover art: Barbara Bingham

Photo credits:
Cover photo courtesy of Library of Congress
LC-MSS-44297-33-001
Pages 1, 30, and 281:
Abraham Lincoln: ©CORBIS
Charles Lindbergh: ©Bettmann/CORBIS
Pages 18 and 281:
Paramhansa Yogananda and Lahiri Mahasaya:
courtesy of Ananda Sangha

Printed in the United States of America
ISBN: 0-9772381-0-5

Crystar Press
P.O. Box 640965
San Jose, CA 95164-0984

Toll free telephone: 866-763-4922
Fax: 408-456-0444
info@crystarpress.com
www.crystarpress.com

Library of Congress Control Number: 2005907188

First Edition

10 9 8 7 6 5 4 3 2 1

What Others Are Saying about *Soul Journey*

"Truth, it is frequently said, is stranger than fiction. Few books have made the case more persuasively than this one. About fifty years ago a great master of yoga declared that Abraham Lincoln had been an advanced yogi in a previous life, and that he reincarnated as Charles Lindbergh. Richard Salva saw in this statement a mystery as fascinating as any our best novelists could dream up. In this book he delves into all that's known about these two celebrated men, and unearths a remarkable array of similarities between them. The psychological portraits he draws will be controversial, but they're creatively argued, and well defended. Mr. Salva has produced a most unusual and thought-provoking book, and has succeeded admirably in his effort to present the material in such a way that the reader can draw his own conclusions."

—SWAMI KRIYANANDA,
author of *The Path: Autobiography of a Western Yogi* and *Hope For a Better World*

"A fascinating account that weaves known history and higher consciousness to show us how the law of karma unfolds the story of life on mystic layers of transformation. The book has much wisdom and insight, encouraging us to take a deeper look at not only the world but our own individual lives and destinies."

—DR. DAVID FRAWLEY,
author of *Yoga and Ayurveda* and *Yoga for Your Type*

"This book is one of the best explorations of reincarnation that I've ever read. Usually this subject is presented ponderously, in a vague way or as an attempt to "prove" that it is real. Mr. Salva's book brings reincarnation alive! It shows, in a delightful way, how the central consciousness and qualities remain much the same from life to life. Soul Journey looks at how a single soul expressed itself in the lives of two great Americans. It also contains a wealth of information on two of the most fascinating characters in American history. I highly recommend it."

—JYOTISH NOVAK,
author of *How to Meditate,* the *Meditation Therapy Video Series,* and the *30 Day Essentials Series*

"Richard Salva presents a remarkable study of two of America's most heroic figures—men of different centuries and seemingly distant dreams—whose histories, until now, have never been so profoundly and convincingly joined. His research into the characteristics and myriad similarities revealed in Lincoln's and Lindbergh's lives is detailed with the depth and detective work of a Sherlock Holmes whodunit. Enroute to this book's overarching conclusion, Salva also imparts a provocative insight into the teachings and methods of Eastern yoga, exploring its ancient ideals as reflected in the feelings, thoughts, and actions of these two extraordinary men. But the reader is finally left to ponder the evidence of his findings. To those who question the soul's journey of countless incarnations and karmic tests, this book may prove to erase all shadows of doubt."

—JAMES CONTI,
manager of East-West Bookshop, Mountain View, California

To Swamiji, with gratitude.

Preface

What happens after we die? Oblivion? Eternity in heaven or hell? An infinite reward or punishment for the finite actions of one brief lifetime?

Or is life a school that we attend over and over, learning and growing, receiving an equal and just reward or punishment for our good and bad actions, moving from one grade to the next as we pass through many lifetimes, until we graduate and return to our blissful home in Spirit?

In hope of bringing greater clarity to these questions, and to increase the reader's understanding of how reincarnation and karma works in his or her daily life, I offer this study of one soul's several incarnations. In it, I highlight the connections I perceive between Abraham Lincoln, Charles A. Lindbergh, and the teachings and practices of Himalayan yogis. (The basis for this study is explained in Chapter One.)

Part One considers the karmic links between Lincoln and Lindbergh via a chronological trip through the life of Lindbergh, with appropriate Lincoln anecdotes interspersed. Part Two explores the yogic connections in the lives of Lincoln and Lindbergh via a quick tour through the teachings of yoga, with appropriate Lincoln and Lindbergh anecdotes interspersed.

A multilifetime study of famous subjects has an advantage in that a wealth of information widens the number and type of connections. By reading the past-life ties between famous people, we can learn more about the connections in our own lives, for the principles of reincarnation, if they exist, must function just the same for famous people as they do for us "average Joe"s.

Readers may experience another benefit from this book, for it indirectly addresses the question: How is greatness achieved? One hears stories of historic figures like Abraham Lincoln and wonders how it is possible to become like them. Part Two of From Lincoln to Lindbergh presents a point-by-point analysis of Lincoln's greatness, and explains how that greatness was gained by a conscious, focused application of spiritual principles in a past life. These principles, listed in this book, are universal and can be adopted by everyone. In fact, even those with no interest in reincarnation can find inspiration and instruction in Part Two.

All of the Lincoln and Lindbergh quotes and anecdotes are derived from their histories and their actual words. Every detail related to Himalayan yogis is based on their lifestyle and the ancient spiritual science of yoga.

For the yogic teachings, I borrowed heavily from the writings of Paramhansa Yogananda and Swami Kriyananda as published by Crystal Clarity Publishers in Nevada City, California.

For excerpts from Lindbergh's writings, I kept the wording exact; for Lincoln and Lincoln sources I often edited the original text for clarity or brevity, but without changing the meaning. For both characters, I sometimes combined things said at different times to emphasize a recurring trend of thought. At times, I portrayed individuals speaking or thinking words they had written.

The reader may notice that the Lincoln anecdotes are supported by more direct quotes than the Lindbergh ones. This is only natural, since everything Lindbergh wrote is protected by copyright. If the reader is interested in learning more about either Lincoln or Lindbergh, he or she may consult the source list in the back of the book.

Acknowledgements

Many people helped with the development of this book. To everyone, I express my deep and sincere thanks.

I would like to mention my appreciation toward:
The Lincoln Library in Springfield, Illinois, for copies of newspaper articles on Lindbergh's visit in August 1927.

The on-site historians and staffs at: Ford's Theater and the Smithsonian Institution in Washington, D.C.; the Cooper Union Foundation Building in Manhattan, New York; the Lincoln Boyhood National Memorial in Indiana; Lincoln's New Salem in Illinois; and the Charles A. Lindbergh House in Little Falls, Minnesota.

John Downey, for computer help and suggesting the tie-in between the two Annes.

Rammurti and Sita Reed, who recommended the anecdote format.

My wife, Laura, for all that words cannot express.

For timely suggestions or other assistance: Swami Kriyananda, Hotranatha Ajaya, Asha and David Praver, Frank Monahan, Tom Cerussi, Drupada MacDonald, Rambhakta Beinhorn, Sheila Rush, Terry Strom, Sue Mann, Frank DeMarco, Mary Kretzmann, Bob Silverstein, Karen Gamow, Stephanie Sandin, Robert and Sharon Clark, Carol Whiteley, Carol Susan Roth, Latika Parojinog, and Jon Parsons.

I would especially like to thank Swami Kriyananda and Crystal Clarity Publishers for allowing the liberal use of quotes and paraphrases. Without their generous help, this book would not have been possible.

Contents

PART II: FROM BRAHMA TO ABRAHAM (LINCOLN)

A Multilifetime Chronology
of events mentioned
in this book

Abraham Lincoln

1809	February 12	Born in Kentucky.
1816-29		Moves with family to Indiana. Mother dies. Father remarries (Sarah Bush Johnston). First Mississippi flatboat trip to New Orleans.
1830		Moves with family to Illinois.
1831		Leaves home. Second Mississippi boat trip to New Orleans. Moves to frontier town of New Salem, Illinois.
1831-36		Black Hawk War. Becomes New Salem shopkeeper and postmaster.

Proposes marriage to Anne Rutledge, who dies soon after. Studies law. First political forays. Attends state legislature in Vandalia. Passes bar exam. Meets and woos Mary Owens.

1837-60

Moves to Springfield. Fails to wed Mary Owens. Practices law. Meets, courts, and weds Mary Todd. Buys a house, raises his children. Takes on William Herndon as law partner. Short stint as U.S. congressman in Washington, where he attacks President Polk for Mexican War. Rides circuit court. Pursues political career. Debates with Stephen A. Douglas. Visits Manhattan, gives Cooper Union talk. Elected president of the United States.

1861-65

Moves to Washington. Presides over a divided nation during the Civil War. Son Willie dies.

Signs Emancipation Proclamation. Gives speech at dedication of Gettysburg Cemetery.

| 1865 | April 14 | Shot while attending a play at Ford's Theater. |
| | April 15 | Dies at Petersen House, Washington, D.C. |

Charles Lindbergh

1902	February 4	Born in Detroit, Michigan.
1906		Father becomes congressman.
1918-19		Tries to run family farm.
1922		Attends flying school in Nebraska.
1924-25		Becomes air cadet in army flying school.
1926		Flies airmail.
1927	May 20-21	Flies Atlantic, landing in Paris, France.

May 28-June 3	Visits Belgium and Britain. Returns to France.
June 4-11	Sails for America.
June 11-12	Reception in Washington, D.C.
June 13	Manhattan parade.
July 20-October 23	Makes cross-country U.S. tour by air.
August 15	Visits Springfield, Illinois.
December 14-28	Visits Mexico City.
1928-29	Courts and weds Anne Morrow.
1932	Son is kidnapped and killed.
1933	Visits Russia.
1935	Gives testimony at the trial of Bruno Richard Hauptmann. Moves with family to England.
1936	Tours Luftwaffe airfields and factories.

1937		Visits India.
1938		Buys home on French island of Illiec.
1939		Returns to America.
1939-41		Gives speeches against American involvement in European war.
1941	December 7	Pearl Harbor bombed.
1942-43		Works for Henry Ford.
1944		Flies 50 missions against Japanese in South Pacific.
1945		Visits postwar Germany.
1946-54		Works for the U.S. military at the Pentagon and other locations.
1953		*The Spirit of St. Louis* is published.
1954		Made brigadier general. Receives Pulitzer Prize.
1962		Attends reception with Kennedys at White House.

| 1972 | | Visits Tasaday Indians in Philippines. Diagnosed with cancer. |
| 1974 | August 26 | Dies in Hawaii. |

CHAPTER ONE

Soul Journey

"Abraham Lincoln [in a past life] had been a yogi in the Himalayas who died with a desire to help bring about racial equality. His birth as Lincoln was for the purpose of fulfilling that desire. He has come back again in [the twentieth] century as Charles Lindbergh."

This statement was made by Paramhansa Yogananda, a master of yoga and one of the pioneer teachers of meditation in the West (best known for his spiritual classic, *Autobiography of a Yogi*).

I first read these words in 1977 when they were published in Swami Kriyananda's autobiography, *The Path*. Twenty years later they returned to my mind, and I wondered, considering the wealth of historical detail recorded from the lives of Lincoln and Lindbergh, what hard evidence existed to support Yogananda's words. I felt that my own, extensive study and practice of the teachings of Himalayan yogis would aid my search.

The results of that search are in your hands. In this book I draw hundreds of connections that span every aspect of human individuality, connections that link Abraham Lincoln with Charles Lindbergh and the lifestyle of Himalayan yogis. Not only that, but these connections demonstrate how past lives affect you and me in countless ways on a daily basis, and how we evolve in wisdom as our souls make the journey from lifetime to lifetime.

Was Yogananda right? Was Abraham Lincoln a Himalayan yogi in a past life? And did he return to his beloved America as Charles Lindbergh?

I don't ask you to accept what Yogananda said at face value. Read this book, weigh the facts, and make your own judgment.

Paramhansa Yogananda

CHAPTER TWO

The Past-Life Clues Revealed

[Note: this chapter contains keys that will help you understand the rest of the book. Please read it before starting Chapter Three.]

How can you tell who you were in a past life? There are hidden clues in everyone's life that indicate who or what they were in the past, for those who know how to read them.

In this chapter, I will summarize these past-life clues so that you can recognize them in the stories of Lincoln and Lindbergh, and in your own life.

Physical Traits

When we leave our physical bodies at death, who we are remains much the same. Our spirits, temporarily freed from physical limitations, expand somewhat in the astral world, yet our thoughts, habits, and emotions endure. And when we return to earth we carry them with us into our new bodies.

One thing we bring with us is our self-image. And since our consciousness does not change that much from one life to the next, when we reincarnate, our faces often resemble the faces that were ours in the past, or we share other physical traits—height, weight, shoe size, etc.—with those incarnations.

When we enter the body, it's like putting on a new coat. The garments we wear conform themselves to our contours; similarly, each new body will fit the contours of our self-image.

In the next chapter of this book, you will see how Lincoln shared similar bodily traits with Lindbergh.

"Deja Vu All Over Again"

You know the saying, "Those who ignore history are doomed to repeat it"? The same principle applies in reincarnation. Like Bill Murray in the movie *Groundhog Day*, we are destined to repeat similar experiences over and over until we learn whatever lessons are contained in them. At that point, we are freed from those particular tests.

In the stories in this book are many instances of situations repeating themselves.

The Long and Winding Road

Reincarnation is the long path our souls walk—a path that leads from a baser awareness to a higher one. On a spiritual growth chart, we start off at Point A near the bottom left-hand corner and work our way up to Point Z at the top right-hand corner. It takes a long time to get from A to Z—thousands of incarnations. Since the purpose of life is soul growth, you might expect the average spiritual growth chart to look like this:

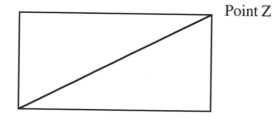

Point Z

Point A

But, actually, the growth line is almost always less direct. It usually resembles more of a reasonably successful business's financial chart, and looks something like this:

Point Z

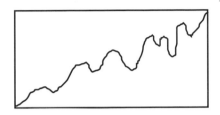

Point A

Why? Free will. We can take as much time as we want to go from A to Z. It's not recommended. It's more painful that way. But we have been given the freedom to make mistakes.

On this second chart are peaks and valleys. The peaks represent lifetimes in which our strengths are showcased, our faults are minimized, and we do something wonderful for our fellow man. It usually takes lifetimes of spiritual effort to manifest such a glowing life. Abraham Lincoln's life was a peak on his soul's reincarnational growth chart. His previous life as a Himalayan yogi (according to Yogananda), filled no doubt with much prayer and fasting, prepared him for his role as the Great Emancipator.

In Part Two, we will explore the signs of yogic development in the lives of our two American heroes. Surprisingly, Lindbergh matches Lincoln pretty closely. However, in Part One, you may notice that Lindbergh sometimes fell short of Lincoln's lofty standards—his secret second family in Europe, for instance. In fact, I've often thought while working on this book that Lindbergh was Lincoln *on vacation*.

The small section of this soul's growth chart that represents the three lifetimes of this study probably looks like this:

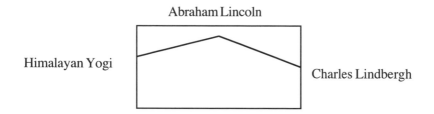

However, given this soul's strong overall moral and spiritual development, I would wager that, in his next life, the growth line will swing upward once again.

Soul Families

As we journey from lifetime to lifetime, we gravitate toward others who are also stuck on the ferris wheel of rebirth. We bond deeply with these people, who become part of our extended soul family.

Members of soul families often incarnate at about the same time and place in order to work out karma, learn lessons together, and generally raise a ruckus. Not everyone joins in on these group migrations every time, but many do.

Have you ever met someone for the first time and felt like you have known them forever? That is likely to be a member of your soul family. You have known her or him for a long time. And meeting them again in this life is like unexpectedly spotting a good friend sitting at a desk two rows ahead of you in high school physics. Cherish and develop that relationship, so that you will grow together.

Everyone in your birth family is a member of your extended soul family. In the lives of Lincoln and Lindbergh, we see evidence of soul family members coming together once more.

The Power of Desire

Every desire that comes into your heart must eventually be fulfilled or transcended. That's the way it works, and that's why we keep coming back. The desire to marry a particular person. To become a millionaire. To drive that shiny new convertible. Even the desire for a dish of gelato ice cream. Any of these can make you reincarnate. Desire is a powerful thing.

But the desires that have the greatest effect on our future lives are those that arise just before we pass on. A mental obsession that comes while one is on one's deathbed can determine the precise conditions of that person's next life. So, be careful what you wish for. Somehow, sometime, you will inevitably get what you want. Even if you don't really want it anymore, or consider the timing inconvenient.

In the pages of this book, we'll see many past-life desires fulfilled.

The New New Thing

Have you ever eaten so many blueberries that you felt sick of them and thought that you never wanted to eat another one? Whenever in any lifetime you experience something that fully, you lose the taste for it.

Say, for instance, you long to become a famous musician and are reborn as a Beatle. Let's say that that desire is fulfilled in spades, so in your next life you probably won't show that much interest in music—even if you have a natural talent for it. Instead, your passion might be sculpture, or gymnastics, or medicine.

The soul's nature is ever-new joy, and this spring-like attraction to something new and different is an expression of that quality.

Reincarnation is not about just doing the same things over and over; it is a blending of the old and the new, the already-tried and the exotic. It is starting from the foundation of the familiar, and reaching out to new horizons and possibilities.

Variety is the spice of life, and we observe in Charles Lindbergh a movement away from the life in politics that Lincoln had mastered, toward a vocation that jibed well with one of Lincoln's hobbies. We will also see that he brought forward other Lincoln interests.

"There You Go Again"

As I mentioned earlier, when we enter a new lifetime we carry our habits of thought and behavior with us.

Let's face it, we all like to do things a certain way. These habits of behavior are our comfort zone, our life patterns, and other people tend to define us by them.

In this book, you will see some dramatic instances of Lindbergh doing and saying things that were strikingly similar to what Lincoln did or said in similar situations. You will also observe occasions when people described Lincoln and Lindbergh, or they described themselves, in almost the same words. Lindbergh's tendency to mirror Lincoln's habits extended even to his sense of humor and the kind of wife he chose.

More Than a Coincidence

One thing I found especially fascinating while working on this book was the number of seemingly coincidental ties with Lincoln in Charles Lindbergh's life. Are there similar connections in our own lives? And if so, why is this the case?

When we reincarnate, we carry from past lives subconscious images of familiar experiences. Our souls have great spiritual power, though that power is often hidden. On a subtle level, we interact with the material world, and in a new lifetime, we often magnetize surroundings and experiences related to our past lives, almost as if we were "advertising" them.

In his book, *The Holographic Universe,* Michael Talbot relates scientific and medical evidence that the universe conforms itself to our conscious or subconscious expectations.

I found many of these "past-life advertisements" in Lindbergh's life, and have included some of them in these pages.

The Big K

There is a lot of talk about karma these days. The other evening, within an hour's time, I heard people on two different "reality" shows using the term in general conversation.

But what does karma really mean?

Most folks, I suspect, equate the word with punishment. But karma means simply "action." The karmic law is that whatever you do, good or bad, comes back to you in equal measure. "What goes around, comes around."

This book offers numerous examples of the karmic

law at work—where something Lincoln did came back to bless or bite Lindbergh.

What's the Big Idea?

One of the main purposes of reincarnation is to clarify our understanding. To reach a pinnacle of comprehension regarding any essential truth takes more than one lifetime. Fortunately, once we really learn something, that knowledge stays with us forever.

In Chapter Thirty-Five, I show how Lincoln's obsession with death was reborn in the mind of Lindbergh, and clarified.

The Righting of Wrongs

Christ said, "He that lives by the sword will die by the sword," but we don't often see such perfect justice in the world. Good people are abused, and criminals die peacefully in their beds.

Reincarnation gives the karmic law time and opportunity to function, and in these pages we see certain injustices of Lincoln's life made right in Lindbergh's.

Places We Remember

Home, we say, is where the heart is. Some places in our lives carry a deep meaning for us, and if we are deeply attached to those places, reincarnation gives us the opportunity to revisit them.

Have you ever traveled to a city or country you've never visited before and felt immediately at home? In Chapter Ten, we find that Lindbergh had a similar feeling while visiting Lincoln's home town. In addition, Lindbergh's early reactions to Washington D.C. mirrored Lincoln's feelings at the end of his life.

Hail to the Chief

Some lifetimes make a greater impact on us than others. A life where we work a 9 to 5 job, have three kids, and live to a peaceful old age doesn't leave the same impression on our psyche as one in which we play some great role on the stage of life.

Have you ever seen a young child lording it over the other toddlers, like Lucy in the Peanuts cartoons telling Charlie Brown and the gang what to do and demanding that they obey her decrees? That child probably held an authoritarian position in a past life; and in Charles Lindbergh we see presidential attitudes, ideas, and ways of looking at the world, surrounded by the trappings of power.

A Question of Ethics

Despite the fluctuations of the average spiritual growth chart, we can expect some moral continuity between lives. A Mahatma Gandhi will not be reborn as a mass murderer, and death will not transform an anarchist into an angel.

In Part Two, we will see how Lindbergh almost perfectly matched Lincoln, virtue for virtue.

A Note About the Format . . .

This book is filled with paired stories from the lives of Lincoln and Lindbergh that illustrate the principles I've listed above. I have placed dividers in the text that will tell

you when these paired stories begin and end.
The dividers look like this:

* * * * *

In Part One, for instance, most of the pairings go thus:

* * * * *

[a Lindbergh story]

[a comparable Lincoln story]

* * * * *

Occasionally, I have added a second relevant Lincoln
story, or my own commentary before closing those
connections with a divider. Also, some of the Lindbergh
stories had such obvious Lincoln connections that I left them
without comparisons. At times, too, I enclosed one of my
commentaries with dividers when I thought it merited
separate attention.

In Part Two, the dividers are used less frequently in
the first chapters, which are filled with narrative text, but
then the format goes something like this:

* * * * *

[an experience or teaching known to Himalayan yogis]

[a comparable Lincoln story]

[a comparable Lindbergh story]

* * * * *

You'll get the idea as you go along.

PART ONE

From Lincoln to Lindbergh

"Be it my proudest plume, not that I was the last to desert [America], but that I never deserted her."
— Abraham Lincoln

"Lindbergh would have been at home in [a] pre-Civil War environment; . . ."
— Brendan Gill

CHAPTER THREE

The Hunt Begins: Two Bodies, One Spirit

Let us begin our comparisons of Lincoln and Lindbergh with their physical forms. We will start on the outside and work our way gradually within, until we plumb the depths of the person.

I suspect that many people who'd like to know who they were in past lives have opened up art books and studied the portraits of men and women who lived in centuries past, searching for someone they resemble. Occasionally, this technique brings results, but not often.

For one thing, of the many millions who have inhabited the planet in past centuries, relatively few have had their portraits done. And of the portraits that were done, many were lost in the washing machine of time.

If, however, you were one of the few who found a portrait of your past incarnation, would you recognize yourself? In the transition between lives, our appearance may change. We may become taller or smaller, thinner or heavier; sometimes, we even change gender, as the soul's essence is neither female nor male.

Fortunately, in our study, we are dealing with men who shared many physical similarities, and they were famous enough to have left us many portraits.

If we study the photos of Lincoln and Lindbergh, several things stand out. For one, the two men look to have been roughly the same height. Abraham Lincoln stood at a little under six foot four, while Lindbergh was just an inch shorter: almost six foot three. Lincoln had been very tall when compared with the average man of his day. Lindbergh didn't have quite the same advantage, but he was still taller than most.

If we look at the group photos, we observe that both subjects usually stood head and shoulders above the others. We can identify Lincoln or Lindbergh as "the tall one."

Looking more closely, we notice that there is something in the way Lindbergh stood that is reminiscent of Lincoln. Lindbergh hunched his upper back slightly; Lincoln had the same physical habit.

As we continue with our study, we see that both men were about the same weight. They were both tall and slender. In fact, Lindbergh was called "Slim" by his aviation buddies.

Like Lincoln, Lindbergh kept his weight down into middle age. Unlike Lincoln, however, he failed to maintain a svelte physique until the end.

Of course, Lindbergh lived longer. Lincoln died at fifty-six; Lindbergh lived to be seventy-two. So, Lindbergh had more time to manifest bodily changes. Besides, the stress of being president during the Civil War was enough to keep anyone's weight down. Lindbergh's life wasn't nearly as stressful, notwithstanding his workaholism and near-constant travel.

On the other hand, souls often change habits from lifetime to lifetime. That's part of what reincarnation is about: trying out new things, evolution and growth.

Returning to the pictures, it is clear that the faces of the two men didn't really look all that much alike, although in old age they seemed to share a similar, bemused expression.

A quick comparison of the shape of the head tells us that both men had wide, medium-high, sloping foreheads.

Then, too, there was a similarity about the way they *held* their heads, cocking them at a certain angle as they stared at the camera.

The eyes are interesting. Both men had a deep, calm, penetrating gaze. And looking deeply into the eyes themselves, one observes that they looked the same.

Yogananda agreed with the old saying that "the eyes are the windows to the soul." In other words, when we look into a person's eyes, we touch the mind, the spirit, the inner being. There is a look in the eyes of each person that is unique and cannot be duplicated. It is as individual as a thumbprint. Therefore, it makes sense that when souls reincarnate they keep the same expression in the eyes, even if the face, body, or sex changes. And here, if you look at the photographs, is proof.

Again, from the photographs, it appears that, like Lindbergh, Lincoln's eyes were a light shade. Looking it up, we discover that Lincoln and Lindbergh both had eyes that were described as light blue or blue-gray. Not only had Lindbergh kept the look in the eyes, but the color as well.

And there is more. Both men's eyes were deeply set—Lincoln's more so, but Lindbergh's eyes nonetheless resembled Lincoln's in the way they were cast into shadow by the depth of their placement.

* * * * *

While reading a biography of Abraham Lincoln, we learn of his unique smile. Dr. James Miner referred to it as a quick grin that lit up Lincoln's face. He often looked gray and somber, but when he smiled, it brought his features to life like the evening sunlight reflecting on a cloud bank.

Turning again to Lincoln's photographs, we find only

the merest traces of the smile that Dr. Miner described. Because of the limitations of photographic equipment in the mid-eighteen hundreds, fleeting facial expressions couldn't be captured.

Wouldn't it be wonderful to see the joy twinkling in Lincoln's eyes while that great grin swept across his face? The smile that had vanished in the tides of history.

. . . or had it?

"Aw, c'mon Lindy!"

The New York paparazzi had Lindbergh focused squarely in their cameras. They were coaxing him to smile, but the flier wasn't one to perform like a trained seal.

And then a reporter repeated an amusing story he had heard the previous day. And when he got to the punch line, Lindbergh's marvelously sweet and spontaneous smile broke over his face like the sun clearing the horizon.

Flashbulbs popped. And the trademark grin of Charles A. Lindbergh was displayed on many front pages, making it familiar to millions. His childlike joy was so evident that the people couldn't help but love him.

* * * * *

Continuing with the physical comparisons, we find similarities between the two men's hair (both black at birth, although Lindbergh's became lighter as he grew older—also, both had problems with unruly hair and slicked it back with water or gel); mouths (both pursed the lower lip out, as if in deep thought); chins (both had a cleft, though Lindbergh's was more pronounced); ears (substantially large by the end of their lives); legs (for both, quite long in proportion to the rest of their bodies); arms (same as legs); hands (large and powerful); and feet (very large: Lincoln's were size fourteen; Lindbergh, twelve-and-a half—both looked clownish with big feet at the end of their long, thin legs). Even their stamina was similar: though slender, both men were hardy.

* * * * *

These physical correlations point to a continuity of consciousness. The way one holds ones lips, for instance, can be traced to an attitude of mind. Yet we may ask why, if this is a case of one soul manifesting in two bodies, the faces didn't look more alike. Why did he keep all those other physical traits, but not the facial ones? Why did he appear so unlovely in one life and so attractive in the next?

As we ponder these questions, let us consider these images. A tall young Hindu with soft skin and a pleasant face hikes into the Himalayas and settles in a cave. Over the years, the freezing winds and intense sunlight gradually transform the Hindu's features until they are as craggy as the Himalayan landscape that shapes them. Time wears on. In his later years, the Hindu's forehead becomes lined with furrows, his cheeks chapped and leathery, his hair long and unruly, his beard stiff from the harsh elements.

Then, the image morphs slightly. Everything stays the same except for the garb and the length of the hair, and . . .

Abraham Lincoln really did resemble a Himalayan yogi.

Next, we see Lincoln repeatedly entering the doors of photographic studios. Later, Lincoln dies, but his photos live on. After his passing, his face becomes familiar to millions throughout the world. The mere sight of him suggests to people higher values like truth, compassion, unity, and brotherhood. This process takes place while Lincoln's spirit is resting in the astral world.

Yogananda taught that the instrument is blessed by that which flows through it. Abraham Lincoln offered up his image as a channel for blessings to flow into the world, and —if the karmic law is true—that act, which took place almost entirely after his lifetime, must have had a beneficial effect. Whatever else might happen, in Lincoln's next incarnation his face would be transformed into a more attractive one. In a very real sense, the handsomeness of Lindbergh's features reflected the beautiful qualities that Lincoln had represented.

* * * * *

A few more thoughts on the subject. Lincoln's looks were highly singular. There would have been a commotion if Lindbergh had looked exactly like him. And Lindbergh was born with a life path very different from Lincoln's. When a soul experiences something fully, it's time to move on. There was no reason for Lindbergh to look just like Lincoln. Just the opposite.

CHAPTER FOUR

Roots

For the remaining chapters of Part One, we will begin with Lindbergh's birth in 1902 and follow his life chronologically until his death in 1974. Significant moments will be juxtaposed with corresponding events from Lincoln's life.

But before we start in on the life episodes, let us compare some of the mundane details of their lives.

Charles Lindbergh was born fewer than thirty-seven years after Abraham Lincoln's death. In reincarnation studies, such a brief interruption often provides more correlations than if centuries separated them. More than that, both men were born and, for the most part, lived in America. Associations of place, language, and custom may have drawn similar responses from them.

Let us look at their birthdays. Lindbergh was born on February 4; Lincoln's birthday was February 12.

Astrology teaches that people born near the same time share certain characteristics. We may find that this soul, born so close to his old birthday, brought with him a similar mentality.

Lindbergh was born in southern Michigan, Lincoln in Kentucky. Considering all the possible places in America where he might have been born, Lindbergh began his life not far from where Lincoln had started his.

Lindbergh's first and middle names were Charles Augustus. They were almost the same as his father's, but maybe there is more to it.

For one thing, Charles was the name of a king. Then too, Augustus was the name of an emperor who lived at the time of Christ. These points are significant when we consider that Lincoln was a president, the closest thing America has to a ruler.

Looking in a dictionary of names, we see that the name Charles means "manly." That makes sense, for both Lincoln and Lindbergh were manly men.

Augustus means "venerable." Looking up *venerable* in a dictionary, we find that the definitions include "worthy of reverence . . . . Exciting reverential feelings because of sacred or historic associations" and "a title . . . for one who has passed the first stage of canonization."[1]

If we reflect on how the American public honored Abraham Lincoln after his passing, Augustus is a very fitting name for his reincarnation.

* * * * *

Other Lincoln connections may be found among Lindbergh's ancestors . . .

Charles Lindbergh's paternal grandfather, born in Sweden in the early 1800s, worked his way to a high position in government and was a man of non-violence. Later he left Sweden and moved to Minnesota, the very edge of the American frontier. There, he took an axe, felled some trees, and fashioned a log cabin homestead for his family.

At one point he had to move his family to a stockade to

[1]The meaning of the names and this definition are from *The Reader's Digest Great Encyclopedic Dictionary,* copyright 1966.

escape the rampages of Chief Little Crow and his Sioux warriors. The dramatic stories of those early days of 1862, told to Charles as a child, made a strong impression. In Lindbergh's later years he recounted them in his autobiography.

President Lincoln sat alone in his White House office. After careful study of the facts, he formed a list of thirty-nine warriors who had been part of the 1862 Sioux Indian uprising in Minnesota. Those on the list would be punished with death, but it was a much smaller number than the original 300 plus recommended by the military authorities.

Lincoln paused in the writing of his autobiography. He remembered the tales of his ancestors he had heard in his younger days. Some he had forgotten, but one had left an indelible impression. "My paternal grandfather," he wrote, "emigrated to Kentucky where, a year or two later, he was killed by Indians."

* * * * *

Little Charles Lindbergh was struck by the fact that two of his paternal aunts and one of his uncles died while very young.

Abraham Lincoln wiped away a tear. It was hard, losing a child. First, little Eddie died before he was four years old. Now Willie, only eleven and beloved of them all, had passed on. Half his brood had perished young.

* * * * *

In spite of the pains of frontier existence, Charles

loved to hear stories of the rough-and-tumble lifestyle of his ancestors. He looked out the window. It all happened here, on these Minnesota prairies.

Reading of his debate with Stephen Douglas in a New York newspaper, Abe Lincoln was pleased to see that it had merited front-page attention. "The Prairies Are On Fire!" screamed the headlines.

* * * * *

Of interest to Charles was that his maternal great-grandfather and grand-uncle had enlisted in the Union Army during the Civil War—the elder man perishing in the conflict.

* * * * *

Charles enjoyed the companionship of his father, C.A. Lindbergh. Lindbergh senior was suited to his son's nature. They shared an affinity in thought and temperament.

After growing up in a prairie cabin, C.A. Lindbergh studied law. He apprenticed for a time under an established attorney before hanging his own shingle.

After years of learning the trade under more experienced lawyers, Lincoln finally made his first rent payment on an office. Picking out the location was easy; there was a space open across the street from the State Capitol building.

* * * * *

Charles listened solemnly as he heard of his father's rise from the law to state government.

Abraham Lincoln stared at his desk, his companions, and the room he was sitting in. He had made it to the capital city of Vandalia and was an active member of the Illinois State Legislature.

Stretching his arms and interlacing his fingers behind his head, Lincoln put his feet up on the desk. He'd come a long way from studying law in the fields of New Salem.

* * * * *

C.A. Lindbergh was against the physical punishment of children. Charles never knew the pain of spanking. His father disciplined him by other means.

Abraham Lincoln sat and listened to his wife complain about their son Tad, who had hitched a goat to a cart and driven it through the White House while Mary was entertaining guests. Lincoln chuckled, and Mary shook her head. Their boy was worse than a wild Indian.

A few moments later, Lincoln strode the hallways of the Executive Mansion with a smile on his face. He sometimes used sweet reason on his sons, but no physical deterrence. He and Mary had chosen this gentle approach, and they had never seen fit to change it.

* * * * *

C.A. Lindbergh was instrumental in exposing young Charles to Capitol Hill and Pennsylvania Avenue when he went to Washington as a Republican congressman.

The Whig Party under which Lincoln had served as a congressman was dying. It was time to move on, but Lincoln wasn't sure where to go.

In the end he went with the newly formed Republican Party. It was carrying forward ideals that Lincoln approved of. And, as a new party, it needed leadership. The Republican Party was the key to Lincoln's future.

* * * * *

You've probably heard the saying, "We didn't choose our families, but thank God, we can choose our friends." But on a deep soul level, we did choose which family we would be born into, and our parents.

Lindbergh, before he incarnated, chose to have a harmonious father. This would have been a natural decision, given that Lincoln and his father were often at odds. It is quite possible that Lincoln finished his life with a longing for a happier relationship.

On the other hand, looking further into the past, if he had been a yogi who renounced fatherhood (most Himalayan yogis are celibate)—maybe even entertained negative thoughts about it—then that decision might have resulted in Lincoln's difficult relationship with his father.

Lincoln was loving and kindly to his sons, especially the younger ones. Given the law of karma, he was bound to attract a father who would treat him well in his next life. In accordance with Yogananda's words, that was exactly what happened.

* * * * *

Now, we turn our attention to Lindbergh's mother . . .

Evangeline was C.A. Lindbergh's second wife. His first wife died young, at the age of thirty.

Nine-year-old Abe Lincoln stared uncomprehendingly at a wooden cross, freshly planted in the earth. It was hard for him to believe that his mother, Nancy Hanks Lincoln, was truly gone. It didn't seem right. She had been so young, only thirty-four. He didn't see how he could live without her.

And yet, life did go on. After a short while his father married again. And Sarah Bush Johnston became a second mother to Abe.

* * * * *

Evangeline Lindbergh informed her son that President Lincoln's first commanding general, Winfield Scott, was in their family tree. Perhaps for this reason, she enjoyed singing and playing this Civil War song on the piano for Charles:

> . . . and there were Union men
> Who wept with joyful tears
> When they saw the honor'd flag
> They had not seen for years;
> Hardly could they be restrained
> From breaking forth in cheers,
> While we were marching through Georgia![2]

* * * * *

[2]From "Marching Through Georgia" by Henry Clay Work.

Charles was close to his mother. During his early years, she was often by his side. They shared a remarkable friendship in which age seemed to make no difference.

Sarah Bush Johnston herded a group of gawking children out the door of the log cabin while her stepson, Abe, sat in a corner studying. Abe's new mother was a godsend. She respected him, and they shared a deep rapport. She understood the importance of his studies and encouraged him, thus earning his love and gratitude.

* * * * *

Unfortunately, Charles's parents separated while he was still young. Although he had two stepsisters, genetically speaking, he was an only child and felt like one for most of his childhood.

When Abe's stepmother moved in, she brought two daughters and a son. Abe was glad of their company. Their presence was all the more welcome because Abe had only one blood sister (his brother, Thomas, died in infancy), and she died before her twenty-first birthday. For most of his life, Abe was the only surviving offspring of his parents' union.

* * * * *

Lindbergh was born in Detroit, and one of his early experiences in that city helped shape him . . .

A young Charles Lindbergh stared at an illustration of an upright ape that his grandfather, a dentist, had hung on his examining room wall. His grandfather had patiently explained to Charles the theory of evolution: that many thousands of years ago man had evolved from creatures like these. After considering it for a time, Charles accepted the theory. It made more sense than the creation story told in church.

Disillusioned with religion at an early age, Charles turned to science as his source of inspiration. Its clarity and breadth fascinated him. Although in time the limitations of science would disillusion him, Lindbergh believed in evolution the rest of his life.

William Herndon stepped into his law office. He found his partner at his desk with his feet up and a book in his hands. "What's that you've got there?"

Lincoln showed him the book. It was called *Vestiges of Creation*. The two men discussed the idea of a universal law of evolution until a client's entrance interrupted them.

Lincoln's interest in evolution wasn't unusual: he was intrigued by science and dabbled in astronomy, heredity, philology, and other subjects.

CHAPTER FIVE

Little Falls

Some of the events in Lindbergh's life while he was growing up in Minnesota demonstrate the principle of "past-life advertising" described in Chapter Two . . .

Just before Charles was born, his father built a house on a piece of farmland in Little Falls, near the source of the Mississippi River. The Mississippi was just a two-minute stroll from the back door—a sight Charles was to know from the age of six weeks, when he was brought to Little Falls from Detroit.

A young Abraham Lincoln stood on the deck of a steamboat as it arrived at St. Louis, Missouri, looking down at a waterway that was very familiar to him. In a way, his life up to that point could be seen from the perspective of the Mississippi River. He was born south of one of its tributaries, grew up near it in southern Indiana, and traveled on it several times since then.

* * * * *

At the house that his mother dubbed "Lindholm," little Charles spent his summers playing either in the woods out back or in the front yard next to the rather unusual oval driveway.

President and Mrs. Lincoln decided to go out for the evening. They put on their overcoats and hats and walked out the front door of the White House. There, they saw that the horse-drawn carriage was already on the oval driveway.

* * * * *

As Charles pushed his toy automobile up the driveway, he caught a whiff of flowers. He glanced to one side and smiled. His mother had seen to it that fragrant lilacs grew along the driveway.

Walt Whitman entered his room after a walk in the countryside. He laid the sweet smelling blossoms he had picked on a table and filled a vase with water. After carefully arranging the flowers, he stood back and gazed solemnly at the display.

It was the anniversary of the day that President Lincoln had been shot, and Whitman was commemorating his death. The flowers he had gathered were lilacs; there were many lilacs blooming that terrible night.

It was spring when Lincoln fell, and the white and purple blossoms were in full display. Their fragrance so permeated the air that, in future, many who had experienced those traumatic days were taken back to them every year by the poignantly sweet scent of lilacs blooming in the springtime.

Whitman wrote about this experience:

When lilacs last in the dooryard bloom'd,
And the great star early droop'd in the western sky in the night,

I mourn'd, and yet shall mourn with ever-returning spring.[1]

* * * * *

Charles roamed the woodland path behind his house until it brought him to the river. He spent many happy days playing by the banks of the Mississippi.

One summer Charles and his father paddled a rowboat down the lakes, streams, and inlets of the Mississippi's headwaters. Charles had so much fun! He enjoyed leaning over the side of the boat and watching the trees, fields, and houses as he and his father drifted by. The trip was wonderful, and they spoke of how exciting it would be to take the great river all the way south to Louisiana and the exotic city of New Orleans on the Gulf of Mexico.

Abe Lincoln stood and stretched. New Orleans! This was the second flatboat trip he had taken down the Mississippi. He enjoyed the richness of New Orleans with its French people and their accents. But above all he found pleasure in floating past fields, woods, and towns to Louisiana and the gulf.

* * * * *

Charles was still very young when his father taught him how to wield an axe. He was given the chore of chopping wood for the fireplace, and Mr. Lindbergh observed that Charles had a natural affinity for the job.

---

[1]From "When Lilacs Last in the Dooryard Bloom'd".

While working on a brief autobiographical piece, Abraham Lincoln contemplated how, in a few words, he could condense the experience of his boyhood years.

He wrote, "Though very young, A. was large for his age, and had an axe put into his hands; and from that time until his twenty-third year, he was almost constantly handling that most useful instrument."

* * * * *

C.A. Lindbergh was worried. He had instructed his five-year-old son to wait at a certain place in the woods while he went exploring, but he came back to find the boy missing. The elder Lindbergh was planning a search party when he arrived home; but there was Charles, standing at the gate with his hands in his pockets, explaining how he had used the sun to guide him through the trees.

Young Abe Lincoln strolled nonchalantly through the woods of southwest Indiana. It was growing late, but he was unconcerned. Even in areas he had never seen before, he always managed to orient himself. He was becoming a true frontiersman.

* * * * *

From boyhood, Charles Lindbergh surprised people with his adult mannerisms. He was serious, self-assured, responsible, and always listened closely to important discussions.

He had the face and eyes of an old soul. While talking with him, one might be excused for imagining that he was of a more mature age.

One might expect such qualities in the reincarnation of Abraham Lincoln, but it is interesting to note that Lincoln, too, had a reputation for maturity in his youth.

* * * * *

Little Charles awoke. He'd had a strange dream in which he climbed to a high spot, then fell to his death. This was a scary dream for a little boy, but Charles turned over and went back to sleep. In his dream, his spirit had survived the plunge that destroyed his body.

Young Abe sat up in bed. Was it a vision he had had, or a dream? He wasn't sure. It was a frightening image.

In his dream or vision, Abe saw himself ascending to a high position in life, then falling from it to his death.

* * * * *

In 1918, when Charles was sixteen, the war in Europe freed him from school. With his father away, he was the master of the house. The country's need for farmers meant that Charles could enjoy life on the homestead.

On a typical morning Charles woke early and, whistling happily, went outside to do the milking and feeding. Only when the chores were done did he return to the house for breakfast.

Later, he hitched a plow to the tractor and turned over a section of farmland. In the afternoon he helped an older man notch and lay logs for the pig shed.[2] After supper, he

---

[2]Lincoln helped his father build two log cabins in Indiana, and one in Illinois.

bedded down on the screened-in veranda. As he fell asleep with the night sky for a companion, he heaved a sigh of contentment.

This, he felt, was the life.

Abraham Lincoln got up while it was still dark, dressed, chopped logs into kindling, and got the fire going under the water boiler. He fed the horse, milked the cow, and carried the pail of warm milk into the house. Then he washed up and ate breakfast before heading to the law office.

Isaac N. Arnold wrote about the last morning of President Lincoln's life:

After the cabinet meeting he went for a drive with Mrs. Lincoln. "Mary," he said, "we have had a hard time of it since we came to Washington. But the war is over, and with God's blessing we may hope for four years of peace and happiness, and then we will go back to Illinois and pass the rest of our lives in quiet." A picture of a prairie farm on the banks of the Sangamon River rose before him, and once more the plow and the axe were to become as familiar as in the days of his youth.

Arnold's words were poignant, for Lincoln never realized his dream of a prairie farm.

* * * * *

It seems fitting that a war freed Lindbergh to pursue the lifestyle that Lincoln had longed for at the end of his life. It was a war, after all, that had taken Lincoln away from it.

* * * * *

Charles Lindbergh pulled a new machine out of its box and looked at the instructions that came with it. He went over every detail very carefully before hanging the shiny metal contraption under a milk cow and sliding the suction cups onto the teats that hung pendulously from her udder. Then, after plugging in the machine, he turned on the switch.

The milking machine chugged away. The cow seemed to find the sensation irksome at first, but after awhile the sucking action relaxed her and she turned her attention back to the grain in her manger.

Lindbergh nodded. These labor-saving devices — engines and other machinery — were the future of farming, and he felt the call to convince his neighbors to try them.

Abraham Lincoln glanced over his speech — "Modern Discoveries and Inventions." It was his wish to expound on "the wonderful new improvements in machinery, the arts, and sciences."

Lincoln himself had an idea for a new invention. It had to do with using a steam engine to plow the earth. He could visualize his mechanical contraption laying multiple furrows in the soil. Such a device would save the backs of many farmers. Lincoln had sweated under the sun in his younger days, and his sympathy rested with those whose livelihood depended on manual labor.

* * * * *

Charles Lindbergh hefted a box of leaflets and carried it to the car. His father was on the campaign trail, and Charles was helping him. Together they met the constituency, with

Mr. Lindbergh delivering the talks while his son passed out the leaflets.

March 6, 1960. Abraham Lincoln yawned. He had been on the campaign trail in New York and New England for the past week, and the traveling and speechmaking was starting to get to him.

He drifted off to sleep. Almost exactly one year from this time, he would be giving his presidential inaugural address, thanks in part to his helpers back home in Springfield.

CHAPTER SIX

Washington, D.C.

From our perspective, there is much of interest in Lindbergh's early experiences in the District of Columbia . . .

Charles Lindbergh walked down the street, moodily kicking a stone. He hated Washington. Being there felt like a form of incarceration. He didn't like the schools or the weather, and he had no friends and no quiet places.

Every winter Charles's father brought him to the nation's capital while the House was in session. Other than being near his father, Charles found no joy there. For ten years he endured it, each year looking forward to going home to Little Falls.

Abraham Lincoln shook off his boots and lay on a White House sofa like a dead man.

What a job! In spite of his willingness to serve, he felt a resistance welling up. Like many presidents before and since, Lincoln saw the nation's capital as little more than a gilded prison. Whatever glamour there had been at the outset had long since faded away. In this place he'd watched his son die. Here he'd sent friends to war and received news of their crippling injuries or deaths. Here he'd waged battles against political adversaries.

Lincoln sighed. He looked forward to the end of his term, when he could return to Springfield, his friends, and his home. But as long as he had a job to do, he was willing to fill the big chair.

＊ ＊ ＊ ＊ ＊

It was spring, and seven-year-old Charles Lindbergh, accompanied by his father, stood on the White House lawn waiting for the start of the Easter egg roll.

He was staring at the Executive Mansion when the starting signal came. Charles moved quickly, passing another boy, and the race was on.

Returning from a stroll, Abraham Lincoln stared at the White House. Something seemed different about the place. What was happening up on the roof?

The president smiled. His sons Willie and Tad, with the help of some friends, had constructed a fort atop the Executive Mansion. Now they were raising the Stars and Stripes.

Shaking his head, Lincoln continued his walk up the driveway. He was glad that he had allowed his sons free rein in and around the White House. Boys should have the freedom to be boys, no matter where they lived.

＊ ＊ ＊ ＊ ＊

A Washington politician almost bit his tongue. In the midst of an important discussion, Mr. Lindbergh's boy had jumped onto his father's back. The politician fumed when, instead of chiding his son, Lindbergh gave Charles a piggyback ride that lasted several minutes.

William Herndon felt like screaming. The noisy entrance of Willie and Tad had brought a halt to work on an important lawsuit. Lincoln casually let the brats turn the office upside down while Herndon fumed. Finally, the boys wandered off to find their mother and peace returned.

* * * * *

Charles had caught the collecting bug. He was making the rounds of the House of Representatives, seeking autographs.

Seeing the House Speaker, Charles requested, "Excuse me, sir. Would you sign my autograph book?"

The jovial congressman looked at the solemn boy. With a twinkle in his eye, he decided to give this autograph hound more than he bargained for.

"I will sign it, young sir, if you wish. But I should warn you that my signature isn't very valuable. In fact, it isn't worth much even when it's written on one of my personal checks!"

The congressman shouted with laughter and Charles, thoroughly embarrassed, made his getaway. He decided to find a safer pastime.

Abraham Lincoln sighed. An autograph request, from a young clerk in Philadelphia. Well, he couldn't refuse, but maybe he could discourage people from asking . . .

Two minutes later, Lincoln read the words above his autograph: "Your note, requesting my 'signature with a sentiment,' was received. I am not a very sentimental man; and the best sentiment I can think of is that if you collect the signatures of all persons who are no less distinguished than I, you will have a very undistinguishing mass of names."

* * * * *

Standing in a museum, Charles Lindbergh gazed through the glass at a long saber, gleaming in the light. The weapon had belonged to General Philip Henry Sheridan, a Union hero of the Civil War.

Abraham Lincoln was aboard the *River Queen* near City Point, Virginia, when he spotted Philip Henry Sheridan. Taking the general's hand, Lincoln shook it with emotion. Sheridan's exploits in the Shenandoah Valley had shortened the war, and Lincoln wanted to express his appreciation.

"General," he said, "before the war started, I told people that I considered something close to my own height of six foot four to be a good stature for a cavalryman. But," he paused, "I want you to know that I've changed my mind. *Five* foot four will work in a pinch!"

* * * * *

Mrs. Lindbergh pulled at her son's hand, but Charles stood staring at the Arlington grave marker with the words "General Philip Henry Sheridan." It wasn't only that the tombstone reminded Charles of the sword he had seen. Standing there, he sensed the ghosts of Sheridan and the other Union generals, and other people from America's past, hovering beside him.

* * * * *

Charles Lindbergh walked with his mother through the Latrobe Gate that marked the entrance to the Washington Navy Yard. They went from one exhibit to another, enjoying the displays of old naval ordnance. When it was over, Charles looked forward to their next visit to the old military site.

Francis Burns waited while the president seated himself in the carriage, then he flicked the reins and yelled "Hee-yah!" The horses trotted around the oval curve of the driveway and the White House disappeared slowly behind them.

When Mr. Lincoln had asked Francis to take him for a ride, Francis knew where the president wanted to go. Lately it was always the same. Mr. Lincoln sought friendship and the pleasure of inspecting the new naval ordnance.

Before long they were passing through the Latrobe Gate. And there was Admiral Dahlgren, standing in front of the Commandant's Office with a broad grin splitting his face.

* * * * *

Charles Lindbergh gazed up at Woodrow Wilson and returned the president's greeting quietly.

"Weren't you excited?" Mrs. Lindbergh asked Charles later that evening.

"No," he answered, much to her surprise. "The president is just a man like anyone else."

* * * * *

Mrs. Lindbergh watched her son as he slept. There was a purity about him, never more apparent than in his adventure today in the streets of Washington.

While walking through an empty lot, Charles saw two groups of boys playing at war. Deciding to take part, Charles joined the side nearer him and picked up some stones to heave at the other group. After a few throws, one of the boys surprised Charles by crying out, "Hey, look at the white kid fighting with the niggers!"

Mrs. Lindbergh shook her head. Charles hadn't noticed that the groups were segregated by skin. He was color blind. And she had to explain the ways of the city streets to her son.

As Frederick Douglass stepped out of the White House, he felt light and happy. What an extraordinary experience! Meeting the president hadn't been at all what he had anticipated.

The former-slave-turned-diplomat had experienced most white people's reactions. There were those who hated him and tried to hinder him. Others felt uncomfortable and avoided him. And some supported him, but many did so in a way that was demeaning. Almost everyone made adjustments, if for no other reason than that they had never met such a capable black man.

But Lincoln was different. He was unperturbed by Douglass's intelligence and related to him just as he was. He didn't talk down to him. He seemed, in fact, not to have been aware of Douglass's skin color at all, except as it had to do with the topic of conversation.

Douglass felt liberated. It was freeing to meet someone who cut through superficialities and related to the vibrant and equal spirit that dwelled within.

* * * * *

Charles Lindbergh's face mirrored disbelief as he viewed the slave quarters and work areas at Mount Vernon. It was hard for him to reconcile the fact that George Washington, the Father of the Country, had been a slaveholder.

* * * * *

Charles Lindbergh shot out of his seat and cheered with the crowd. Attending an airshow not far from the nation's capital, he was thrilled by the aerobatic displays. The sight of planes speeding overhead filled him with joy. He wished he could soar with them—and a powerful thought was sown.

Lindbergh's life work had its beginning in Washington, D.C.

Late at night, John Hay, former president's aide, sat alone in the White House. He drank some wine, then wiped the moisture from his eyes. The marvelous chemistry between Lincoln and himself had ended too soon. Their work had really just begun.

But now the president's toils were over. The life work of Abraham Lincoln had ended in Washington, D.C.

CHAPTER SEVEN

The Army and the Airmail

"Flying airplanes! *That's* what I want to do!"

This realization arose as Charles Lindbergh contemplated his future. After doing a little research and talking with his parents, he prepared to attend flying school. He would begin at the Lincoln Flying School in Lincoln, Nebraska, and he would start by flying the airplanes known as Lincoln Standard Tourabouts.

* * * * *

While listening to a mechanic describe the workings of an aircraft engine, the image of that motor materialized in Charles Lindbergh's mind. The firing pistons, the spinning camshaft . . . everything was there and in perfect proportion.

This extraordinary knack of comprehending engines was an unexpected bonus for a would-be pilot. It was part of what would build his reputation as the best pilot in the world, and he remained an aviation expert to the end of his days.

A railroad engineer smiled as Lincoln and his son entered his railway cab and requested a ride. Tad asked his father how a locomotive functioned, and the engineer prepared to correct Lincoln's account. But Lincoln's explanation needed no corrections.

* * * * *

Standing at the army cadet school firing range, Charles Lindbergh took a deep breath. He had come in his off-hours, determined to free himself from something that had haunted him since his first day of training school. Why should the loud noise a gun made frighten him?

Well, he intended to fix it. It was a bad habit to jerk his hand when he fired his gun, and it messed up his scores.

He stood at the firing range, firing shot after shot. He practiced until his arm muscles ached from the strain.

In time, he was able to fire his gun without jerking. The problem never bothered him again.

Ford's Theater was dark except for the stage lights. The sound of the actors' voices drowned out every other noise.

Abraham Lincoln leaned forward in his chair, and . . .

Suddenly, a gunshot exploded right behind his ear. A brief spark of pain, a very brief and natural reaction of fear, then peace.

* * * * *

Upon hearing his name, Charles Lindbergh stood up. Striding forward with head held high, he approached the podium to accept his award: first place in outdoor sharpshooting.

Charles had always been good with a gun. As a boy, he hit the first bird he shot at, and it felt good to receive this confirmation. Walking back to his seat, he carried the trophy gun reverently.

Ping!

"Good shot, Lincoln!"

"Thank you. I've always had a way with a rifle. Did you know that I hit the first bird I fired at? Your turn now."

"All right!" came the nervous shout from behind. "Put your guns down and your hands up in the air where I can see them. Don't you know this is a restricted area . . . Mr. President!"

"Good morning, men. Are you arresting me?"

"We didn't recognize you, sir! What are you doing out here behind the White House?"

"Well, Will Stoddard and I thought we'd amuse ourselves by having some target practice on that old lumber pile. I hope you don't mind."

"No, sir. Not at all, sir. It's just that, it would help if we was to know ahead of time, sir."

"That's fine. We'll do that next time, eh, Stoddard?"

The sound of their voices faded as the soldiers beat a hasty retreat.

* * * * *

Charles Lindbergh sat at his desk. His father was dying, and he couldn't go to him.

Charles and his father were kindred spirits who had gotten along like the proverbial peas in a pod. When Mr. Lindbergh had first been afflicted with brain cancer, the army gave Charles leave to see him. During that visit, however, his father was mute. It wasn't possible for father and son to converse together, and they shared instead a wordless harmony.

Now his father was near death, and because of the timing, Charles wasn't allowed leave. Although he desperately wanted to see his father, he had to send a letter instead.

It was all he could do.

Abraham Lincoln sat at his desk in his Springfield home, proofreading. His father was dying, and Lincoln had written a letter.

He and his father had never gotten along. Abraham Lincoln was bright and inquisitive; Thomas Lincoln was roughhewn and unable to comprehend his son. He had thought young Abe's intellectual curiosity a pretentious air and had shown his displeasure by physical punishment. That was one reason why Abe had left home so early and why he seldom returned to visit.

And now that his father was dying, Lincoln couldn't bring himself to speak to him. Instead, he had written a farewell message to be delivered by his stepbrother.

It was the best he could do.

* * * * *

Looking at the grade list posted on the wall of his flying school, Charles Lindbergh smiled. First in his class. He'd worked hard, and hoped he would succeed. But it had taken a little faith.

From kindergarten through college, Lindbergh had floundered with barely passing grades. His lack of scholarship was no surprise. He had bounced around from one city and state to the next. With so many distractions, he had never developed a love of learning.

After he conceived his goal of becoming an airplane pilot, however, he turned into a scholar. Many a night Charles spent poring over his textbooks, anxious to make the grade. And he had succeeded.

All he had needed was an incentive. The rest was easy.

Gazing at the document in his hands, Abe Lincoln smiled. He was a bona fide lawyer, by jing!

How his success would surprise his family. His early schooling had been piecemeal: attending "A.B.C. schools" whenever one was offered nearby. He reckoned that he'd accumulated less than a full year of classroom study by the time he reached adulthood. He'd grown up an ignorant backwoodsman.

But all that changed when he found his vocation. After he realized that he wanted to become a lawyer, he became an exemplary scholar. He devoured Blackstone's *Commentaries* and other legal works until he could recite what he had learned by rote. And now he had passed his bar exam.

All he needed was an incentive.

* * * * *

Charles Lindbergh hardly noticed the noise the Liberty engine made as he soared over the farms of north-central Illinois. He looked over the side of his plane as he plotted the course he would follow while carrying the airmail. This was his first real job—on another level entirely from farming and barnstorming—and he wanted to make the best of it. So far, he had confirmed Peoria and Springfield as the two stops between Chicago and St. Louis. Now, flying south on the middle leg of his route, he found himself studying the lay of the land, as he often did on these flights.

As his eyes scanned the view, he may have noticed a plot of earth below and to his right. There was nothing special about it—it was little more than a clearing in the woods, a level area above a slope that angled to the Sangamon River. It boasted what looked like a broken-down log building or two, the vague outlines of a small village.

Lindbergh gunned his engine and he turned his sights to Springfield. In the weeks ahead, the contours of central Illinois were to become increasingly familiar to him.

Postmaster Abe Lincoln settled himself with his feet up on the counter. It had been a quiet day, and he was looking closely at what the morning's mail had brought. Another letter to the Bales from their cousins back East. More bills for Sam Hill, the grocer. But nothing for himself today.

That was to be expected. Lincoln was on his own in the frontier village of New Salem—a little clearing in the woods above a slope that led down to the Sangamon River—and he seldom heard from relatives or old friends. He was just starting out, making his way in the world, and the postmaster position was one of the first real jobs he'd had.

*   *   *   *   *

Charles Lindbergh fell onto his cot laughing. He had designed the practical joke very carefully—replacing water in a container with kerosene, then wiping the sides with a clean cloth.

While he was away, an unsuspecting fellow flier had fallen into the trap. When Bud Gurney had come in looking for some water to drink, he spotted the harmless-looking bucket. Bud took a gulp, only to spray out the foul liquid, his face red.

After his laughter had died down, Lindbergh apologized for his actions, but Gurney looked at him askance. All the stories were true. Lindbergh was an incurable practical joker. You never knew what trick he might play on you, and it was best to be wary when visiting his boardinghouse.

For his part, Charles continued to have fun with these

hijinks—even inflicting them on his children when he was well into middle age.

Charles Forbes's face glowed with anticipation. The president had just informed him that the fruit on the tree before them was wonderfully sweet, and the Irishman was eager to give it a try. Lincoln reached into a branch, pulled some off, and gave one to Forbes. Polishing it on his vest, he took a bite . . .

. . . and spit the contents out, his face a study in agony.

Lincoln laughed so hard he thought he might injure himself. The jest had gone off better than he'd hoped. As a foreigner, Forbes could not have known that unripe persimmons are among the most acrid things on earth. Lincoln had discovered it as a young man; now he converted his hard-won knowledge into personal entertainment.

Playing practical jokes was a habit Lincoln had indulged from his earliest days. As a youth he'd held little children upside-down to make muddy tracks on the ceiling, confounding his mother. Later, he had convinced travelers to strip to cross a river when there was no need to do so, and he had connived a bald congressman into accepting a bottle of tonic that he claimed was a miracle cure for restoring hair.

The man wasn't safe, and Lincoln's friends, knowing this fact, watched their steps around him very carefully indeed.

* * * * *

Charles Lindbergh pondered his idea while filling the tanks of his airplane. He thought about it while loading the bags of mail. And it was still in his head when he glided over the trees at the end of the runway.

It was a fantastic notion, flying the Atlantic. He had

read about the contest in the newspaper: A businessman offered a cash prize of twenty-five thousand dollars to the first person or persons to fly an airplane from New York to Paris. For years the Orteig prize had sat, waiting for someone to claim it.

The thought of blazing new trails fired Lindbergh's imagination. He felt sure he could do it. He just needed the ideal airplane, the details of which were already forming in his mind.

Absentmindedly finishing his mail run, Lindbergh continued to plan his assault of the Atlantic by air.

"He said *what?*"

Abraham Lincoln was incredulous as Professor Joseph Henry of the Smithsonian told him of the grand scheme that an inventor, Thaddeus Lowe, had tried to sell him.

"I'm not joshin' nor jestin'. He said he could fly his air balloon over the Atlantic Ocean to Europe. He swore he could make the trip as fast as any clipper and bring the balloon in safely."

"It sounds fantastic. Flying the Atlantic Ocean! What a thought."

"But is it a *workable* thought?"

"That's part of it. But more to the point: is it a *useful* thought? Air balloons might be handy for charting troop movements in the field. But . . . an air trip over the ocean? It seems too risky. I can see why you didn't feel to promote this just yet.

"I'll tell you one thing, though," the president leaned forward and Henry could see that his imagination had been roused. "I warrant we'll see air crossings of the Atlantic and other wonders soon enough. Look at the progress we've made in the last fifty years. Why, just look at the things

we've developed during this war! Humanity is racing into
the future, and modern science is leading the charge.

"I tell you, Henry," Lincoln said, his eyes agleam.
"There are exciting days ahead!"

* * * * *

To Lindbergh, one thought was a given. He must make
this Paris trip alone. It wasn't merely that it was cheaper or
that only one pilot would bring the weight down, thus giving
a greater chance of success. It was that he was unwilling to
risk anyone else's skin. Sink or swim, Lindbergh would put
only his own life in jeopardy.

Seated on a train to Gettysburg, Pennsylvania, President Lincoln listened as a man related how his son had val-
iantly defended Little Round Top before dying a hero's death.

Lincoln's face was a picture of sadness as he told the
bereaved father:

"When I think of the sacrifices of life yet to be
offered and the hearts and homes yet to be made desolate
before this dreadful war is over, I feel at times like hiding in
deep darkness."

* * * * *

While Lindbergh pored over the design layouts, the
chief engineer of the Ryan Aircraft Company studied him.
Lindbergh had arrived in San Diego a few weeks earlier to
work with the builders, and the aviator had impressed the
engineer by objectively weighing each question related to the
construction of the *Spirit of St. Louis*. It was strange that,
though the engineer was the titular head of the operation,

Lindbergh embodied the real spirit of the group. The young man was a natural leader who drew the best out of his helpers.

William Seward stood by as Abraham Lincoln listened to a report from his secretary of war. Months ago, Seward had doubted that Lincoln was up to the challenges of the presidency. But Lincoln had learned to weigh objectively each piece of information, as well as his secretaries' opinions, to arrive at the right action. He was leading his cabinet of strong-willed men, pulling them together despite their differences, and maintaining a clear group purpose. It was no easy task, but somehow Lincoln managed it.

CHAPTER EIGHT

The Flight

Lindbergh named the airplane he used to fly the Atlantic after a saint. One might expect such a decision from a past-life yogi, but is there anything about the life of Saint Louis that relates to this study? . . .

Charles Lindbergh slipped his hand behind his back. While New York news photographers shouted brash questions or requests to pose, he ironically touched his flying machine to ground himself.

The *Spirit of St. Louis*. He had approved that name when it was suggested. And he was content to fly an airplane with those words painted on its side. His aircraft was named for the Missouri city whose citizens were backing the expedition. But the name was also a gesture to the people of Paris who would, he hoped, be greeting him in a day or two.

For Saint Louis was still honored in France. Louis was a medieval hero who combined the traits of holy man and king. He was a national figure who acted selflessly, a political saint who loved and honored his mother, was said to have been unusually tall, was never known to swear, and was compassionate to those who rebelled against his reign. He had problems with the people in the southern part of his country, but showed remarkable wisdom and forbearance in the administration of his duties. He studied law and distributed justice to the people where they lived, invited the poorest of his citizens into his home to hear their pleas for help, and sought at the end of his life to reconcile with his enemies. He studied the Bible and prayed for wisdom; recommended thanking God for His blessings; yearned for Jerusalem with his last breath; and promoted the Crusades even though some of his own people opposed him. Though not possessing the usual qualifications, Louis was canonized by the public; his name was invoked, post-mortem, as a symbol of justice and compassion, and he was said to have acted as a divine instrument. Historians have pointed to his reign as a defining one for the French monarchy, and all future French kings were measured against the almost mythical Saint Louis.

This was the man whose name graced the side of Lindbergh's airplane like a banner. This was the man whose spirit Lindbergh subconsciously evoked when he flew to Paris. And, when he succeeded, he laid a wreath at the foot of the statue in Missouri depicting the holy man of France.

Was it a coincidence that Lindbergh had named his airplane after a man whose life mirrored Abraham Lincoln's in so many ways? All the details listed in the foregoing biosketch apply to Lincoln as well. The parallels are so close that it was as if Lindbergh had put Lincoln's name on his plane.

Maybe, too, this was another incarnation advertising itself in an obvious way: from Louis to Lincoln to Lindbergh. It is certainly conceivable that Saint Louis reincarnated as Abraham Lincoln. And possible also for Louis to have spent a future lifetime or two in the Himalayas seeking God. Remember that the three lives we are exploring are just a few links on a reincarnational chain that extends backward for millennia. We have all lived many lives.

* * * * *

Lindbergh stared with disbelief at a news headline. Another nickname! Why did they do it?

"Flyin' Fool"? There was nothing foolish about his attempt to cross the Atlantic. He had laid his plans with exquisite precision, and still the media had turned him into a clown.

"Why can't they just call me 'Charles Lindbergh'?" he griped. "That is my name, after all . . ."

Abraham Lincoln was dead, and John W. Bunn was sitting at his desk in his place of business in Springfield, thinking of his old friend. As the details of their connection sprang to mind, Bunn recalled how Lincoln had never liked nicknames like "Honest Abe" or even "Abe". Usually, he preferred that people call him "Mr. Lincoln."

* * * * *

Every so often during their lunch together, Charles Lindbergh gazed into his mother's eyes.

The *Spirit of St. Louis* was ready, every instrument checked, every contingency accounted for. It was merely a question of when the weather would break. And then he would be off, flying the Atlantic alone, something that had never been done.

They didn't talk about it. They didn't have to.

Both knew that he might not be coming back.

Abraham Lincoln and his stepmother sat together, enjoying a rich silence in which words were superfluous.

Sarah had just expressed her fear that her stepson

would not return from Washington alive, and Abe hadn't denied the possibility. In fact, that concern had prompted his visit to her.

The two sat quietly, enjoying the last moments they would spend together on earth.

* * * * *

He took off from Roosevelt Field in New York at 7:54 a.m. on May 20, 1927. A few hours later, he was lost to sight over the Atlantic Ocean. And the world wondered if this was the last they would see of twenty-five-year-old Charles A. Lindbergh, captain of the National Guard.

O Captain! My Captain!

The poem's title and words, inspired by Abraham Lincoln, flowed from Walt Whitman's pen.

> O Captain! my Captain! our fearful trip is done,
> The ship has weather'd every rack, the prize we sought is won,
> The port is near, the bells I hear, the people all exulting,
> While follow eyes the steady keel, the vessel grim and daring;
> But O heart! heart! heart!
> O the bleeding drops of red,
> Where on the deck my Captain lies,
> Fallen cold and dead.

> O Captain! my Captain! rise up and hear the bells;
> Rise up—for you the flag is flung—for you the bugle trills,
> For you bouquets and ribbon'd wreaths—for you the shores
> a-crowding,
> For you they call, the swaying mass, their eager faces turning;
> Here Captain! dear father!
> This arm beneath your head!

> It is some dream that on the deck
> You've fallen cold and dead.

Lincoln's only experience of army life had come when, as a young man of twenty-three, he was made captain during the Black Hawk War. With his poem Whitman immortalized that rank, but he converted Lincoln's captaincy to a naval one—allegorically guiding the national ship through the storm of divisive war and into the safe harbor of unity and freedom.

* * * * *

The lively New York audience hushed as the announcer entered the spotlight and walked to a hanging microphone. He paused, then spoke with great solemnity.

He acknowledged that they had gathered to enjoy a prizefight, and said that he would perform the introductions shortly. But first, he suggested that they turn their thoughts to a young man of twenty-five summers, by himself over the clouded Atlantic, with nothing but thin canvas and metal between him and a frigid death. And the announcer asked the audience to pray with him for Lindbergh's protection.

The tough boxing fans bowed their heads. They were joined by millions across America and elsewhere who prayed that the choices of a young man whom a week earlier they had never heard of, would lead him to safety.

Francis Carpenter stood still. He had come to the White House to paint a portrait of Abraham Lincoln, and now he was struck by a mental image so luminous as to approach the visionary. As he later wrote:

I seemed to see lines radiating from every part of the globe, converging to a focus at the point where that plain, awkward-looking man stood, and to hear in spirit a million prayers ascending on his behalf.

* * * * *

Over the Atlantic, Charles Lindbergh sat in his rumbling airship. His awareness was augmented, helping him to notice problems before they became insoluble. His mind was strengthened, so that he wasn't overcome by lack of sleep. Above the coasts of Nova Scotia and Newfoundland the sky cleared, allowing him to keep track of his course. And the tail wind he was hoping for arrived, gently nudging his craft forward.

Heavenly intervention brought a spiritual boon. Lindbergh was transported to a higher sphere and visited by spirits.[1] Meanwhile, his airplane did not stop, did not falter, but continued to soar over the Atlantic.

* * * * *

With a slight jolt, Lindbergh set the *Spirit of St. Louis* down on Paris's Le Bourget field. Opening the door to his airplane, he was about to set foot on French soil when his feet were whisked out from under him.

Lindbergh was carried in a circle on the shoulders of excited Frenchmen shouting his name. They gleefully ignored his struggles to free himself. When he finally touched the ground, he was dizzy for the first time since setting off from New York thirty-four hours earlier.

[1] See Chapter Thirty-Four.

Abraham Lincoln finished his response to Stephen A. Douglas and received a rousing response from the crowd. As he was about to return to his seat hands grabbed at his limbs, and the next thing he knew he was riding on the shoulders of two young Republicans. The revelers ignored Lincoln's protests, and it seemed like forever before he was allowed to set his feet on the ground.

* * * * *

Refreshed by his sleep and wearing a bathrobe, Lindbergh was eating a late breakfast in the company of the U.S. ambassador to France, Myron T. Herrick, and the ambassador's son, Parmely, in the embassy rooms.

"You're going to need a suit," the ambassador said.

Lindbergh considered the point. "I have my flying clothes. I could put those on."

"Not on your life." The ambassador turned to his servant. "Blanchard, do you know of someone who has a proper suit that our guest might borrow for a little while?"

The valet looked Lindbergh up and down. "Yes, Your Excellency. My friend is much the same size. I could fetch it for you, straightaway."

Lindbergh and Herrick chatted while waiting for the suit. Lindbergh put it on; it was a fairly snug fit.

The press entered the room and interviewed Lindbergh. Meanwhile, the sound of voices shouting Lindbergh's name filtered through the window. Parmely peeked outside and chuckled.

"They're out there, all right."

Lindbergh blinked. *"Who're* out there?"

"The Parisians. They've gathered on the sidewalk. They want to see you."

Ambassador Herrick opened the French doors and herded Lindbergh out. The flier stood looking at hundreds of smiling faces below. A great cheer went up. Camera light-bulbs flashed. And the first photographs of Lindbergh as a public hero, wired to news agencies across the globe, showed him wearing borrowed clothes.

"You aren't going to get your picture taken in that getup, are you?"

Abraham Lincoln glanced down at his outfit. "It looks fine to me."

The photographer laughed. "That linen suit is *really* out of date. Besides, I don't think it will show up well on the ambrotype."

"What would you suggest?"

The man thought for a moment. "You'd better wear one of my coats. We aren't exactly the same size, but it will fit you well enough. At any rate, it will look a lot better than what you've got on, that's for sure."

Minutes later, Lincoln sat very still with his borrowed coat on and had his picture taken—one of his early pictures that, decades later, became famous throughout the world.

* * * * *

In an afterword to *We,* Lindbergh's first book about his Atlantic flight, Fitzhugh Green describes the odd and powerful effect the young flier had on large groups of people, beginning with the crowds that greeted him in Paris. Green described this effect as "the phenomenon of Lindbergh" . . .

Charles Lindbergh looked over the balcony railing at the sea of eager faces. He could feel the crowd's interest.

Their expectations reached into him and unlocked a hidden door, and the energy and light that poured out of him expanded his aura so that it filled the city block. In a trice, Lindbergh had become more than the sum of his parts.

The Parisians had waited for hours to see the bright young American. They were excited, but they weren't *too* excited. They were French, after all. They had seen everything.

But now the world changed. As the Parisians stared at Lindbergh, time slowed down. Things started to happen in slow motion.

Lindbergh gazed at them and smiled. He lifted his hand and waved. And the people went into a trance. They were moved as never before. The stoic French felt as if their hearts would burst. One thought filled their minds: It is Him. The Hero, the Great Man Himself. *He has come!*

Lindbergh seemed to them more than human: he was infinitely more beautiful. Some in the crowd wept. Others laughed. And everyone began to cheer. *"Leendbairg! Leendbairg!"* came the exultant cry from hundreds of Parisians.

On the balcony, Ambassador Herrick gazed at the young flier standing next to him. In his long experience of public life, he had never seen anything like this.

Little did Herrick realize that this was just the beginning. The floodgates had opened. The law of karmic restitution, by which the universe is held together, had come into play; and great acts of love must be recompensed with love, here on earth, where it began long ago. The young man with the brilliant aura was fated to be adored wherever he went—Europe, Asia, Africa—but especially back in America, where the people would receive him with open arms, and shower him with honors and gifts.

But all that was to come later. In Paris, Lindbergh was handed two flags: American and French. He grinned as he waved them back and forth. And the crowd was overcome with joy.

* * * * *

After Lindbergh's Paris flight the Europeans treated him with such reverence that it might have been a great American president who was paying them a visit. They lavished him with praise far out of proportion to his actual deeds.

Lindbergh was taken on a whirlwind tour. He was greeted by France's most distinguished people. He addressed the Parisian Council. He became used to hearing "The Star-Spangled Banner" when he entered a building.

Meanwhile, each of his acts was put into a political context. Everything he did was seen in the light of bringing together the American and French people. Similar interpretations would be placed on his deeds for years to come, and he eagerly endorsed those interpretations and sought to further them by any means possible.

After France, Lindbergh flew to Belgium, where he continued to receive VIP treatment. The royal family and prime minister greeted him. And Burgomaster Max, the great World War I general, told Lindbergh, "In your glory there is glory for all men—a victory of humanity."

Lindbergh didn't stay long in Belgium. He wanted to see as much of Europe as possible before returning to the States. From Brussels he flew the *Spirit of St. Louis* across the channel to Britain.

As Lindbergh disembarked from his plane, one hundred fifty thousand adoring Londoners converged on him. Then he was escorted into an automobile for a triumphant ride through the city. He was greeted affectionately by the king (who decorated him) and other royalty and statesmen.

Mid-April, 1865. In the habit of printing strongly worded criticisms of Abraham Lincoln, most London papers were frantically reversing the trend. After the president's assassination, nearly everyone had come to appreciate his greatness. Newsmen splashed praise across the front pages. One periodical published a cartoon of Britannia, a mythical figure in flowing gown, consoling her sister, Columbia, as she wept piteously at the dead president's bedside.

* * * * *

Charles Lindbergh sat solemnly in a Westminster church pew, attending a special service celebrating the American Civil War. He turned and smiled at his neighbor. The old gentleman returned a gaping grin. The aged expatriate didn't have many teeth left, but he could dimly recall marching to the battle of Antietam next to William McKinley, the future president of the United States, who was later assassinated.

* * * * *

A chauffeur drove Lindbergh to the Savoy hotel in downtown London. While bobbies fended off the crowds, he entered the famous building and was greeted by the hotel manager.

"Mr. Lindbergh, sir."

"That's me."

"The newsmen and honored guests are waiting for you."

"Where do I go?"

"Let me take you."

The two men strode down the hall. Then the manager

turned and opened a large door.

"Here you are, sir. The Abraham Lincoln Room."

* * * * *

Lindbergh swapped smiles with the Prince of Wales.

So far, the aviator had been warmly received by royalty in Belgium and England, and this happy state of affairs continued. Wherever he went, the aristocracy honored the man who had flown the Atlantic, and he returned their friendliness with enduring goodwill. In later years, he sympathized with his royal friends' problems.

President Lincoln signed a letter and placed it on the stack of outgoing mail. Some of his correspondence consisted of personal messages to royal families like this one: condolences to Queen Victoria on the death of Prince Albert.

* * * * *

"Captain Lindbergh, welcome aboard!"

"Thank you."

Lindbergh stepped onto the deck of the USS *Memphis*. At the request of President Coolidge, the pilot and his airplane were to be ferried across the Atlantic to Washington on the flagship of the American fleet. Not even the president rode better than Lindbergh.

* * * * *

At the end of its excursion up the Potomac, the *Memphis* settled into its berth. The military aircraft that had kept the cruiser company flew over the city with a roar. As the gangplank went up, cannonfire and rifle fusillades welcomed the long-awaited passenger. The hero of America had come home, and the capital city had sent its cabinet ministers and high-ranking officers, all clad in black silk top hats, to gather him in.

Charles Lindbergh walked slowly down the gangplank, his mother's arm linked with his. Many in the crowd, seeing them reunited, burst into tears.

It was a special moment — somehow, the image verged on the transcendental, yet no one could say why the tableau was so moving.

A group of tourists and Indiana schoolchildren stood before a solitary tombstone with a crest that resembled a cathedral roof.

A tour guide took her place before the gathering. "This is the gravesite of the mother of Abraham Lincoln," she said. "Nancy Hanks Lincoln passed away of a disease called "milk sick" at the age of thirty-four. Although she didn't live to see her son achieve his prominence, although she died before he reached adulthood, her influence on him was very marked.

"The president blessed her memory and said that all that he was or hoped to be, he owed to her. It is no exaggeration to say that it is partly because of her that we honor Abraham Lincoln; and, today, she has achieved the status of a folk heroine.

"Rosemary Benet wrote a tender poem that depicted Nancy Hanks as an earthbound spirit making touching inquiries, trying to discover what had become of her son."

The tour guide proceeded to read the poem. As she did so, some in her audience were moved to tears.

* * * * *

Charles Lindbergh sat in the president's motor-car—which bore the national seal and was surrounded by an honor guard of cavalry—as it made its way down Pennsylvania Avenue.

It was only a few years since he had virtually flunked out of college. He had also been unsuccessful in running a farm. Back then, no one suspected him of greatness. And yet, now he rode through the streets of Washington, prior to being received by the president at the Washington Monument. He was going to be welcomed by military bands, waving flags, and cheering multitudes. He was a world-renowned hero.

Lindbergh shifted in his seat. This would take a little getting used to.

Abraham Lincoln sat in the president's carriage as it made its way down Pennsylvania Avenue. He glanced at President James Buchanan seated next to him. How quickly things could turn around!

Only a few short years ago, Lincoln's life story could have served as a textbook for futility. He had failed in so many endeavors: businesses, courtships, political races. And now, here he was, being driven through the streets of Washington preparatory to being sworn in as president of the United States. He had become a world figure.

It would take some getting used to.

* * * * *

President Coolidge was delivering an introductory speech. Known for his terseness, Silent Cal was giving a longer address than usual.

He had finished his remarks on the history of American aviation, and it was time to say something about the young man whom two hundred fifty thousand people had come to honor. Coolidge was prepared. He had many quotes to choose from.

Among his papers was a note from one of the military men Lindbergh had served under. Looking at the vast audience, Coolidge said, "One of the officers expressed his belief that Charles Lindbergh 'would successfully complete everything he undertakes.'"

In the middle of his speech, Stephen A. Douglas took a moment to look at the crowd. In this, his first debate with Lincoln, he had drawn the long straw. He needed a forceful argument to open the proceedings.

Douglas was a master speaker. He knew how to draw the audience to his side, to work them until he had them in the palm of his hand. One technique he liked to use was openly avowing his opponent's strengths, then undermining them. Now, he thought, was a good time for that ploy.

Which strength to choose? Lincoln had many. But one quality stood out in Douglas's mind.

Douglas said, "Abraham Lincoln is one of those peculiar men who perform with admirable skill everything which they undertake."

* * * * *

Charles Lindbergh stepped up to the microphone. Coolidge's speech had gone on longer than expected, making following it something of a chore.

He cleared his throat, then began to speak in a strange, high-pitched tone.

As Abraham Lincoln stepped up to give his speech on the battle of Gettysburg, he noticed that the crowd had become restless during Edward Everett's lengthy oration.

Clearing his throat, Lincoln began speaking in his high-pitched, reedy voice. His talk was short—so short, in fact, that the audience stood for a few moments in surprised silence before they realized it was over. Then they broke into applause.

Lindbergh's Washington speech shattered records for brevity. Afterward, the audience stood for a few moments in uncertainty before they understood that he had finished. Then, the thunder of their response shook the stands. Several newsmen who were present had the same thought: "That was just like Lincoln's Gettysburg Address!"

* * * * *

The Washington aristocrats steeled themselves. The word on Lindbergh was that he was a hayseed, fresh from the fields of the Midwest. They expected the manners that attend such a person, and were prepared to suffer them willingly in honor of the great deed he had done.

Hours later, the aristocrats were abuzz. Lindbergh was the talk of the town. His manners were impeccable, his grace seamless. Where had this unknown youth picked up his easy way with important people? Whence his unexpected savoir vivre?

The mystery was never solved. Surrounded by big-wigs and high-society types, Charles Lindbergh had risen to the occasion, surprising everyone. From some deep inner well he had tapped the elegance of a social adept. All of Washington was at his feet.

President Lincoln had had enough.

"Yes, Mary. I know where the little spoon goes and not to slurp my soup. I know I must wear my best pants, and I know how to address the ambassador from Paraguay. You and Seward don't have to pound it into me. I'm not a rustic anymore, and I'm not an imbecile."

Mrs. Lincoln was undeterred. "You saw how people viewed us when we arrived a few months ago. They looked *down* on us. They thought we were peasants, fresh from the fields of the Midwest.

"Well, we've changed their minds, you and I. But I want to make sure they never go back to that way of thinking. Because I couldn't abide it."

Lincoln gave his wife a long-suffering look. "Mary, I don't need those fancy manners. I know how to get along with all kinds of people. But I'll do these things, just to keep you happy."

* * * * *

After his speech, Lindbergh ate dinner with the president and his cabinet. The next day he accepted a church invitation from the Coolidge family. Later, he received a medal in front of the Capitol building at an event commemorating one hundred fifty years of the American flag.

President-elect Abraham Lincoln stood on a platform in front of Independence Hall in Philadelphia, Pennsylvania. He was on his way to the White House, but first he had a job to do. Tugging on a rope, he hoisted a new version of the American flag. Kansas had just joined the Union, and Lincoln had been invited to participate in the official flag-raising ceremony.

* * * * *

Lindbergh went from wheelchair to wheelchair greeting World War I veterans at Walter Reid Hospital. As he shook hands with the men, the hospital staff smiled. Lindbergh lifted the men's spirits, and the old soldiers needed such morale boosts.

Lincoln sat at a soldier's bedside. The president was indefatigable in his visits to injured soldiers, often leaving his duties to minister to them in the hospital tents. And the men loved him. Their faces glowed long after he left as they recalled his funny stories and encouraging words.

CHAPTER NINE

Two Processions

After Washington, Lindbergh visited New York City . . .

Lindbergh came across the water, ferried to Man-hattan along the Upper Bay. In the midst of a boisterous tumult of horns and whistles the world-famous pilot, newly returned from France, gazed solemnly at the approaching shoreline.

He came across the water. The body of Abraham Lincoln was ferried to lower Manhattan from the shores of New Jersey. Arriving on Manhattan, the funeral procession made its way along a street with a Gallic name: Desbrosses.
He came by way of a French road.

* * * * *

Arriving in the Battery, Lindbergh was escorted to an automobile. The car turned onto Broadway, then made its way into the heart of the city.
Police on horseback surrounded Lindbergh's car. On all sides the multitudes cheered and waved. Many crowded the rooftops and upper-story windows to watch Lindbergh pass below. Men took off their hats and tossed them into the air. The throng shouted themselves sore and shed tears of joy. White confetti floated on the breeze, blanketing the

streets like a blessing of gladness. The people felt uplifted and ennobled.

Lincoln's hearse, pulled by horses and surrounded by the National Guard, turned on Broadway and made its solemn way up the great wide avenue. Some witnesses watched from upper-story windows and rooftops. People lined the street in silence and bowed their heads. Men took off their hats and held them somberly. Small groups stood off to one side, speaking in hushed tones, grieving for the fallen president. When the casket passed, they turned and followed, walking in the dust of its passage. A light wind lifted the black crepe that lined doorways and windows.

They came with mournful step. They walked slowly, keeping time with the drumbeat. With heads low, with hands clasped to their breasts, they came—wounded souls, weeping in bereavement.

* * * * *

The Lindbergh parade halted at City Hall. Walking up the steps of the old building, Lindbergh noticed that a banner proclaimed "Welcome Lindbergh!" while the white pillars beneath it were festooned with wreaths. On the grandstand, the mayor of New York greeted him emotionally and presented him with a key to the city. The audience cheered. Some wept from sheer happiness.

The funeral cortege halted at City Hall. Uniformed soldiers gently lifted the coffin, carried it inside the building, and placed it on a catafalque in a darkly decorated room. Then they opened the doors to the people gathered outside by the thousands.

By ones and twos they passed the casket, men baring their heads, women whispering prayers. Those waiting outside were distracted by the banner on the front of the building, flapping in the breeze. It read: "The Nation Mourns." Black streamers accompanied the sign.

"We shall not forget him," promised the New Yorkers. Some were ashamed that their city had erupted in draft riots just after the battle of Gettysburg. They wished now that they could show him their love and support, but that opportunity had been stolen from them.

The next day, the procession with Lincoln's coffin continued north up Broadway.

* * * * *

Leaving City Hall, Lindbergh's cavalcade could easily have continued up Broadway, but instead it turned right and traveled up Lafayette Street. It rode past adoring fans for many blocks before it made a left turn at Ninth Street and a right at Fifth Avenue.

Along the way, as he crossed Eighth Street, Lindbergh turned to his right to wave at fans. As he did so, he may have spotted an unusual edifice out of the corner of his eye.

It was as if the event coordinators had determined that, though it was out of the way, Charles Lindbergh should pass within a stone's throw of the old Cooper Union Building.

Abraham Lincoln's funeral procession wound its way up Broadway. Eventually, it would turn left at Fourteenth Street before turning right up Fifth Avenue. But, for now, the hearse rolled across an intersection just a few blocks west of the Cooper Institute where, five years before, Lincoln had made the speech that sent him to the presidency.

The soldiers in the procession continued to march, following the slain president up Fifth Avenue and through Madison Square.

* * * * *

The Lindbergh parade continued north up Fifth Avenue before making a stop at Madison Square. There, Lindbergh knelt to lay a wreath at the base of a white marble monument commemorating American soldiers who had perished in the Great War.

Lindbergh was now an expert at wreath-laying. He had performed similar duties at the Tombs of Unknown Soldiers in Paris, London, and Washington. And, while flying over a Belgium military cemetery, he had tossed a wreath from his airplane.

Lindbergh performed these tasks gravely, with a sober countenance. He seemed to feel it a privilege to honor those who had made the ultimate sacrifice for their countries and for the world.

Abraham Lincoln looked up from his notes. There was no need to read this part of the speech. He had it memorized.

. . . we cannot dedicate—we cannot consecrate—we cannot hallow—this ground. The brave men, living and dead, who struggled here have consecrated it, far above our poor power to add or detract. . . .

Lincoln spoke with emotion. His voice grew in majesty as he urged his audience.

. . . that from these honored dead we take increased devotion to that cause for which they gave the last full measure of devotion—that we here highly resolve that these dead shall not have died in vain.

The people gathered in Gettysburg stood listening in the sunlight.

* * * * *

Madison Square was so crowded that some people straddled tree branches, and even sculptures and monuments, to witness the proceedings. While Lindbergh was laying his wreath at the memorial, a black man lifted himself onto the Lincoln statue that graced the square. Taking a seat on the bronzed knee, he held onto an arm to keep his balance. Then he waved at Lindbergh and lovingly called his name.

The last group in the Lincoln funeral march consisted of two thousand Negroes, some bearing a sign that proclaimed: "Abraham Lincoln, Our Emancipator."

* * * * *

The Lindbergh parade continued north up Fifth Avenue. By the time it reached Central Park, it had lasted four hours. Lindbergh had taken the city like a victorious hero. For him the metropolis had opened wide its doors.

Moving slowly up Fifth Avenue, black-clad mourners followed Lincoln's coffin to Thirty-fourth Street, where the procession turned left for the Ninth Avenue train depot. The procession had taken nearly four hours. The city Lincoln had called "America's front door" mourned their victorious hero.

The funeral train left a city submerged in sorrow, its people yearning for one more glimpse of their beloved leader.

In Central Park Lindbergh mounted a short stairway while the crowd applauded. He stood tall on the stage so that the people could see him. As he spoke, the audience was overjoyed to glimpse the hero.

* * * * *

Writers sought in vain to describe the outpouring of love that engulfed Lindbergh. Yet even their failures furnished examples of the emotion he evoked.

It was an emotion that made no sense. He was a good-looking, good-natured young man who had done a brave thing. But just by looking at him people were moved to their core, and they couldn't say why. It was as if something missing had been replaced or something they didn't know they needed was given to them. They couldn't take their eyes off him. And this reaction was more than a passing fad: it lasted for decades after his flight.

Lindbergh was weary after the hoopla in Manhattan, and all the newspaper pictures (he was the most photographed man of his day).

Alexander Gardner aimed his camera lens at Abraham Lincoln, who sat rigidly upright. Glancing up for a moment, Gardner took in the full impact of the president's gaze. Lincoln's gray-blue eyes, set deep in their sockets, had an uncommon look. It was as if the man no longer existed, but was only a conduit for a greater purpose.

Lincoln waited for the photographer to finish, just as

he had done many times. He was one of the most photographed men of his day.

* * * * *

Charles Lindbergh sat in a New York hall attending a banquet in his honor. His hosts expected him to speak, but what was he supposed to talk about?

Forty years later he summed up moments like this one: "I would not have been embarrassed," he wrote, "if I had had something important to say."

Abraham Lincoln stood on a White House balcony. The hearty group on the lawn wished to hear a few words.

"I believe," Lincoln said, "that I shall never be old enough to speak without embarrassment when I have nothing to talk about."

His audience laughed appreciatively.

* * * * *

Charles Lindbergh was working on a brief chronicle of his flight that was to be published with the title *We*. Everyone wanted to hear the story of his journey from the hero himself. This book, people assured him, would help his readers understand what he went through to get to Paris.

Abraham Lincoln was preparing a brief outline of his life. Now that he was running for president, his advisors told him, people were anxious to know about him. It was important that they understand what he had gone through to reach where he was today.

* * * * *

It almost seems that the universe conspired to make Charles Lindbergh a hero.

The aviator's life was charmed. Though other airmail pilots died in accidents, Lindbergh survived several crashes. Other aviators were considered favorites to reach Paris, yet they experienced difficulties that kept them earthbound, while Lindbergh's time at the New York airfield was, by comparison, swift and seamless. Technicians were unexpectedly onsite to help him. During the muddy takeoff, his plane, though heavily loaded with gasoline, had enough momentum to rise above the telephone wires at the end of the field.

It is astonishing that Lindbergh made it to Paris at all. He could barely stay awake, made numerous heading changes, and his compasses were unreliable—yet he remained almost perfectly on course, beyond what might have been expected with everything going smoothly. And he noticed, fortunately, when ice settled on his wings in time to avoid crashing into the ocean.

Beyond that, Lindbergh's feat came at just the right moment. In the 1920s heroes were lionized with great enthusiasm. One odd fact is that on five previous occasions pilots had made the Atlantic crossing by airplane or dirigible. Yet Lindbergh's passage touched off a mass hysteria while the others did not. Not long after Lindbergh's flight, two pilots flew from New York to Germany. Their accomplishment was ignored.

Finally, Lindbergh's extraordinary rise to fame and fortune fit precisely within a small window of time, between the evolution of technology that would allow a New York-to-Paris crossing, and the stock market crash and depression that happened a few years later.

* * * * *

Everybody loved Lindbergh . . . *why?*

He was humble, unpolished, and honest, and that moved people to tears . . . *why?*

People rolled out the red carpet for him as it had never been rolled out before . . . *why?*

Who in the history of the United States gave a great gift to his country without reciprocation? Washington was appreciated during his lifetime. Jefferson was applauded for his accomplishments. Benjamin Franklin? Alexander Hamilton? John Adams?

Who else but Lincoln died with a huge Payment Due stamped on his forehead? Who else deserved, but never experienced, the reception that Lindbergh received? Only Lincoln.

Abraham Lincoln was the most beloved of all Americans, and Charles Lindbergh received the greatest outpouring of love in America's history. Lincoln's gift blessed the whole world; just so, the love that Lindbergh received was not limited to America.[1] Lindbergh was loved and admired to the same degree that Lincoln, after his death, was loved and admired.

---

[1] Abraham Lincoln is esteemed in many countries of the world, including India.

CHAPTER TEN

Coming Home

Charles Lindbergh turned his thoughts to the invitations he had received from many American cities. With the encouragement of the government and his friend Harry Guggenheim, he made plans for a three-month tour that would take him to every state in the Union. This was to be a pleasurable adventure for Lindbergh, who felt a deep, personal connection with America that amounted virtually to a proprietary interest.

Abraham Lincoln gazed at a map of his United States. The president eyed with interest the states he had yet to see. Given his wanderlust, it was only a matter of time before he visited them—yes, even far-off California.

As he rolled up the map, Lincoln determined to make such a trip as soon as his term was over.

* * * * *

Lindbergh's trip was the first time anyone had made an all-encompassing tour of America by air, and he enjoyed it immensely. He saw America from above like an angel riding a cloud: the Grand Canyon, the Great Plains, the Rocky Mountains, California, and the coastlines; rolling hills, vast grasslands, great cities, and snow-covered mountains. He breathed the air of every state through the open window of the *Spirit of St. Louis*. He reveled in America and loved it. He met millions of Americans in cities and towns across the land. Everywhere he went, the people honored him.

* * * * *

If you place a map of Lindbergh's tour of the forty-eight states next to a map that shows the route Lincoln's funeral train had taken, you will notice a similarity. At the beginning and end of Lindbergh's tour, he visited many of the same American towns, and in the same order, that had held Lincoln funerals in the previous century.

Did Lindbergh come to bring joy to places that had deeply mourned Lincoln? The ties between the two trips are strengthened when we consider that the same number of Americans saw Lindbergh on his tour and mourned Lincoln while his funeral train followed its route: thirty million.

* * * * *

During the first half of Lindbergh's national tour, he visited Springfield, Illinois . . .

President-elect Abraham Lincoln stood on the back of a railway car before a crowd of rain-streaked faces and spoke,

My friends—No one, not in my situation, can appreciate my sadness at this parting. To this place, and the kindness of these people, I owe everything. Here I have lived a quarter of a century, and have passed from a young to an old man. Here my children have been born, and one is buried. I now leave, not knowing when, or whether ever, I may return.

With a few more carefully chosen words, Lincoln left Springfield and his beloved Illinois, and never saw them again.

Congressman Isaac Arnold chronicled some of the last thoughts of Abraham Lincoln:

He spoke of his old Springfield home, and recollections of his early days—his little brown cottage, the law office, the court room, his adventures when riding the circuit—came thronging back to him. The tension under which he had lived for so long was removed, and he was like a boy out of school.

"We have laid some money by," he said to his wife, "but not enough to support us. We will go back to Illinois, and I will open a law-office at Springfield, and do enough to give us a livelihood."

Such were the dreams of Lincoln, the last day of his life.

* * * * *

As I mentioned in Chapter Two, the thoughts one holds while leaving the body have a strong influence on the details of one's future existence. If a man hungers for wealth in his last moments, for example, he will be reborn in a well-to-do family, or in a time and place where he will have opportunities to explore financial gain.

According to Arnold, some of Lincoln's final thoughts were of his home town. With this in mind, Lindbergh's connections with the town of Springfield, beginning when he was a youthful twenty-four, are intriguing.

* * * * *

The sun shone brightly on Charles Lindbergh as he rode in a shiny Lincoln automobile through the crowded streets of Springfield.

One year before, while carrying the airmail from Chicago to St. Louis, Lindbergh had enjoyed the friendships he made with the townsfolk at his scheduled stops. But he had prized Springfield more than the other stops along his route.

Recently, when planning his tour, he had gone out of his way to ensure that he would spend time there. He wanted to buzz Peoria, but stop in Springfield. And today, on August 15, 1927, he brought the *Spirit of St. Louis* down for a landing.

As the mayor of St. Louis read the telegram, his excitement grew. It appeared that the nearby city of Springfield was in need of a nicely appointed hearse for the funeral of Abraham Lincoln. Well, the mayor thought, St. Louis has one that is almost regal, a lavishly decorated carriage.

The mayor responded that it would be the honor of St. Louis to provide the transportation that returned Abraham Lincoln to his home in Springfield.

* * * * *

"Home," Lindbergh thought, as the parade car rolled along. This is what Springfield feels like. Even though I never lived here, this place is home. And that was Lindbergh's answer when, after stepping out of his aircraft, he'd been asked what it felt like to be here. He had come home.

Lindbergh's heart overflowed, and he decided to make special gestures. Even though he had denied similar requests, he allowed Springfield's residents to photograph him. And though he was supposed to stay only one hour, he almost doubled the time—cutting into his tight itinerary to give Springfield the attention he thought it merited.

As he rode slowly down Springfield's streets, Lindbergh saw welcoming posters, flags of red, white, and blue, and smiling faces. The people of Springfield had rolled out the red carpet for a pilot who, by spontaneous affection, they had adopted as their own.

When the nation elected Abraham Lincoln to a second term as president, the people of Springfield felt a glow of happiness. And as the war neared its conclusion, their pride grew. Some of Lincoln's old neighbors and friends were already looking ahead, four years hence, to the return of the beloved hero. What a glad day that would be! Streamers and flags, brass bands and fireworks, parades and speeches—Springfield was going to shoot the works!

Then came spring of 1865 and the news of Lincoln's assassination. A cloud of gloom settled over the people and many hopes were dashed. There would be no parade in Springfield.

* * * * *

Slowly the motorcade rolled along, the two flags on the sides of the automobile fluttering in the breeze. Wending through downtown Springfield, the parade passed within a few blocks of Abraham Lincoln's historic homestead. It turned down roads—Capitol Avenue, Sixth Street—that Lincoln had walked on his way to work. Directly past the law office Lincoln had shared with William Herndon, Lindbergh went, and alongside the State Capitol building where

Lincoln had given his famous House Divided speech—and where, in 1865, the president's body had lain in state.

All along the way, the people of Springfield cheered and waved and Lindbergh returned their greetings, thoroughly enjoying himself.

Ever so slowly, the parade made its way to a quiet place on the north edge of town. There, in the wooded hills, the people had laid to rest Springfield's most beloved son. Abraham Lincoln had once mentioned that he wished to be buried in what he called "a quiet place," and Mary, recalling his words, had stipulated that it should be done according to his wishes.

As Lindbergh's motorcade passed through the gates of the Oak Ridge Cemetery, he glanced up and saw the tall monument that had been erected on an elevated mound: the site of Lincoln's tomb. Sitting quietly, Lindbergh experienced the peace of the place where they had laid the great man to rest.

Lindbergh stepped out of the Lincoln car and, with a small group in procession, walked up the hill to the entrance of the memorial. There was an honor guard of black soldiers. Lindbergh smiled and nodded. The soldiers returned the gesture.

The black residents of Springfield walked solemnly in Abraham Lincoln's funeral procession, their hearts full of emotion. Many had known Lincoln personally and were proud of their association with the man who had brought freedom to their people.

At the same time, some felt slighted. They were made to walk at the end of the funeral march of the man who had showed such love for their race. Lincoln, they thought, would have done it differently. He would have given them a place of prominence.

* * * * *

In the monument's office, the aviator signed his name on the guest ledger, writing it in his habitual fashion: C. A. Lindbergh.

The president scribbled a note to save another soldier from the firing squad and handed it to the mother who had pleaded on his behalf. Glancing at the page, the woman was overjoyed to see the signature that ensured her son's safety.

The president had signed it in his usual manner: A. Lincoln.

* * * * *

Charles Lindbergh walked down the short, cool hallway that led to the place of burial. He halted at the gravesite and stooped his long, thin frame to lay a bouquet of flowers. Then he straightened and, with his calm, light-blue eyes, looked around.

Next to Lincoln were interred the remains of his wife, Mary, and his sons, Willie, Tad, and Edward. Lindbergh was unaware that, due to the threat of grave robbers, Lincoln's remains hadn't achieved a permanent rest in this spot until just a few months before Lindbergh was born.

He closed his eyes and stood for a few moments in silence.

One of his companions shuffled his feet and coughed, breaking the spell. Lindbergh took a breath, inhaling the musty air of the tomb. In a sober mood, he made his way out of the tomb, down the hill, and into the waiting car.

The Lindbergh parade backtracked to arrive in downtown Springfield, halting at the State Arsenal. In the place that honored military greatness, Lindbergh was to address the people of Springfield.

Historians have debated the best way to define the presidency of Abraham Lincoln. Some, as they pondered this question, thought of Lincoln sending telegrams to his generals, asking for updates and suggesting courses of action and attack. Of Lincoln touring battlefields and seeing fallen soldiers. Of Lincoln visiting the wounded and dying in military hospitals. Of Lincoln reviewing troops, lined up in formation.

And these historians concluded that Abraham Lincoln was the greatest war president the United States had ever known.

* * * * *

Throughout Lindbergh's visit the military made a strong showing, as represented by the National Guard, the American Legion, the Veterans of Foreign Wars, the 106th Illinois Cavalry, and the 130th Illinois Infantry. Also attending were the mayor and many prominent citizens of Springfield.

A horn sounded and the mayor and prominent citizens of Springfield turned to look. Around the corner rode General Joseph Hooker, leading a regiment of Illinois' 146th Infantry.

Lincoln's funeral march was about to begin.

* * * * *

A great cheer welcomed Lindbergh as he entered the arsenal building. After he had taken his seat, a priest opened the occasion by invoking "a blessing on heroes past and present." Then he led the crowd in the Lord's Prayer.

Next, the mayor of Springfield informed Lindbergh that "here in Springfield, the home of Lincoln, the capital of liberty, we grant you to ever know, you are welcome beyond all other places." He presented him with a gold Abraham Lincoln watch, saying, "With it goes our city's sincere best wishes."

Lindbergh's speech was on the subject dearest to his heart: aviation. He closed his talk by saying, "I thank you for your interest in the past, in me, and in airmail."

His words were followed by thunderous applause.

Abraham Lincoln's was a strange funeral. There was the weeping and sorrow that one might expect, but white cloth intertwined with the black on the buildings of Springfield.

Recent local shortages of black cloth had resulted in this odd combination. Still, all the white cloth contributed an optimistic atmosphere to an occasion of irreparable loss—as if encouraging the crowds to expect that someday, somehow, the great tragedy might be reversed or made right.

* * * * *

The people of Springfield honored Lindbergh for his historic flight and his visit. As tokens of their affection, they dubbed their little airport "Lindbergh Field." Years later, they kept the flier's memory alive by naming a park and a nearby street after him.

The Springfield residents gathered on the railroad tracks. They were dedicating the train depot from which

Lincoln had departed for Washington. From now on it would be known as the Lincoln Depot.

CHAPTER ELEVEN

The Price of Fame

Pausing before rendering a speech on commercial aviation, Charles Lindbergh looked at the audience. From the lapels of men's suits and the brims of women's hats, many circles of light reflected, identical in size. The circular pins had Lindbergh's name and image stamped upon them.

Election day, 1860. The line of voters stretched outside the Springfield courthouse and down the block. Little pins glittered like stars on many lapels, all sporting the name and face of candidate Abraham Lincoln.

* * * * *

Charles Lindbergh walked quickly away from a blaring radio. He had heard some of the many melodies written in his honor, and deplored them all, thinking them foolish. As he strode along, the corny song followed, as if to torment him.

In front of the State Capitol building in Springfield, Illinois, a band started up, intending to rehearse for the upcoming election.
The song began:

Hurrah for the choice of the nation!
Our chieftain so brave and so true;
We'll go for the great reformation,
For Lincoln and Liberty too. . . .[1]

* * * * *

A young black couple were "cuttin' the rug" on a dance floor in Harlem. It was the height of the Lindbergh era, and the hero's fame had cast a rainbow aura of bliss that made people want to celebrate.

The band was playing an energetic piece, and the couple began to improvise. No one had ever seen their moves and variations on the old standards. The other dancers stood back and clapped. Finally the song ended, and the duo, wreathed in smiles and bathed in perspiration, walked off the floor to a crescendo of applause.

"What do you call *that?*" asked one of the other dancers.

The couple looked at each other and shrugged. Suddenly, a man in the back cried out, "It's the Lindy Hop!"

Soon, bodies crowded the floor, all trying the Lindy Hop.[2] The dance caught on fast: a physical manifestation of the joy of the hour.

Abe Lincoln stopped for a moment to catch his breath. He was trying to get the hang of the clog dance the black laborers were demonstrating next to the docks of Troy, Indiana. Many doubted he would succeed.

But Lincoln's determination hardened, and, after watch-

[1]From "Lincoln and Liberty," authors unknown.
[2]In 1860, when Lincoln was running for president, one of the songs written to promote him was the "Lincoln Quick Step."

ing their movements carefully, he was finally able to copy their steps. His instructors grinned and the people cheered as Lincoln, red-faced and dripping with perspiration, finished the dance perfectly.

* * * * *

The people of America honored Lindbergh's heroic Atlantic crossing in verse. Among his many tributes, citizens dedicated to him more than five thousand worshipful poems.

The decades following Abraham Lincoln's demise produced thousands of poems written about him.

There were short poems, long poems, poems by famous writers and poems by schoolchildren. Many hundreds of muses were awakened by the inspiration of Lincoln's great life.

* * * * *

Charles Lindbergh was elevated to near-godly status. The public, observing his moral character, revered him with an almost religious devotion. They accepted each new story of his excellence with perfect faith. He had become a symbol, almost Christlike, of everything pure and uplifting.

They believed that Lindbergh was goodness itself, and that nothing could ever sully him.

On Easter morning, one day after Lincoln's passing, pastors throughout America stood at lecterns within crowded churches and told their congregations that Lincoln was a new Abraham: a father of multitudes. They spoke of his essential goodness, and pointed out that Lincoln's assassination occurred on Good Friday: considering his character, nothing could have been more appropriate.

The people bowed their heads in prayer. Abraham Lincoln had become, very nearly, an object of worship. He was the symbol of everything good and noble, and the American public knew beyond a doubt that he deserved such elevation. In decades to come, other leaders' reputations might tarnish, but Lincoln's Christlike halo would not fade.

* * * * *

Unhooking the latest medal from his lapel, Charles Lindbergh placed it in a box for safekeeping—another cross.

Lindbergh was becoming a connoisseur of crosses: Distinguished Flying Crosses, Grand Crosses, and Crosses of Honor. American crosses, and crosses from foreign lands . . . his box seemed full of them, and yet more were given to him.

Nearly everything in his life these days seemed out of place. The man with the long white beard who had pinned the latest medal on Lindbergh's breast was a famous jurist. Of the two of them, it was the legal expert who had seemed more honored by the exchange. And what logical reason could a distinguished university have for making Lindbergh an honorary Doctor of Law?

President Lincoln stared at the paper on his desk and shook his head. He was now a Doctor of Law. The Columbia College of Law had conferred the title on the president soon after he took office.

Although it was an honorary degree, Lincoln appreciated the gesture. He had spent his life studying and serving American law and justice, and this token of esteem seemed appropriate.

* * * * *

As she read the morning paper, Evangeline Lindbergh wiped the moisture from her eyes. There on the front page was a photo of her son being decorated again. This time Charles was receiving the Congressional Medal of Honor—the first noncombatant in history to do so—at the Executive Mansion, from the president himself.

Evangeline smiled through her tears. She had felt a similar pride when learning that the government had created a new medal—the Distinguished Flying Cross—so that America might present it to her son.

Abraham Lincoln studied the document in his hands. It was a good piece of legislation, one that would bring recognition to the thousands of unacknowledged heroes of the war.

And the president wrote his name, approving a bill authorizing the creation of the Congressional Medal of Honor.

* * * * *

Charles Lindbergh stared at a telegram. Another offer of riches. He had had so many such promises in the past few months that he could have become a wealthy man. As it was, the proposals he felt he could conscientiously accept would put him in a very stable financial position, one that would allow him to withstand the depression that would soon overwhelm America. He put the telegram aside for later consideration, setting it on top of the medals he'd been given in the past year.

It would be difficult to fit all his medals on one suit. And he would need a massive key ring to hold all the keys to cities he'd been given. Did the people really think that his flight was that important? Apparently they did. Although the publicity was good for aviation, the public's reaction seemed crazily excessive, to Lindbergh's orderly way of thinking.

While working on his biography of Abraham Lincoln, Isaac N. Arnold wrote:

> If Lincoln had lived, what would have been his future? Would he have passed, like other ex-presidents, soldiers, and statesmen, into comparative obscurity? How differently great public services are rewarded on the other side of the Atlantic. There, titles and wealth are sure to follow great public service. Would Lincoln, the savior of his country, have been left to earn his living by the practice of law, or would the republic have honored him and itself with honors and wealth?

* * * * *

William Randolph Hearst stared into the fireplace, where a contract had gone up in smoke. Earlier that day, Hearst had offered Charles Lindbergh half a million dollars if he would allow Hearst to produce a movie based on Lindbergh's flight. Unfortunately, Lindbergh had declined.

Hearst didn't have the best reputation—he ran a controversial newspaper empire—but he also did things for humanitarian reasons—like saving New Salem, the town Abraham Lincoln had lived in as a young man.

Hearst was a Lincoln enthusiast, and it had been a joy for him to purchase the abandoned frontier community for posterity. He was a businessman, but he had a heart. And in a spurt of generosity he sent Lindbergh a valuable pair of silver objets d'art that the pilot had admired during his visit.

* * * * *

At the age of twenty-six, Charles Lindbergh was handed that which most people prized. Fame and fortune were his . . . and he cared for them not at all. What others might spend a lifetime learning—that a high worldly role means nothing, and that one's inner spirit is everything—Lindbergh seemed to have known from the cradle. The impossible dream of the huddled masses was to him a worrisome burden.

Ward Hill Lamon listened as Abraham Lincoln paced back and forth across the White House carpet, listing the problems of his presidency.

It was clear that the president had no illusions left about the glory of fame.

* * * * *

The newspaper columnists of Lindbergh's day faced a dilemma. The problem with Lindy was that he didn't share much about himself. He talked for hours about aviation or mechanics, but regarding his personal life—his innermost feelings and aspirations—he was a cipher.

It wasn't as if the reporters hadn't tried to draw Lindy out, but the flier persisted in holding his cards close to his chest. And they had finally realized, if not accepted, that he wasn't going to change.

And so, the choice they had was to report the most bland material on America's darling, or to make stuff up. Many chose the latter course.

Some of Lincoln's friends were reminiscing about their fallen comrade.

"One thing I noticed about Lincoln," said Herndon. "He just didn't talk about himself. He was a man of infinite silences. The word shut-mouthed sums him up. In fact, I'd go so far as to say that he was thoroughly and deeply secretive, uncommunicative, and close minded as to his wishes, hopes, and fears. He received everybody's confidences and rarely gave his own in return."

"From what I recall," added Leonard Swett, "he always told only enough of his plans to induce the belief that he had communicated everything, yet he reserved enough to have communicated nothing. He told all that was unimportant with a gushing frankness, yet no man ever kept his real purposes closer."

The men nodded their heads in silent agreement.

* * * * *

Charles Lindbergh was a world-renowned celebrity, and his instinctive reaction was to control the situation. He would decide what was written about him and surrender to the press only what was absolutely necessary. Although the media often circumvented this agenda, Lindbergh applied it diligently throughout his life.

Abraham Lincoln sat in the White House discussing a problem with Secretary of War Edwin Stanton. The situation—a democracy struggling through a civil war—was unprecedented, and called for careful consideration. Catastrophe loomed, given the freedom of the press. One piece of information casually printed could spell the difference between a

Union victory or defeat.

Lincoln and Stanton decided to strictly control the flow of information to the newspapers. By maintaining a heightened security, perhaps they could avoid disaster.

* * * * *

Fame, of course, also has its benefits. This is true even on a spiritual level, for it offers opportunities to give . . .

Charles Lindbergh crossed the wide driveway and shook hands with the man waiting for him. "Well, Paul, here it is!" he said, casually gesturing at the large object behind him. Paul Garber, who was later to become the first curator of the aeronautic branch of the Smithsonian Museum, beamed.

It was Garber's influence that led to today's great moment. Looking over Lindbergh's shoulder, he saw what he knew would be a star attraction at the Smithsonian for years to come. Lindbergh had generously donated his best-loved aircraft, the *Spirit of St. Louis,* for perpetual display.

Lincoln also had a positive connection with a Smithsonian official . . .

Abraham Lincoln turned to Joseph Henry, the first secretary of the Smithsonian Institution. The president had developed a rapport with Henry based on their mutual interest in science. During the visit, a man accused Henry of treasonous support of the Confederacy. Lincoln manufactured a frown to tease the professor, and Henry saw through the facade.

Lincoln spoke sternly: "Well, Henry. What about it?"

Somehow the scientist kept a straight face throughout his inquisition and held it in place until the suspicious man left the room.

CHAPTER TWELVE

Anne

Charles Lindbergh glanced out the window of his aircraft. He was on his way to Mexico City, where President Calles and Ambassador Dwight Morrow had invited him to visit.

After his arrival, the Lone Eagle took the Mexican president for his first airplane ride. He also attended the opening of a Lincoln Library and a bullfight, where he had a front-row seat with the Stars and Stripes draped in front of him.

President Lincoln walked through the audience at Ford's Theater. In moments he was seated in a balcony adorned with the American flag and a Treasury flag with a large, lone eagle splayed across it, wings spread wide as if in flight.

* * * * *

At the bullfight, Lindbergh sat next to Will Rogers, who was also visiting Mexico City.

Rogers had a curious history. He was born in a log cabin, and was a newspaper columnist as well as a political comedian. His style was casual; he shared wise and witty thoughts in a down-home manner. Although some of his verbal jabs hit hard, he was patriotic.

Rogers had a Western prairie accent, and he laughed at his own jokes. He had encouraged people to pray for Lindbergh during the flight to Paris, and, when they met, they recognized each other as kindred spirits. For his part, Lindbergh thoroughly enjoyed Rogers's sense of humor. They became lifelong friends.

Abraham Lincoln laughed so hard that he almost dropped the book he held. He got a kick out of Petroleum Nasby and often read the humorist's writings when the pain of war struck most deeply.

Lincoln first met Nasby (David Locke) in Quincy, Illinois, and liked him immediately. Nasby was a newspaper reporter as well as a humorist, and his outlook on life and politics jibed with Lincoln's. Lincoln thought so highly of Nasby that he said he'd give anything to write like him. The two men stayed friends throughout their lives.

Lincoln also had a comedic gift—evoking belly laughs with his droll outlook on the goings-on in Washington and elsewhere. Then, too, his laughter at his own jokes was infectious. He looked at America and its people and, with his Midwestern drawl, lightly poked fun at their foibles.

* * * * *

Charles Lindbergh was enjoying Mexico City. He liked visiting with the Morrow family. They had traits he could appreciate, and an interesting history.

Mr. Morrow had been in the banking industry, having worked with J.P. Morgan and Associates for many years. Within the Morrow family tree were distinguished lawyers and statesmen. Furthermore, the Morrows were people of high character. There was a refinement and sobriety in the parents, and a natural simplicity in the children, that Lindbergh found charming. And it seemed the ambassador was taken with Lindbergh.

Abe Lincoln sighed as he sat on the front porch of the Rutledge Tavern. This place, he decided, was a home away from home.

He liked Mr. and Mrs. Rutledge and their daughter Ann. In fact, he liked the entire Rutledge family. They were good people, with a sober quality that he admired. And they came from a refined background, which Lincoln—whose parents were low on the social scale—could appreciate.

The Rutledges counted a governor and several judges among their relatives and ancestors. And Mr. Rutledge had a good head for business. His tavern did well in the rustic confines of New Salem.

Also, Mr. Rutledge returned Abe's esteem. He had chaired some of the literary society meetings Lincoln attended, and had spoken encouragingly of Lincoln's speaking ability and potential.

* * * * *

As I said earlier, our close relations in this life have been close in the past. In that case, Lindbergh must have known Anne Morrow before. Was it possible he had known her in his lifetime as Lincoln? If so, who was she in that life?

One might assume that a reincarnated soul will marry the same woman in successive incarnations, but this isn't always the case. Plus, it hardly seems likely from what we know of Lincoln that he would have wanted to marry Mary Todd again, or necessary for him to have done so.

Anne Morrow—her writing, thinking, and personality—doesn't seem a match for Mary Todd. They share a few superficial qualities, but their natures are too dissimilar. And even the similarities might be attributed to Lincoln-Lindbergh's taste in women.

I was beginning to wrestle with this dilemma when a friend suggested another idea . . . is it possible that Ann Rutledge (Lincoln's first sweetheart) reincarnated as Anne Morrow?

Perhaps there is more here than just a coincidence of name. We will study this possibility as we go along . . .

* * * * *

Anne Morrow listened as Charles Lindbergh tore her sister's argument to pieces. She was startled by this side of Charles—the way he marshaled his facts, point after point, each unanswerable, indisputable in its logic. He defended his position with such ease, then attacked with so much verve and humor, that you were forced to agree with him—or wanted to strangle him—or both. Poor Elisabeth was completely deflated, while Anne found herself unable to speak.

President Lincoln looked solemnly at the card in his hand, then at the job applicant who sat before him. He spoke.

"You say you want a job as House doorkeeper?"

"Yes, sir," the man replied.

"Have you any past experience in doorkeeping?"

"No, sir."

"Have you studied doorkeeping in school?"

"No. I can't say that I have."

"Are you familiar with the *theory* of doorkeeping?"

"No."

"Then, perhaps, you have read the recommended texts on the art and science of doorkeeping?"

"No, sir. I'm sorry to say that I haven't."

"Well then," said Lincoln, as he came to the final thrust of his argument, "wouldn't you have to agree that you are severely underqualified to serve as House doorkeeper?"

"Yes, sir," the man stammered, "I guess I would have to, at that."

The applicant left, chance victim to the razor-sharp humor and arguing skills that had served Lincoln so well in the Illinois county courthouses. There, his opposition learned to its dismay that Lincoln's reasoned arguments were so pithy and forceful as to be virtually unanswerable.

* * * * *

Charles Lindbergh was at dinner at the embassy when the sounds of guitars and voices wafted in on the evening air. He allowed the ambassador to steer him to the front door, where he said a quick hello to a small group of Mexicans, then upstairs and through the French doors.

Lindbergh stood on the balcony of a building that resembled the White House and scanned the crowd. Many people had assembled to serenade him. When they spotted him, they cheered and called his name affectionately. He heard several songs, then bid them good night.

"They're out there again, Mr. President," John Hay said. Lincoln looked up. He was seated on a couch, where he'd been relaxing with an after-dinner book.

"Another serenade?"

"Yes, sir."

The president put aside the volume and angled himself to his feet. "You lead the way, John."

The crowd on the White House lawn was in a festive mood. When Lincoln stepped through the French window, a cry of delight went up. After an extended cheer, Lincoln raised his hand for silence. He spoke of the brave soldiers and their commanders on the field of battle. Then, calling for a rousing cheer on their behalf, he bade them good night.

* * * * *

Anne Morrow sat at the dinner table, despairing. The dashing Colonel Lindbergh was paying more attention to Anne's older sister Elisabeth than to her. Of course it was a foregone conclusion that he would like Elisabeth more. Soon they would be going out together. Anne could see it happening. And she would be left out and forgotten.

It always happened that way. Even though she loved her sister, Anne hated this aspect of their relationship. Elisabeth always outshone her. It just wasn't fair.

Mary Todd sat in her sister Elizabeth's parlor and studied the man who had come to see her. Although she had been spending time with Stephen Douglas, lately she was feeling more drawn to the taller, awkward man who sat on her left. True, it wasn't that long ago that Mr. Lincoln had courted her older sister Frances, but that wasn't necessarily a bad thing. Perhaps Frances had interesting things to say about this intriguing man who couldn't keep his eyes off her.

* * * * *

Charles Lindbergh gunned his engine, then took off from Mexico City. He was bound for other Central and South American countries to dine with their generals, governors, and foreign ministers.

As he flew, he began to think that it was time he found a wife. He had met quite a few young women in his travels. Many had been attractive, but he hadn't fallen for any of them. If he had, he would have begun his courtship, no matter her skin color. It was the individual he cared about, not her racial background.

* * * * *

Lindbergh mentally reviewed the many eligible young women who had smiled coquettishly at him while shaking his hand. They all seemed so superficial, so silly, so frivolous! Not for me, he thought.

In the woods of Indiana, a youth watched his friend Abe Lincoln whittle away at a piece of wood.
"You got a girlfriend yet, Abe?"
Lincoln looked at his friend and blushed.
"Naw."
"How come?"
"They're too frivolous!"

* * * * *

Lindbergh had preferences regarding the woman he wished to share his life with. He knew instinctively what he wanted. More important, he knew what he *didn't* want. For one thing, his future bride should come from healthy stock. There should be, for example, no instances of mental illness in the family.

As Lindbergh banked his aircraft, he mused that it would be best to make sure before he committed himself to any young lady. Above all, it was important that he not allow himself, in a time of emotional vulnerability, to be lulled into a mistake by a pretty face.

Abraham Lincoln cut a comical figure as he ran, bobbing and weaving, through the backyards of Springfield. He glanced behind him. His wife—still clutching a butcher knife and with a maniacal gleam in her eye—was gaining on him.

Mary was ill, he knew. A weakness in her mind or constitution had left her with the tendency to become hysterical over the least little thing. It made her exceedingly difficult to live with, but there was no use griping over what couldn't be helped. Still, there were times when he wished that he had had the sense years ago to step back and see through Mary's good looks to the emotional imbalance that boiled beneath.

* * * * *

Another thing vital to Lindbergh was that his future bride be truthful. He needed to be able to depend on her word without hesitation. He didn't think he could live with someone who might lie to him.

Lincoln was furious. He had just discovered through conversation with a Springfield merchant that his wife had run up a large bill while he was away. And just that morning Mary had assured him that she was strictly following the budget they had agreed on.

Lincoln flushed with rage. He expected people to lie when he cross-examined them in the courtroom, but he never expected such treatment from his wife! How could he live with someone whose word he couldn't trust? Of all the misfortunes man could fall prey to, an unstable spouse who lied must rank among the highest.

* * * * *

As he flew into the night, one young woman's image flitted repeatedly through Lindbergh's mind. For some reason Anne Morrow had left a mark on him.

Anne lay awake in bed, hugging her pillow. She couldn't stop thinking of Colonel Lindbergh. The young pilot with the serious demeanor and wry sense of humor had made a lasting impression.

A young man held his beloved's hand and kissed it. Her life was fading, and it was time to say what was in his heart. He spoke of his undying love and the troth they had pledged each other. Perhaps, if God was good, they would find each other in the life after death.

She looked at him. Unable to speak, a light came into her eyes. Though it cost her pain, she nodded her head. And Abe Lincoln knew that Ann Rutledge had committed herself to the vow he had spoken.[1]

* * * * *

The evidence seems to suggest that Anne Morrow was Ann Rutledge in a past life.

Some of Lincoln's contemporaries believed that he never stopped loving Ann. He himself said, late in life, that he loved and would have married her. And Herndon maintained that Lincoln nearly went mad when she died. It makes sense that these sundered lovers would come together again in their next lives.

Not only is it poetic and karmically appropriate, but the desire for fulfillment in love with a particular person must

---

[1]This anecdote is based on William Herndon's supposition that Lincoln and Rutledge exchanged lovers' vows at their last meeting.

be worked out, like any other desire.

* * * * *

Lindbergh continued his tour of Central and South America. The capital cities went by in a blur, but the scenario remained much the same. He switched off his engine and his plane was engulfed by huge crowds of enthusiastic natives, barely held in check by police or soldiers. A band played the "Star-Spangled Banner" and high officials handed him bouquets, escorting him to a large, open automobile decorated with an American flag. They drove down the main route of the city with thousands of people lining the street, shouting and waving. His escorts dropped him off at a palace or government residence, where he met the ruler who decorated him with a symbol of the nation's esteem. Then he gave a speech. After a sumptuous meal, he attended an entertainment, or inspected the troops. Finally, making excuses related to his itinerary, he boarded his plane with invitations to return any time that suited his plans.

If Lincoln hadn't been killed, how would he have spent his later years?

Certainly he had plans to return to his law practice and to travel. Was it also possible that he, like Lindbergh, might have become an unofficial ambassador to other countries? Such a role would have been his anyway if he, a former president, were to have visited France, England and Germany as he'd planned. He would have been asked to meet heads of state, attend formal banquets, and the rest.

Even though Lincoln, at the beginning of his second presidency, was already looking forward to some time off, we can imagine him swiftly losing interest in petty legal squabbles.

After his White House duties, he would have been about sixty years old and still vigorous. Perhaps, like Benjamin Franklin, he might have served his country into his eighties.

* * * * *

To many people, the military aspects of Lindbergh's visits would have become monotonous. Almost everywhere he went, soldiers stood at attention, rode horses in his parade, or guarded him as he spoke. Generals, admirals, and enlisted men saluted and honored him. Secretaries of war and navy shook his hand, sent army fighters to accompany his airplane, and eagerly invited him to inspect guns, planes, and ships.

Abraham Lincoln sat uneasily atop his galloping horse. While passing the front ranks of a company of soldiers, he was having trouble with his mount. It was all he could do to stay in the saddle.

The soldiers struggled to keep from laughing. Seeing their leader's simplicity, they loved him all the more for it.

CHAPTER THIRTEEN

Marriage

Charles watched Anne as she slipped into the automobile. She was attractive in a shy sort of way—with her dark hair, blue eyes, and pale skin. Anne was petite, standing only five feet two and slim of build. She was delicate like a china doll. She was twenty-two, and he was twenty-six.

Charles knew Anne was the one for him. He was going to ask her to marry him.

Tonight. On their second date.

Abe Lincoln sat next to Ann Rutledge as they ate a picnic in the fields of New Salem. Abe openly stared at Ann as she ate. She was a delicate beauty, with auburn hair and blue eyes, slender and not too tall at five feet two inches. She was twenty-two years old, and he was twenty-six.

Ann was everything Abe had dreamed of. And he was going to ask her to marry him.

* * * * *

Dwight Morrow was filled with concern. He had just heard that Charles Lindbergh wanted his daughter's hand in marriage, and this sudden announcement made him review his opinion of his potential son-in-law. In his own mind and to others, he began asking pointed questions about Charles. He doubted that Charles was worthy of his daughter. Charles and Anne came from two different worlds.

It was past midnight, and Abraham Lincoln sat alone in his law office, staring at his desk. He had asked Mary Todd to marry him, but Mary's family, including her father, opposed the engagement. They had cruel things to say about his family and his lack of a future. Clearly, he was not worthy of a Todd. Mary stood up for him, saying that he was going to be president someday. But her relatives refused to back down. It was up to them, they said, to look after her welfare, and they could not agree to this unwise betrothal. Obviously, the pair did not suit each other.

* * * * *

Charles and Anne stood before a minister in the house of Anne's parents. After his years in the public eye, Charles was sensitive to the public's unquenchable thirst for information. It was best, he said, that they marry in a secure place, surrounded by a handful of loved ones. He felt much safer celebrating this special occasion at a private location. Afterward, they would announce their marriage as a *fait accompli* to a world taken by surprise.

"I now pronounce you man and wife!"

The minister smiled his blessings as Abraham and Mary sealed their union with a brief, chaste kiss. The small gathering of friends and relatives applauded appreciatively. The ceremony had been an entertaining one, marked by the groom's nervousness.

Lincoln sighed. He was finally married. But there were disruptions from the start of their courtship. So they kept their meetings secret and held a spur-of-the-moment wedding ceremony in the home of Mary's sister.

And he was glad of these decisions. The world wasn't safe. It was best to keep these developments from public scrutiny—and to see the surprise on their friends' faces afterward, when they were told of the knot already tied.

* * * * *

Charles Lindbergh smiled at his wife. Anne was charming and sweet—and intelligent. She had attended Smith College, where she had majored in English literature. She was quite a scholar, and spoke passable French. Charles was aware that Anne had prominent individuals in her ancestry, and that Anne's father had been a well-to-do banker, as well as a U.S. ambassador.

Abraham Lincoln gazed at his wife and smiled. Mary was vivacious, attractive, the life and soul of any social gathering. And smart, too. A tutor had educated her at home, and she had received secondary schooling at a time when women normally did not. She was knowledgeable in many subjects and could converse quite easily in French. And it didn't hurt that her family was so prominent. Her father was a bank president; before long, he would be a U.S. senator. And in her family tree there were governors as well as a Revolutionary War general.

Lincoln tended to feel attracted to intelligent women. Ann Rutledge had been a scholar, too, having attended the Jacksonville Female Academy.

As she sat next to her husband, Mary Lincoln may well have wondered what life with her lawyer-husband would be like. Would he, for instance, use courtroom terminology in everyday conversations?

Anne Morrow Lindbergh smiled her pleasure at her husband. Charles had a rare sense of humor. Just now he had crowed that "the family, the whole family, and nothing but the family" had been present at their wedding ceremony.

* * * * *

Charles and Anne Lindbergh, on their honeymoon, held each other while fighting the rocking motion of their boat. After only a few days, the reporters had found them. Charles refused their demands for an interview and photos, asking only that they be left in peace, and one of the stymied reporters had begun running his launch around the couple's vessel. Anne felt harassed. Charles was incensed.

Setting his jaw, Charles made his way forward to the control station and the ignition switch.

Abraham Lincoln, Secretary of War Edwin Stanton, and Secretary of State William Steward were in the War Department discussing a distressing situation. A pair of New York newspapers had made the mistake of printing a forged letter by someone purporting to be the president. During the meeting with Stanton and Seward, Lincoln ordered the arrest and imprisonment of "the editors, proprietors, and publishers" of the offending papers.

* * * * *

Click. Pop. Clack.

The photographers fell over themselves trying to get the best picture. This was their chance to get the Lindberghs on film, and they didn't want to waste it.

As they framed their shots, the reporters noticed the

marked difference in height between the pair. Charles stood six feet three inches tall, with his clear, direct gaze, while Anne, about twelve inches shorter, had dark hair and a pleasant smile.

In Pennsylvania Station, on their way to the White House, Mary Todd Lincoln exited the rear door of the caboose and stood next to her husband at the railing. Side by side the couple waved to the people, who smiled at the sight of the tall president-elect, at nearly six feet four inches, standing beside his dark-haired wife, who was a foot shorter.

Mr. Lincoln told the crowd, "Now you've seen the long and the short of it!"

* * * * *

The newlyweds had flown to Haiti, and Anne was riding slowly with her husband in an open-topped vehicle down the main street of Port-au-Prince. As they went along, she was struck by the ebony-skinned multitude that surrounded them. She and Charles would have looked strange from overhead: the light-colored heart of a surging throng. But the most memorable thing was the love the Haitians were showering on her husband.[1]

It was the evening of New Year's Day, 1865, and a reporter from the New York Independent was recalling what had occurred earlier that day at the White House. It was a spectacle that touched his heart.

[1]Lincoln's Springfield barber, William Florville, was Haitian. In addition, Lincoln was the first American president to receive an ambassador from that country.

The president had grown weary of greeting visitors, when he noticed a group of black folk who had waited timidly for hours to be with him. When he saw them, he advanced forward and welcomed them with such heartiness that they became wild with joy. They laughed and wept—exclaiming, through blinding tears: "God bless you! God bless Abraham Lincoln! God bress Massa Linkum!"

The reporter smiled. He could still see the president surrounded by those black men and women, rejoicing with them.

* * * * *

A strange man had just been spotted on the Lindbergh property, and Charles Lindbergh was discussing security with his friend, Donald Keyhoe.

"You've got a real problem here," Keyhoe said. "There are plenty of unscrupulous people who'd like nothing better than to get in the news by associating with you. You have to think not only of yourself, but of your wife and your baby boy."

"No. I won't have it. How can Anne and I relax with guards toting guns around the place? What sort of home would that be? I'll tell you what. We'll get a dog, but no guards."

Keyhoe shrugged. "Suit yourself."

The Lindberghs tried this strategy for awhile, but eventually they followed Keyhoe's advice and hired a guard.

"Does he have to sit there like that?"

Abraham Lincoln was talking with his friend and bodyguard, Ward Hill Lamon, about a cavalry officer stationed at the White House gates.

"You need protection, Mr. President. You and your

family both."

"I know. But, it's just that I feel so uncomfortable with him sitting there. I'm a president, not an emperor.

"I'm sorry, Hill, but he has to go."

Lincoln fought against keeping guards, but ultimately he surrendered to the logic of his friend's argument.

* * * * *

"Oh, Charles!"

Anne Lindbergh held a piece of paper gingerly, as if it were dipped in sewage. Charles took one quick look at the death threat and shoved it into his pocket.

It was just one piece of hate mail among many that they had received.

"Soon after I was nominated," President Lincoln told Francis Carpenter, "I began to receive letters threatening my life. The first few made me uncomfortable, but so many have come my way that they have ceased to bother me."

Carpenter shook his head. "How can you remain so calm when you know that people are wishing you dead?"

Lincoln smiled. "There's nothing like getting used to things!"

* * * * *

The baby was gone. Little Charles had been kidnapped, and the Lindbergh home was converted into a police barracks, with troopers camping out in the living room and Charles Sr. in conference upstairs with detectives and police officers.

For her part, Mrs. Lindbergh stayed in her room as

much as possible. The martial atmosphere, in addition to the loss and worry, threatened to overwhelm her.

America was embroiled in a civil war, and the White House had abandoned any pretense of a family residence. It was impossible to hold that illusion while soldiers camped in the downstairs rooms, uniformed men roamed the halls, troops set up tents in the yard, and military bigwigs met with Mr. Lincoln from dawn until dusk.

For the most part, Mrs. Lincoln stayed in the private apartments set aside for her and the children. Later, she went on a shopping trip to New York to get away from it all.

* * * * *

Anne Morrow Lindbergh shut her eyes. She was unfamiliar with seances, but if there was the slightest chance that this medium could locate her boy, or say if he were alive, then it was worth it.

Closing her eyes, Mary Todd Lincoln prepared herself for the seance. Her son Willie had died, and she was asking a spiritualist to help her communicate with her lost boy. Although seance messages were often vague, she wanted to do it anyway. Anything was better than silence.

Seated across the table, her husband looked at her sadly and shook his head.

* * * * *

Charles Lindbergh looked at his son's remains. Others had identified the body, but he had come to the mortuary to confirm their statements.

As he gazed at the pitiful form, he remembered his little boy. He said a prayer for his spirit and wished him peace.

Abraham Lincoln gazed at the body of his son. Willie had been buried days before, but Lincoln felt the loss so keenly that he opened the casket once more so that he might see Willie's features again. His poor boy, Lincoln wept. His poor little boy. How he missed him. He said a prayer, imploring God to grant Willie peace.

Little Willie Lincoln had died in the White House of typhoid fever, and it was a crushing blow. His mother was devastated; but for Lincoln, too, the bereavement was intense. And it was difficult to comfort his wife and continue with his duties while ensconced in the public eye. It took all his strength just to get out of bed in the morning and go to work. But he set aside time every Thursday for grieving.

Willie had been special from the start, born less than a year after Eddie's death, almost as if volunteering to take his brother's place. He was also the apple of his father's eye. He was like a miniature version of him; the son unconsciously mimicked his father. If ever the ideal father-and-son relationship was manifest on earth, it had been theirs.

And now, after so few years together, death had stolen Willie away. For a long while, Lincoln could scarcely bear the loss, until a Christian minister reminded him of the biblical teaching that all souls live after death. After this, he no longer wept for his boy, and the thought of death didn't disturb him nearly so much. But he still missed Willie, and dreamed of him at night.

Lindbergh's son was dead. Charles Jr. had died of a head wound during the kidnapping attempt.

Fame had dealt a grievous blow, but Lindbergh

weathered the storm with unexpected strength. He turned his energies toward helping the authorities locate the guilty parties, and to comforting his wife, who was devastated. Although Anne grieved for many years, and on some level never got over the death of her boy, Charles rebounded more quickly. It wasn't all that long before he felt the joy of living once again. Still, it had been difficult to lose a son and launch a doomed attempt to retrieve him while in the public gaze.

Part of what broke the spell of bereavement for the Lindberghs was the arrival soon after of Jon. The new baby stirred Anne from a quagmire of shock and grief. As Jon grew, he brought a special pleasure to his father as well.

Little Jon's nature was very much in harmony with his dad's. The two were often seen playing, working, or just spending time together. In some ways, the son imitated his father. Happily, their relationship spanned more than four decades, until Charles's passing in 1974.

* * * * *

It was no use. The Lindberghs had to get away from that house. For the sake of Anne's sanity, they needed a break from Hopewell, with its reminders of Charles, Jr. While they started looking for a new place to live, they set up a temporary camp at the home of Anne's mother.

It was no good. The Lincolns had to get out of the building. The White House held too many depressing reminders of Willie. For the sake of Mary's sanity, especially, it was necessary that they find another place to live until their grief abated.

Fortunately, the president found such a place: a pleasant cottage near the Soldiers' Home, several miles from downtown Washington, seemed an ideal respite for the grieving couple.

* * * * *

Charles Lindbergh was reading in his room in Anne's mother's house, when a maid knocked on the door and asked if it was all right for her to dust. He agreed, and while the maid worked, he put down his book and spoke with her. By the time she left the room, Lindbergh had made another friend among the servants, much to the dismay of Anne's mother.

Seeing the black servant girl carrying a load of laundry behind the Lincoln home, Mrs. Lincoln rose and followed her.

Mary Todd was used to domestics; in her childhood home in Lexington, their family had had a full staff.

But Mr. Lincoln had an unusual approach to servants. He was very considerate, and treated them not merely as people, but as friends.

Maybe some of this rubbed off on Mary, for over time she became more caring and thoughtful. She was determined to talk to this new girl, inquire after her situation, and lend any aid she could.

* * * * *

During the trial of Bruno Richard Hauptmann, the accused kidnapper, Charles Lindbergh sat in the witness box and gave his testimony. He was perfectly calm and poised and answered each question with a simplicity that permitted no question as to his integrity. In the courtroom, he radiated a self-confidence and authority beyond belief.

After a difficult session, the defending attorney, Edward J. Reilly, ended the cross-examination. Clearly, it had been foolish to call Charles Lindbergh to the stand as a hostile witness.

One reporter laughed into his hand. Leaning over, he told a crony, "I think *Reilly* withstood the cross-examination very well."

At a public debate, the audience broke into enthusiastic applause. In his speech Abraham Lincoln had answered Stephen Douglas's charges in a masterful manner.

As the crowd dispersed, an old woman remarked, "When Douglas first began to speak, I felt sorry for Lincoln. But now, after hearing Lincoln, I feel sorry for *Douglas!*"

CHAPTER FOURTEEN

Odes of the Spirit

Charles Lindbergh approved a plan that he and Anne had debated. Although living in the States had its advantages, the situation had spiraled out of control. It was only a few years after the discovery of their first son's body, and already they were receiving death threats against Jon. For the sake of everyone's well-being, it seemed wise to embark for Europe, stopping first in England. (The Lindberghs' brother-in-law, Aubrey Morgan, lived in Wales).

Charles and Anne hoped to be treated better in the Old World, and both were interested in distant lands. It would be a kind of extended vacation, a respite from the American media-machine.

To a large degree, their wish came true. As they settled in their new home in England, they began to enjoy themselves again.

At the end of his first term of office, Abraham Lincoln shared with Ward Hill Lamon his plans for the future.

"I hope that I may never have another four years of such tribulation and abuse," he said. "My only ambition is to put down the rebellion and restore peace; after which I want to go abroad, take some rest, study foreign governments, see something of foreign life, and in my old age die in peace with the good will of all of God's creatures."

* * * * *

Since the death of his firstborn, Charles Lindbergh had thought about spirituality with a deeper intensity. He contemplated the possibilities of immortality and wondered about that area where physical and spiritual bodies meet. It seemed to him, from conversations he'd had, that the Himalayan yogis understood these questions, and he decided to investigate the subject. Luckily, there were books on yogis in a London library.

With the death of Willie, Mary Todd Lincoln noticed that her husband had begun to think more about the spiritual realm. He talked about the afterlife and scanned the Bible for references. He was especially intrigued by stories relating to how the material and spiritual worlds meet in visions or dreams.

* * * * *

Anne Morrow Lindbergh smiled. Charles and Jon were reciting the introduction to "The Shooting of Dan McGrew" by Robert Service:

> "A bunch of the boys were whooping it up in the Malamute
> saloon;
> The kid that handles the music-box was hitting a jag-time tune. . . ."

Abner Ellis was recalling the words to a song Lincoln liked to repeat to the boys in New Salem. He used to stand in front of the gang in that store he kept, and recite from memory:

The first factional fight in old Ireland, they say,
Was all on account of Saint Patrick's birthday,
It was somewhere about midnight without any doubt,
And certain it is, it made a great rout. . . .

* * * * *

Charles Lindbergh loved Robert Service above all other poets. Service's verses were about the rough life on the Alaskan frontier. They consisted of stark tales of daring the elements, combined with a childlike wonder at the beauty of nature.

Even the titles of Service's poems reflected these themes: "The Lone Trail," "The Woodcutter," and "The Little Old Log Cabin."

Abe Lincoln channeled his muse onto a sheet of paper. His was a poem that captured the life of the woodsman. It had to do with the great outdoors and spoke of the grandeur of nature, the nearness of death, and the hardiness of men who dared to live in the rough frontier.

It was titled "The Bear Hunt":

A wild-bear chase, didst never see?
    Then hast thou lived in vain.
Thy richest bump of glorious glee,
    Lies desert in thy brain.

When first my father settled here,
    'Twas then the frontier line:
The panther's scream, filled night with fear
    And bears preyed on the swine.

But woe for Bruin's short lived fun,
    When rose the squealing cry;
Now man and horse, with dog and gun,
    For vengeance, at him fly. . . .

* * * * *

Charles Lindbergh recalled the first time he was introduced to Robert Service's work, back when he was young. He'd been paging through the *Minneapolis Tribune* when he spotted an article. The writer quoted "The Cremation of Sam McGee," and Charles enjoyed it so much that he memorized that poem and "Dangerous Dan McGrew," which was to become his favorite. It was about life and death, but it was also humorous, and it gave him joy to recite it to himself and his son.

Abe Lincoln stared at a Midwestern newspaper. On the page was a poem that spoke to his soul. The author (William Knox) had expressed clearly and poignantly the ephemeral quality of life that Lincoln often mused on. It was, he decided, a masterpiece.

In years to come, Lincoln would memorize "Mortality" and recite it to himself and his friends. It would become his favorite poem.[1]

---

[1] A friend, Dr. Jason Duncan, first gave Lincoln this poem to read. But it was while reading it a second time in a newspaper years later that Lincoln felt a deep connection.

CHAPTER FIFTEEN

Rumors of War

At one point during this study, I ran into a proverbial brick wall. Questions had been gnawing at me since the beginning of the investigation, and I had to answer them before I could go any further.

Why did Lindbergh, who embraced nonviolence but was not a pacifist, take a stand against America's helping to stop Hitler? And why, during an address he made at Des Moines, Iowa, in September 1941, did Lindbergh speak against the Jews?

These incongruities made me seriously doubt that Lindbergh had been a reincarnation of the Great Emancipator.

How could a soul of Lincoln's quality not recognize the evil of Nazism? And why would he do an about-face from one lifetime to the next—promoting a righteous war as Lincoln, then fighting adamantly against one as Lindbergh?

Meditating on these questions, I knew that I could not finish this project until I had found answers that fully satisfied me. And I wondered whether there were answers to be found.

However, a return to the history books unearthed facts of Lincoln's life that seemed to intersect perfectly with my questions about Lindbergh, like pieces of a jigsaw puzzle. The connections were logical and profound; eventually, they silenced my doubts.

Proceeding with Lindbergh's life, let us review some of the events that led up to World War II . . .

Charles Lindbergh read the letter he'd been sent, considering it carefully. The Nazis had asked him to make an inspection tour of their facilities in Germany, the invitation having come through the U.S. diplomatic corps.

He didn't think long—of course he would go. His answer was prompted by patriotism. America might go to war with Germany in the near future. If such a terrible event came to pass, it behooved America to know as much as possible about its enemy's strengths.

Lindbergh deeply identified with America and worried about its future. Therefore, he intended to act as his nation's eyes and ears and report back everything he learned. He would absorb the information obligingly supplied by the Luftwaffe and infuse it into his understanding of the Nazi war machine. He would become, in a short space of time, an expert on the German capacity to wage war in the air.

And he would later register shock when the authorities yawned over his findings.

President Lincoln read intelligence reports on Confederate arsenals, supplies, and manpower. He was anxious to know as much as possible about the Confederate situation.

Lincoln had perfected this tactic in his law office. While preparing a case, he had studied the opponent's position with greater energy than his own. He believed that a clear understanding of the other side was vital to success. In front of the jury, he often pleaded the opposing side better than the opposition could before he unraveled it. He'd seldom known this technique to fail.

Now, he was president. In many ways, he identified with his country. Its survival was paramount. And so he adopted the approach that had worked in the courtrooms. And it worked again.

His success in this grand undertaking solidified the habit to such a degree that it is probable that, if ever in future he was confronted by a hazard, he would turn to it immediately, without thinking.

* * * * *

The Nazi general came to a halt. Turning, he lifted his arm and spread his hand in a gesture of pride. Behind him, Lindbergh saw a fleet of bombers stretching into the distance. He watched as a crew worked on the plane nearest him. Their energy and stamina were noteworthy, and this was but the latest example of Teutonic industry he had seen.

In spite of their leaning toward war, Lindbergh commended the Germans for their industry and will power. Not very long ago, Germany had been devastated—driven to its knees in the aftermath of the Great War. They had turned things around in a remarkably short time, and Lindbergh thought that worthy of praise.

Little did he know how much trouble and misunderstanding his admiration would bring.

"Goo-ten tock."

Abraham Lincoln smiled as he tried to pronounce the German words that Henry Remann was teaching him.

"Ja! Sehr gut. You will learn quickly, I think."

Mr. Remann lived on the same street as the Lincolns, and he and his wife often visited them, sometimes bringing their daughter Josie, of whom Lincoln was particularly fond.

Lincoln enjoyed the company of German people, and they seemed to feel the same way about him. One of his presidential secretaries, John Nicolay, hailed from Bavaria. And once, while on a trip with a friend in Illinois, he was pleased that they had to stop for the evening in the town of Highland, because he had heard reports that it was "a little Germany." The Highland residents received him as one of their own.

Lincoln believed in self-effort as the means of achieving prosperity. He was always for those who were willing to work, and it may be that he liked the Germans because they were industrious, efficient, and able to focus their minds on their goals. For whatever reason, he thought they represented the best of the ethnic groups that had made their home in America.

* * * * *

Anne Morrow Lindbergh was surprised. While her husband was performing an invaluable service by going to Germany and sharing his findings with the government, many Americans were criticizing him and giving the credit for his work to the U.S. Embassy.

Anne bristled at the unfairness, but Charles shrugged it off. He didn't mind if the embassy got the credit. The important thing was that vital information had been sent to those who needed to know.

"Dear General Meade, . . ."

President Lincoln paused. He wanted to give Meade an order, but worried about the ramifications of following that order. How could he command Meade to move his troops without risking the general's reputation?

After finishing the letter, Lincoln added a postscript on a separate page: "The order I inclose is not of record. If you succeed, you need not publish the order; if you fail, publish it. Thus, if you succeed, you will have all the credit.

If not, I'll take the responsibility."

* * * * *

While flying to India, Anne leaned over from the copilot's seat and looked down to where Charles was pointing. It wasn't possible to stop at Jerusalem, but the sight of the city, spread out below them, filled her with joy. They were both glad that their route allowed them to fly over Palestine.

A few minutes later, Jerusalem was behind them and Anne leaned back in her seat. She and Charles had seen many places in the past year. Jerusalem from the air. Their house in England. The great cities of London, Paris, Berlin, and Rome, and other places in northern Europe. And the Will Rogers ranch in California.

Mary Todd Lincoln was drinking coffee in a hotel in Rome during a tour of Europe, years after her husband's death.

She and Mr. Lincoln had spoken of traveling: to California, for instance. On the night he died, he had also mentioned his desire to see Jerusalem. But it was Europe that had highlighted their post-presidential plans, and they had looked forward to seeing the countries they had read about. Now, Mary visited London, Frankfurt, Paris, Rome, and other European cities without him.

* * * * *

Anne Morrow Lindbergh gazed affectionately at her husband and brother-in-law as they argued. Charles had brought up some of the blooper moments from England's past, while Aubrey kept referring to America as "that former British colony."

Charles had the ability to speak as an American representing America. He was remarkably assured while talking politics with ministers, presidents, and the aristocracy. He had a vision that embraced the great issues—a vision that one usually sees only in world leaders.

President Lincoln quirked his lips as he told a British visitor to the White House, "Your people made sad work of this mansion when they came up the Potomac in 1812. Nothing was left of it but the bare walls!"

The Englishman acknowledged the verbal thrust, then came back with an appropriate retort.

* * * * *

In Russia, Charles and Anne Lindbergh listened as a Soviet woman, keen on selling socialism, had the floor. She had presented dubious claims for quite awhile and was building to a crescendo.

"Today," she said, "many formerly separate republics are part of the Soviet Union. And let me tell you, Mr. Lindbergh, that they will be so, *forevermore.*"

Looking her in the eye, he replied mildly, "How long is *that?*"

Abe Lincoln had a twinkle in his eye as he listened to an Indiana neighbor. The man tended to exaggerate when describing a personal triumph, and he was running true to form. "I rode this horse," he said, "all the way from Gentryville; and let me tell you, in the last mile, she *never took a long breath.*"

Giving his friend a bland look, Lincoln asked, "How many *short* breaths did she take?"

* * * * *

During his stay in Europe, Charles Lindbergh kept an eye on America. His country had some long-term problems, including racial tension. He was keenly aware of its large population of Negroes, and worried about their future. He wrote in his nightly journal, "The Civil War did not settle the Negro problem by any means."

* * * * *

The nations of Europe were moving inexorably toward war, and Lindbergh was riveted. He was on the phone constantly, seeking updates on Italy's invasion of Albania and other news. He was engrossed in the bloody struggle, anxious to know how it might affect his family, and also the world.

Lindbergh seemed singularly qualified to deal with the situation, as if he knew exactly what needed to be done if a war were to arrive on his doorstep.

Abraham Lincoln waited impatiently at his end of the telegraph line. It was past midnight, but he had forgotten about time. He was expecting news from his commanding general that could send his family packing. With Washington an oasis of peace surrounded by battlefields, it seemed only a matter of time before it, too, was invaded.

The intense situation was bringing out the best in Lincoln, showcasing his strength. Somehow he would lead his country and take care of his family. The dual role was exhausting, but he was up to the job.

* * * * *

To Lindbergh, the idea of America going to war was crazy. The Nazis were too strong. They were a fierce people; they would be a determined foe. A war with such an enemy would probably take many years, with real doubts in the end that anyone was the victor. The ruin it would bring to the land and to European civilization, not to mention to the United States, would be incalculable.

No, he thought, better for America to do everything in her power to avoid the conflict.

Abraham Lincoln wiped the sweat away while he read of the latest casualties. Dear God.

His Northern side had started out so confident. They had every advantage. They should have won easily. But they had underestimated the fighting spirit of the South.

Lincoln meditated on the destruction the war had brought to America's cities, farms, and families. The struggle had already lasted for years, and now, God only knew how much longer it would take.

He sat for a long time, holding his head. This Civil War was searing his soul. He wished it was over. And he never wanted to experience anything like it again. Ever.

* * * * *

As Lindbergh read news reports of Germany's expansion into Czechoslovakia, he shook his head. This situation should never have happened. At the end of the First World War, the Allies should have brought Germany to its knees. This thought seemed blatantly obvious. Make it impossible for the enemy to come back at you in the near future. People's memories were long; enmities could last for generations. But if you take away a nation's ability to engage in warfare, you give the people time to reflect on the blessings of a lasting peace.

The alternative would have been for the Allies to befriend Germany. But that was a course of action few nations were willing to explore in the aftermath of a conflict.

President Lincoln stood and gazed out of a White House window. General Sherman had begun his march to the sea. The heart of Georgia was going to be devastated, so that the Confederacy would lose its ability to wage war.

Lincoln sighed, and turned away from the view. He wanted so badly to befriend the South and welcome them back into the Union. But he could do so only after he had removed the guns from their hands.

CHAPTER SIXTEEN

The Pull of the Past

The years before Pearl Harbor were busy ones for Charles Lindbergh, recently returned from Europe to his native America . . .

Across the dinner table, Carl Sandburg smiled. He liked the Lindberghs, and they seemed to like him. He was glad the Harcourts had introduced them.

Sandburg had become a famous author. His magnum opus on the life of Lincoln was now considered the Lincoln biography and was quoted by many. Sandburg had brought Lincoln alive to many thousands of readers; he had effectively channeled the spirit of Lincoln, a man he deeply admired.

Sandburg himself bore similarities to his hero. Both Lincoln and Sandburg were tall and strong. Both wore their frames humbly. And Sandburg's features, although not what one might call handsome, reflected an inner beauty as Lincoln's had. Even his outfits sometimes seemed borrowed from Lincoln's wardrobe.

And now, as he looked at Charles Lindbergh, Carl Sandburg sensed a friendly spirit. Lindbergh grinned at him, and Sandburg smiled back.

* * * * *

Charles Lindbergh paced the U.S. Capitol grounds before meeting a senator. As he walked, he noticed the litter accumulating in the gutters, the graffiti on the walls, and the overall lack of attention given to the lawn.

Lindbergh worried that these blots symbolized a deterioration of patriotic spirit; if true, he wanted to reverse it.

President Lincoln gazed with concern at the wide avenue that stretched from the Capitol building across the heart of Washington. The avenue was intended to be a beautiful outdoor mall, but right now it looked like a swamp.

The situation was bad. The surroundings were supposed to reflect the pride Americans had in their country. Especially now, it was important that the nation's capital look its best. Lincoln had already made sure that the work on the Capitol Dome continued in spite of the war, and now he intended to see to it that the grounds were well cared for as well.

* * * * *

"And so, my fellow Americans . . ."

Charles Lindbergh listened for a time; then he turned off the radio, thus silencing Franklin Delano Roosevelt.

Roosevelt sometimes mentioned Abraham Lincoln in his speeches. These references to Lincoln weren't unique. A number of politicians quoted the Great Emancipator with reverence. Lincoln's reputation had reached its peak, and the American people equated him with the noblest qualities a public servant might aspire to.

But Roosevelt made overt attempts to identify himself with Lincoln, especially trying to equate himself with Lincoln's image of nation-saver and spiritual instrument. FDR even read from Carl Sandburg's *Lincoln: The War Years* to point out the similarities.

As Lindbergh listened to Roosevelt's speeches, his distrust grew. The president seemed dishonest, insincere—a political opportunist, lacking in moral fiber. To Lindbergh, FDR seemed the cagey, crafty politico who had left behind, in pursuit of fame and power, the whispers of his conscience. He did not fit Lindbergh's mental image of what a president should be.

* * * * *

In Washington, Charles Lindbergh walked out of an office. He had just been offered the newly created job of secretary of air in the president's cabinet.

Lindbergh was aware that his intention to speak against war was making FDR nervous. Apparently, Roosevelt wanted to head Lindbergh off before he could hurt his plans. But did Roosevelt really think he could purchase Lindbergh's allegiance? Did he think he could silence him or stop him from stating his mind, when the president made an error in judgment? If so, he had another think coming.

President-elect Abraham Lincoln was making a list of whom he should invite to help him when he came to Washington. Most people in his situation would fill their cabinet with friends and colleagues, but Lincoln's thought was to have the best men in each position, whether they liked him or not.

Accordingly, Lincoln tentatively wrote the names of William H. Seward and Salmon P. Chase, recent political rivals, as candidates for his cabinet of secretaries.

* * * * *

As he read each day's newspaper, Charles Lindbergh felt a growing unease. He didn't like the way things had shaped up in Europe, and he didn't like the way Roosevelt was reacting to the situation.

What was he trying to do? Push America into the conflict? Didn't he realize what war was like?[1]

It was almost more than Lincoln could stand. Every day he read telegraphed reports, and month after month, year after year, he watched the numbers accumulate. More than twenty-two thousand dead and wounded in a single day at Antietam. Fifty-one thousand casualties at Gettysburg. Shiloh. Fredericksburg. Chickamauga . . . the list went on and on.

When would it end? When would this detestable war be over?

Every day Lincoln felt as though he could bear no more; and yet, he continued to call for more soldiers. To prevent the loss of a nation, the sacrifices must continue. But, for Lincoln, the sacrifice was immense. His anguish tore him apart. His nonviolent heart felt pierced by swords.[2]

It was an experience no man should ever have to go through. And it was an experience his soul would never forget.

---

[1] In 1940, referring to the European soldiers dying in the trenches, Lindbergh told his wife, "I know what hell is going on there." At that point in his life, Lindbergh had had no direct experience with war, so how could he "know"?

[2] In Chapter Twenty-Two, we will study Lincoln and Lindbergh's habitual harmlessness.

The longer Lindbergh studied the situation, the more it looked as if America was likely to be drawn or forced into fighting in Europe. And that, he thought, would be the biggest blunder imaginable. Every part of his being told him so.

He just knew that if his country were involved, American casualties would soar into astronomical figures. Millions would perish. The devastation would be incalculable. This war would be, without a doubt, the deadliest in the history of America and perhaps the world.

Lindbergh had seen Germany's warplanes. The potential for destruction—he could almost see the bodies and rubble piling up—was immense. And the idea of that devastation coming to America was . . . he shuddered.

It was too horrific for words.

Abraham Lincoln walked a battlefield with his head held low. A shudder shook his frame.

He knew the new weapons were efficient killers, but *this!* The sheer number of casualties, the terrible wounds on those who survived, the cartloads of amputated limbs—this was the harvest of the machinery of war that both sides had perfected. This American Civil War was one of the bloodiest conflicts humanity had known.

One of Lincoln's duties was to forward promising gun designs to army developers. As commander in chief, he saw many inventions that were fresh from the drafting table. It was his encouragement that helped send some of the best weapons to the battlefields—and he was seeing the fruit of their handiwork.

Abraham Lincoln presented the ironic spectacle of one of the most nonviolent men of his day, promoting against opposition his country's bloodiest war. And not just any war, but an internecine conflict: brother fighting brother. This surprisingly gentle man had to stand up and declare the need for it. It was his job to draft thousands of men, young and old, to join in the fighting.

I had no choice! he repeated silently as he stared at the battlefield. And still, more than any military leader in history, Lincoln took responsibility for the death toll.

Back in the White House, he walked the halls a wounded man. He confided, "If there is someone who suffers more than I do, I pity him."

Francis Carpenter described the president's pain:

In repose, it was the saddest face I knew. There were days when I could scarcely look into it without crying. During the first week of the Wilderness battles he scarcely slept. Passing through the domestic apartment, I met him, clad in a long morning wrapper, pacing back and forth, his hands behind him, black rings under his eyes, his head bent upon his breast—altogether such a picture of sorrow, care, and anxiety as would have melted the hearts of his adversaries.

When a congressman berated Lincoln for telling jokes, he retorted: "If it were not for these occasional vents of humor, I should die." And he told someone else, "I laugh because I must not weep—that's all!"

Lincoln commuted dozens of death sentences to bring relief to his heart; he could scarcely bear the thought of another man's death. For those who obviously deserved it, he condoned their execution—but for those whose guilt was unclear, he sought a reprieve. Generals argued, but Lincoln said, "There are too many weeping widows. For God's sake don't ask me to add to the number, for, I tell you, *I won't do it!*"

In one of his worst experiences, Lincoln tried to telegraph a reprieve with the soldier's female relations at his side—only to read the return telegram saying the execution had already been carried out.

When a woman whose son he released said, "I shall probably not see you again till we meet in heaven," Lincoln's mournful response was, "I am afraid I shall never get to the place you speak of."

At times he recited a speech from *Hamlet* of a king whose guilt threatened to unseat his reason. Excessive, unreasonable remorse seared Lincoln's soul.

"But, I've only done what I had to do!" his mind pleaded.

"Tell that to the dead," his heart mocked.

Thus his head and heart struggled. And always his head won. But his heart was not overthrown. Biding its time, it would have its way. It would have its say. And reason would topple, and look to rule another day.

"I will not be responsible for promoting bloodshed. There is no way on earth that I will allow myself to do that."

Charles Lindbergh spoke aloud as he paced the floor of his living room. The mere thought of helping promote America's involvement in a war conjured up an overpowering emotion. It was a feeling that originated in the deepest core of his being, and there was nothing to do but honor it.

The war process had to be stopped, he told himself. That's all there was to it. And he had to stop it.

Lindbergh stood still. Yes. That was it. He would do everything—he had to do everything in his power to prevent this war from happening and America from taking part.

* * * * *

Given Lincoln's extreme pain from the carnage of the Civil War, it would have been only natural for a desire to grow in his heart to balance or erase his necessary but lamented promotion of that war. How could he do this? By protecting his fellow Americans and all people from devastation, sorrow, and loss, and by dedicating himself one-pointedly to the endorsement of peace so that wars like that one need never take place again.

There is evidence to show that that desire did exist: In his Second Inaugural Address, for instance, Lincoln spoke wistfully of the end of the conflict and of bringing warring brothers together in compassion and understanding. He spoke of these things again on the last day of his life. Lincoln's hopes were a dream of personal and national healing.

When Lincoln died, soldiers were still fighting, and that dream lingered in his heart. He had no chance to resolve his sense of partial responsibility for the deaths of thousands of American men. Such intense commitments of energy do not disappear with death; they are only postponed. Somehow, sometime, in the vast scheme of things Lincoln's great desire must find fulfillment or release . . .

Lindbergh made a vow. "I will not encourage participation in this war; I will do just the opposite!"

His excitement grew as a plan of action came together. "People listen to what I say. My words affect them. Therefore . . . I will speak of nonviolent solutions, of protecting America from destruction. They will listen to me," he told himself. "They *must* listen! I will do my best to preserve my country from war. It's the only thing to do. After all, the antagonists in Europe are really . . . our *brothers.*"

The thought took hold. "Of course!" he cried, "We have the same cultural roots! Americans are descended primarily from European stock. The English, French, Germans, and Italians are our hereditary brothers and brothers to one another as well. The countries of Europe are really like the states of one nation. Not only should we not fight them, but they shouldn't fight one another. The only result would be senseless destruction. There has to be another solution, and I will find it and make it plain to the American people!"[3]

Lincoln's frown deepened when he heard that two brothers had fired at each other in a recent battle. "Fratricide," he said, shaking his head. "That's what this war is. Fratricide."[4]

The people of the many states of the Union—mainly European immigrants—were meant to remain as one. He had to find a way to win this war before it tore the country apart, family by family.

* * * * *

Lindbergh proceeded to view American involvement in World War II solely from the perspective of avoiding it. He seized and expanded everything that bolstered that viewpoint, and ignored everything that said the opposite. Everyone who agreed with him was his ally. Anyone who disagreed was deluding himself. He was absolutely convinced of the rightness of his cause, and with that certainty fought with all his energy.

[3]In the first national radio address he made on this subject, delivered in Washington, D.C., Lindbergh strongly emphasized the importance of keeping the country out of any but the most necessary conflicts so that fewer Americans would die.

[4]One of the nicknames for the Civil War was "The Brothers' War." As Lincoln put it: "Let us at all times remember that all American citizens are brothers of a common country."

Lindbergh couldn't be silent; he felt so keenly that he had to speak against the course of action being discussed. He had to fight it—and so he lectured on nonintervention, vigorously promoting his ideas from coast to coast. By doing this, he greatly altered his national reputation.

After hearing of the repeal of the Missouri Compromise, which had limited the spread of slavery, Lincoln was unable to be silent. He felt so keenly that he must speak against the course of action being discussed. To pursue it threatened grave repercussions. He had to fight it, and he did so: giving speech after speech up and down Illinois and beyond. By the end of his efforts, he had greatly altered his national reputation.

* * * * *

Charles Lindbergh became deeply involved in the Great Debate: whether the United States should take part in the war in Europe. It was an issue that the American people argued, a dilemma that split the country politically.

The most visible proponents were President Roosevelt on one side and Charles A. Lindbergh on the other.

Abraham Lincoln was now involved in the Great Debate: whether the United States should allow slavery in new territories under the auspices of "popular sovereignty." This was an issue that drew passionate feelings from the American people. They followed the debates closely in the newspapers and argued among themselves. The dilemma divided the country, and its most visible proponents were Stephen A. Douglas on one side and Abraham Lincoln on the other.

* * * * *

At a noninterventionist meeting, Lindbergh called for unity and cooperation among the groups, with their various agendas. Holding fast to the core idea that had brought them together, he declared, would influence America more than a dozen groups pushing slightly different ideals. His words helped bring harmony and stability to the gathering.

"Unity!" Lincoln cried, and the people of the Northern states put aside petty squabbles in lieu of the greater issues at stake.

"Unity!" Lincoln pleaded, as he watched the Southern states abandon, one by one, the Union he held dear.

"Unity," Lincoln breathed, like a prayer, as the war came to a close. A united America would withstand many trials a divided nation could never hope to survive.

* * * * *

Before joining the America First Committee — a fledgling organization dedicated to the prevention of American intervention in Europe — Lindbergh meditated on the move. He didn't want to be pressured into taking charge of any group. Besides, he disagreed with the views of some of the anti-war people. Finally, he decided the organization's goals were close enough to his to support it. Soon, he was the committee's poster boy.

Before joining the fledgling Republican Party, Lincoln contemplated the move. After carefully weighing his options, he decided that their goals were close enough to his. Not long after, he was the Republican Party's poster boy.

* * * * *

Seated on a speaker's platform, a veteran politican stared enviously at Charles Lindbergh. Lindbergh drew the sort of response—wild applause, people hanging on every word, spontaneous cries of support—that the politician would have given his eyeteeth for. But he had to acknowledge that, in spite of a lifetime of effort, he was probably destined to receive only a fraction of the popular sentiment Lindbergh evoked without trying.

Lincoln stood on a White House balcony and waved. The war was nearly over, and people were starting to appreciate the leader who had brought it to a successful conclusion.

Lincoln recalled that, when he first entered politics, it had taken a lot of work to get people to listen. Now, as he smiled and nodded at the crowd, he had reached the opposite end of the spectrum. Not only were they hanging on every word, but now all he had to do was appear for the audience to acclaim him.

He raised his stovepipe hat and a thunderous cheer issued from the crowd.

* * * * *

John T. Flynn, America First Committee member, was incensed. An unsavory man was trying to associate himself with the committee, and Flynn was ready to tell him where to get off.

In a calm voice, Lindbergh spoke to Flynn. Cool down, he cautioned him. Let your anger subside. Then, state your objection. This moderate approach, he said, would bring Flynn the results he desired.

Abraham Lincoln listened to the angry objections of a group of fiery abolitionists. Then, he calmly advised moderation. "You can better succeed with the ballot than with the bullet," he said. "Peaceably redeem the government through your votes, voice, and moral influence."

* * * * *

Charles Lindbergh was drafting a telegram to the *Baltimore Sun*. In it, he declared America First's intention to use methods that were in harmony with the U.S. Constitution, and nothing else.

Abraham Lincoln was ending his address to the Young Men's Lyceum of Springfield. "General intelligence," he said, "sound morality and, in particular, a reverence for the Constitution . . . Upon these let the proud fabric of freedom rest, and 'the gates of hell shall not prevail against it.'"

* * * * *

America First's steering group was discussing a change of leadership. For the job of chairman, the name of Charles Lindbergh topped the list. Not only did he command great respect from the American people, not only was he an international hero, but he had qualities—a calm, clear head in a storm, the ability to inspire others, lucid speech—that everyone recognized as essential for the leader of a new political entity.

The Republican Party representatives gathered to discuss who should represent them in the presidential election.

The choice was crucial to the future of the party. They needed to make a strong showing. They had lost their first election in 1856; they must try to win this one. The person they chose must give them the best possible chance for success.

In the end, they selected Abraham Lincoln. He had many qualities—a calm and clear head under fire, the ability to inspire people with his vision, lucid thought and speech—that the politicians recognized as necessary for their leader.

* * * * *

Lindbergh's mouth was set in a firm line as he wrote in his diary. Why did people insist on trying to draw him into politics? Couldn't they see he just wasn't interested? Sure, he would continue to speak against American intervention, but that was all.

Lindbergh had seen the political life while watching his father, the congressman. It consisted of wearing a permanent groove in your chair, writing letters, and talking and shaking hands with everyone. And then, too, a politician had to confine his words to approved topics. Who in his right mind would want to do *that* for the rest of his life?

Once a politician, always a politician. Once you started down that road, it was hard to change. People tended to picture you in that role forever. And he could see himself, decades from now, mired in an office like his father, or out making carefully worded speeches . . .

He shuddered. No, sir. Not for him. He preferred ditch-digging over politics.

Abraham Lincoln collapsed on a couch and closed his eyes. He was trying, unsuccessfully, to forget his duties.

Greeting Washington politicians, composing and signing letters and proclamations (while getting the wording so precise that there would be no misunderstandings and the fewest people would be offended), hearing complaints, shaking hands until his palm was swollen, dissuading office-seekers from wasting his time, attending banquets and cabinet meetings, dousing flames of ill will among cabinet members, exhorting generals to greater efforts—*huff! puff!* He had meant it when he told someone that shortly after moving into the Executive Mansion, he had felt like finding a good stout rope and hanging himself.

CHAPTER SEVENTEEN

Releasing the Mantle

Brring! Lindbergh answered the phone. Working with an organization was necessary if he was to have a national impact. And so, he personally answered all phone calls from America First Committee headquarters in Chicago.

"I'm off, Mary!" Lincoln yelled as he strode out the door.

"Yes, dear!" Mrs. Lincoln answered from where she sat in the parlor, having tea with her sister.

"That man of yours seems to be always on the run these days," said Elizabeth.

"It's true," Mary responded, with a blush of pride. "They may nominate him for president. At least, that's our hope. So now he's gone downtown to await the telegrams he will receive from the Republican convention in Chicago."

* * * * *

Some individuals in the America First organization tried to induce Lindbergh to accept their help in writing his speeches, help that he didn't want or need. He knew what he wanted to say better than anyone, so he always wrote his own drafts—though he often discussed them with his wife.

President Lincoln stared at the speech draft that Secretary Seward had sent him. Lincoln often consulted Seward while composing his speeches. On the other hand, the final copy always bore the president's imprint.

After reading the draft, Lincoln folded it and quipped, "I like that speech. It has the merit of *originality.*"

* * * * *

Standing under an America First Committee sign, Lindbergh launched his denunciation. Franklin D. Roosevelt, he said, was behaving more like a dictator than a president. He was acting precipitously, drawing the United States into the European war through a deliberate step-by-step process, putting American lives at risk without a care for the expressed desire of the American people. Clearly, new leadership was needed.

January 1848, the U.S. Capitol, the House Chamber. Congressman Lincoln of Illinois had the floor.

Lincoln was denouncing President James K. Polk for what he considered Polk's precipitant actions in initiating a war with Mexico over disputed Texas territory. In his forthright manner, he called on Polk to answer for his actions to the American people, without evasion. It was his assertion that Polk was endangering the lives of American soldiers for no valid reason.

If, Lincoln later added, the president refused to answer these important questions—if he didn't feel he was accountable to the American people—then he was taking on the powers of kings and tyrants and not behaving as a duly elected leader.

At the White House breakfast table, Mrs. Lincoln pushed a newspaper under her husband's chin.

"Have you seen how the press is treating you? A tyrant, they call you. And here's a cartoon showing you with a crown on your head. The caption says, 'King Lincoln'!"

"I know," the president answered, waving the paper away. "Leave me be, Mary. I don't have to read it. I hear about it from you and everyone else."

* * * * *

While reading Lindbergh's speeches for nonintervention, I was struck by the similarity between some of his phrases and those that Abraham Lincoln had employed during the previous century. Placing them side by side, it seemed almost as if Lindbergh were paraphrasing Lincoln. This "paraphrasing" illustrates again how our mental habits remain much the same as we enter a new lifetime. When placed in a situation that Lincoln knew well—that of public speaking and debate—it was only natural that Lindbergh would subconsciously draw on the ideas and terminology that had worked so well in the past.

Unfortunately, for this first edition, I did not have time to request permission to use sentences from Lindbergh's speeches. I hope to include a few comparisons of both men's wording and ideas in later publications of this book.

* * * * *

Although not everyone in Lindbergh's audience shared his beliefs, they had to credit the aviator's earnestness and directness. It was obvious Lindbergh believed what he was saying, and people were swayed by his words.

As he listened to Lincoln speak during a public debate, Stephen A. Douglas winced. He knew Lincoln was tough to beat, and precisely for this reason. It was Lincoln's damnable earnestness and directness that was giving Douglas so much trouble.

* * * * *

Seated in an auditorium, Anne Lindbergh was content. Watching her husband on the podium satisfied something deep inside.

It wasn't that Anne wished for her husband to accede to public office. He was Charles Lindbergh: that was enough renown for anyone. Furthermore, something about a crowd's intense emotions made her uneasy. At times, she worried about her husband's safety. Fearsome images flashed through her mind of an assassin stealing up to him and pulling a gun. And yet, in spite of this, she was pleased at his success in the arena of public debate.

Ann Rutledge scolded her beau: "Now you listen, Abraham Lincoln! You have to stop moaning about your lack of schooling. You've got a great future in politics, if you'd only dare try. You can do anything, once you've set your mind to it!"

Lincoln felt the embers of ambition burst into flame. Ann's words gave him the courage to go out and speak. It was partly due to her encouragement that he won seats in the Illinois State Legislature, the House of Representatives, and ultimately, the Executive Mansion.

But Ann died before she got to see the results of her heartening words.

* * * * *

Anne Lindbergh frowned. Her husband's speech was going well, but . . . what was he doing with his voice? Somehow, it had ascended until it was almost falsetto. He was squeaking his words.

Then, too, Charles had began using a Midwestern accent, sounding like someone who had just stepped off the prairies. He normally didn't speak like that. It sounded strange.

Any visitor from the East Coast who attended a Lincoln-Douglas debate might have concluded that Lincoln had a queer way of talking. It wasn't only his Midwestern accent. It was the fact that Lincoln's timbre rose while addressing the crowd, becoming high-pitched.

* * * * *

Lindbergh listened carefully as a man explained that the America First presentation in Oklahoma City would have to be canceled. The owners of the auditorium had decided that they didn't want such a controversial gathering in their building after all.

Lindbergh's response was immediate and amusing. "Tell them that we'll gather in a cow pasture instead!"

Abraham Lincoln was being notified by messenger that Mr. James Shields, having taken offense at something Lincoln had written about him, was demanding satisfaction. It was still the age of duels, and Shields was determined to preserve his honor.

"What will be your choice of weapons?" the messenger asked, with deadly seriousness.

Lincoln thought for a moment. "How about cow pies at five paces?" he said.

* * * * *

Charles Lindbergh looked as if he'd been poleaxed. He had just heard that Roosevelt had accused him of being a Copperhead—a term used in the Lincoln administration to refer to Northern traitors to the Union cause.

He read the words over and over. Finally, he came to his decision. He had to hand in his commission in the U.S. Army. It was the only possible response. He had shrugged off other insults from the Roosevelt administration, but not this one. The Copperhead label had struck a nerve that the others hadn't.

* * * * *

Lindbergh studied an anonymous letter. Since he started giving lectures, the hate mail had begun to pile up again. This one referred to him as "Nazi Lindbergh" and warned that dire consequences would be suffered by his family.

Just arrived in D.C., Abe Lincoln picked up his latest piece of hate mail. If he were the type to be frightened by such things, he supposed he would be scared. As it was, perhaps it was best that Allan Pinkerton, the detective, had accompanied him on his train trip to Washington.

The writer addressed him as a "Black nigger" and threatened mortal injury.

* * * * *

July 1940. The Lindberghs were contemplating a move to the Pacific Northwest. In Oregon they might enjoy the peace of a secluded corner of the country. On the other hand, such a step meant turning away from society when the couple felt it needed their input.

In the end, they decided not to go ahead with their plan.

"Oregon?" Mary Todd Lincoln inquired with a frown.

"Yes," answered her husband. "They've asked me to be governor."

It was soon after Lincoln's term in Congress, and the Lincolns were discussing the offer that had just arrived of a political post in a distant territory.

"What's in Oregon?" she asked.

"Nothing much, I grant you. Still, the job is nothing to sneeze at. And I hear it is pleasant out there among the redwood trees. We could make trips to the ocean, or go south to California from time to time . . ."

"No."

"What's that?"

"I am not moving to Oregon. I am not going to leave our nice house and move to some Godforsaken part of the country where we might get eaten by wild Indians or who knows what. And you are not going to throw away your political career by hiding in some wilderness hole where no one will see or hear from you again.

"You are going to be president some day, and I am going to be the president's wife. And that will never happen if we go to Oregon."

"All right, Mary," Lincoln capitulated.

* * * * *

Lindbergh had relatives in Cleveland, and had participated in air races there. Yet in 1938 he was lambasted at a public function in that city by Harold Ickes, FDR's secretary of the interior, for receiving an award from Nazi Germany. And now, in August 1941, the Cleveland police had x-rayed Lindbergh's room out of concern for his safety.

They no longer seemed to like him in Cleveland.

"They had a demonstration against you in Cleveland yesterday."

President Lincoln glanced up as a friend relayed the bad news. The only time he had been in Cleveland was when his train stopped there on his way to Washington. Back then, it had seemed that the people of the city supported him.

"What happened?"

"Well, thousands were supposed to show up, but it says that four hundred men attended a meeting in which they spoke against your reelection."

A sudden thought occurred to Lincoln. "How many men did you say?"

"Four hundred."

The president pulled out his Bible. Paging through it, he stopped when he came to a certain passage. Then he quoted, with satisfaction:

And everyone that was in distress, and everyone that was in debt, and everyone that was discontented, gathered themselves unto him; . . . and there were with him about four hundred men.[1]

* * * * *

[1] I Samuel 22:2.

In Lindbergh's journals, he practically threatened to make a politically disastrous public statement if pushed to become a politician. By the time he was preparing for his Des Moines appearance, the cry that he assume public office was loud and insistent . . .

"Our next president!"

Charles Lindbergh winced. There had been many shouts of support from people attending his speeches, but none of those cries had affected him like this one.

"Our next president!"

The first time he'd heard it, he shrugged it off. But with each speech, the shout grew in volume. Each time it was repeated the uneasiness grew in Lindbergh's soul—and with it, the need for escape.

"OUR NEXT PRESIDENT!!"

What had he gotten himself into?! He had been making public appearances for . . . how long? Two years? He needed to change direction before it was too late.

Above all, his subconscious knew that he must erase the image of himself as a public servant from people's minds. The only question was how to do it. It had to be done in such a way that he would never hear that cry again. And it must be done soon.

Abraham Lincoln was on his way home from his debates with Stephen A. Douglas. He had mastered the business of politicking.

It wasn't so hard, really. The trick was to present your ideas in such a way as to make them acceptable to your audience. There were many ways of expressing the same thoughts—ways that brought applause, surprise, or denunciation. It all depended on how you phrased it. Once you'd mastered the rules of speaking, you could evoke whatever response you wished.

As Lindbergh glanced over the headlines, his subconscious mind, which had been controlling his thoughts and actions, relaxed. Just those few politically incorrect words in a speech in Des Moines, Iowa—including the Jewish people in a short list of those pushing America to enter the war—had turned the tide.

People were drawing away from him in droves. Never again would the American public look to him for political leadership. The heavy mantle of herodom that had weighed so heavily was off his back.

But his conscious mind, unaware of the subconscious control, and still intent on turning America from war, was bewildered that the public ignored the main thrust of his speech and focused on a few sentences out of context.

* * * * *

Charles Lindbergh's Des Moines speech was a striking example of how a past-life influence can bring confusion into the present. Instead of seeing what was in front of him and reacting objectively, Lindbergh's intense emotions, triggered by past experiences, obscured the picture and made him act in a way that was foreign to his nature.

When Lindbergh's children grew to adulthood, they were confused when they compared their father's Des Moines speech with his everyday attitudes and the way he'd taught them to behave. Putting aside the fact that when he made the speech the worst of the Holocaust was still a little in the future, and his predisposition was to think well of

Germans and therefore discount rumors of Nazi atrocities, this contradiction was still a hard thing to reconcile.

Lindbergh was aware that an imbroglio might result, yet he couldn't stop himself from mentioning the Jews in his speech. The subconscious mind, where past-life memories are stored, had taken over and had overriden any conscious objections. Simply put, Lindbergh felt unequivocally that he had to do what he did. The fact that in his later years he still bemoaned the public's reaction to his speech hinted at how unaware his conscious mind was of what his subconscious had done. Yet, on some level, his soul must have understood that this was a personal karma, because Lindbergh, in his last days, tried to protect his wife from the backlash of his speech.

Lindbergh's life showed many effects of past good karma, but perhaps the greatest example could be seen in the *results* of the Des Moines speech. Far from pushing America away from war, it nudged America closer to it, and away from anti-Semitism. Not only was that a healthy direction for any nation; it subtly added to America's fervor to fight the Nazis after Pearl Harbor.

Lincoln had the good karma of arguing *for* a righteous war and *succeeding;* Lindbergh had partial good karma in that he argued *against* a righteous war and *failed.* And his failure indirectly helped the war effort.

Both Lincoln and Lindbergh appealed to people's prejudices in public speeches for what they considered good causes. To assure his listeners that he wasn't really an abolitionist, Lincoln stated that "[the black man] is not my equal in many respects—certainly not in color, perhaps not in moral or intellectual endowment." Lindbergh, though certainly not trying to start an anti-Semitic movement, encouraged his Des Moines listeners to think that, "Although most of the Jewish segment of our American population is pushing for war with Germany (and who can blame them!), we who do not wish to join the war in Europe don't have to go along with that idea."

In conversations and writings, Lindbergh used words like "the Jewish problem"; similarly, Lincoln worried over "the Negro problem."[2] Those phrases were common parlance in the mid-nineteenth and mid-twentieth centuries. If Lindbergh had been Lincoln in the past, it would have been natural for him to adopt a similar phrase to a similar dilemma: how to resolve a situation of racial tension. In both instances, the two men canvassed important people about their particular issues and energetically sought solutions.

It is interesting to note that one of Lincoln's early solutions to "the Negro problem" was to send freed slaves to Central America, the Caribbean, or Africa. He told a group of black leaders that blacks and whites were better off separate. In like manner, at this time of his life Lindbergh was of the opinion that the various races of the world should remain apart, culturally and genetically. Later, he changed that notion.

In our more enlightened times, some of Lindbergh's words, common in his era, smack of racism or anti-Semitism. Similarly, Lincoln used to swap "nigger jokes" with his friends, just as others did in his day. Yet, in their personal interactions neither man showed any prejudice.

* * * * *

"Oh, Charles. It's horrible."

[2]You may recall from Chapter Fifteen that Lindbergh, too, showed concern over "the Negro problem."

Anne Lindbergh was reading a speech Carl Sandburg had given. The writer had rebuffed Charles, saying that his actions regarding the European war were contrary to the high ideals Lincoln had espoused. He specifically cited Lincoln's Gettysburg Address and Second Inaugural in his rebuttal. Sandburg ridiculed Charles with great skill, painting him as a fool at best and a traitor at worst.

This was especially painful because Anne and Charles liked Sandburg. They respected the man and his work. Charles was deeply impressed with the painstaking effort Sandburg had put into his Lincoln biography. He wrote very highly of Sandburg in his diary.

For her part, Anne thought that Sandburg bore a similarity to her husband: like Charles he was old-fashioned. The poet was a model of time-honored values like reverence and humbleness.

And now he was attacking her husband. She was shocked that Sandburg, who so deeply understood Abraham Lincoln, would misunderstand what Charles was trying to do. Didn't he realize that Charles wanted what was best for America? Although she didn't know Sandburg well, it felt like a betrayal. At any rate, it was definitely a trial by fire to have the acclaimed Lincoln biographer publicly berate them.

She turned to Charles for comfort, and he seemed to know just what to say. "Isn't it wonderful," he murmured, "that perfection can come out of imperfection?"

It was clear that her husband felt no resentment. Charles extended the same goodwill to Sandburg that he had offered a year and a half ago. In spite of his attacks, Charles never considered Sandburg, the Lincoln devotee, his enemy.

* * * * *

Pearl Harbor had been bombed and America was at war with Japan. After a short reflection, Charles Lindbergh printed a response in the newpapers. Although he had fought America's involvement, he wrote, now that the twisted hulls of U.S. ships were lying at the bottom of Hawaiian waters, all such discussions were moot. He encouraged Americans on both sides of the debate to band together and support the war effort, to furnish American military forces with the best resources for the greatest possibility of success.

In spite of these conciliatory words, most Americans were slow to forgive Lindbergh. The thirty-nine-year-old aviator had lost whatever political clout he had. By fighting against war and opposing the president, he had committed political suicide.

William Herndon held a letter written by his friend in Washington: thirty-nine-year-old Congressman Abraham Lincoln. In his letter, Lincoln explained why he had enthusiastically voted for supplying American troops in Mexico while publicly decrying the actions of President Polk that had brought the war about.

Herndon dropped the letter, picked up an Illinois newspaper, and read a scathing indictment of Lincoln. Herndon shook his head. His friend had made a grave political error.

Herndon doubted that many of Lincoln's political peers were likely to forgive his attacks on President Polk. Lincoln would leave the nation's capital having lost whatever clout he'd come in with. His unpopular stand against the war in Mexico was a form of political suicide.

CHAPTER EIGHTEEN

The Patriot

Following the Japanese attack, Lindbergh immediately wanted to help defend his country. Before Pearl Harbor, he had put one hundred percent of his effort into saving the nation from war. Now that the country was engaged, he wanted to give a hundred percent to help win it.

During his verbal duel with Roosevelt, Lindbergh had resigned his commission in the army. After Pearl Harbor he hoped to resume his duties, but was denied by the Roosevelt administration. Thus stymied, Lindbergh agreed to assist Henry Ford, whose plant in Willow Run, Michigan, was involved in the production of bomber planes.

Henry Ford took Lindbergh, his new technical advisor, on a tour of his museum in Greenfield Village, Michigan. The museum housed some fascinating curiosities, including an old courthouse that Ford had brought from Illinois because Abraham Lincoln had tried cases in it, and another prized possession, the chair in which the Great Emancipator was assassinated.

There may have been another reason besides pride of ownership for this tour: Ford appreciated Lindbergh's generosity in donating his old car to the museum.

* * * * *

Charles Lindbergh stood in the corner of a crowded room, nursing a ginger ale. The room was full of partygoers, drinking wine, telling crude jokes, and laughing raucously.

Lindbergh had been a teetotaler all his life. Yet he didn't denounce those who liked to drink. He merely thought it sad that people demeaned themselves in search of fun. Many in the gathering were headed for hangovers in the morning, and he didn't envy them for it.

Abraham Lincoln stood in front of a temperance group and gave a talk. As a well-known teetotaler, he had been asked to address them. Lincoln was pleased to do so, because he wanted to speak on how to relate to alcoholics.

In Lincoln's view, no good could come from denouncing those under liquor's sway. If they truly wished to help those unfortunate men and women, they should use encouragement and kind words. Honey, he said, catches more flies than vinegar.

* * * * *

General Douglas MacArthur sat at his desk wrestling with a problem. Charles Lindbergh had angered FDR so much that the president had ordered that no one should involve Lindbergh in any war operations.

He considered the situation. Permitting the famous aviator to participate was a risky proposition, but his boys in the Pacific could use the man's help. Lindbergh knew aircraft like no one else. And just knowing he was working with them was a boost for their morale. Still, it was risky.

The general closed his eyes. Then he opened them and smiled. He knew what to do. He would let Lindbergh stay and help.

Perhaps MacArthur's decision was inspired by the actions of one of his lifelong heroes: Abraham Lincoln. MacArthur knew all about Lincoln's life, and how the president had opened his heart to people who wanted to contribute, no matter their past. He gave people a second chance. Lincoln had done that with several of his generals, and MacArthur may have been inspired by Lincoln's goodwill in his decision to help Lindbergh.

* * * * *

A pilot in the army air force watched the aging flier leaning next to him against the fuselage. Lindbergh was a bit on the old side, but no one could deny that his heart was in it.

The pilot had watched Lindbergh maneuver as he shot down a Japanese plane at nearly point-blank range. And just now, on landing, the old-timer had charmed them all with his grin.

Months before, Lindbergh had test-flown a new fighter plane and almost lost his life when the oxygen gave out. But that wasn't enough. He wanted to see battle. This need was almost an obsession.

And it finally happened. The call came for him to risk his life for America. He faced death beside his countrymen. He had fulfilled the sternest duty like a real soldier. He was content.

If only I could be one of them, Lincoln thought. If only I could be a common soldier in the Army of the Potomac—standing on the field of battle, risking my life for my country—instead of sitting at this desk.

He envied the soldiers who slept in their blankets near the Potomac. He would trade places with them in an instant.

Lincoln wondered how he would stand up to the test of death—to see if, after all, he had the same "cowardly legs" he'd forgiven in many soldiers.

If only it were possible . . .

* * * * *

It was early morning on a South Pacific island. Charles Lindbergh grabbed a canteen and slung it over his shoulder. After checking his sidearm, he exchanged greetings with a few soldiers, then wandered into the hills above the base camp.

Lindbergh had an easy camaraderie with the enlisted men. They seemed to genuinely enjoy being with him. They took his presence so much for granted that Lindbergh felt they had made him an honorary member of their company.

It was a good feeling.

After Lincoln's passing, Walt Whitman's muse was stimulated by the memory of the sweet and friendly relationship he had observed between Lincoln and his Union soldiers. Whitman dipped his pen and wrote,

> Hush'd be the camps to-day,
> And soldiers let us drape our war-worn weapons,
> And each with musing soul retire to celebrate,
> Our dear commander's death.
> .　.　.　.　.　.　.　.　.　.
>
> But sing poet in our name,
> Sing of the love we bore him—because you—dweller in camps,
> 　　　　　　　　know it truly.
>
> As they invault the coffin there,
> Sing—as they close the doors of earth upon him—one verse,

For the heavy hearts of soldiers.[1]

* * * * *

It was decades after the end of the war and Lindbergh was reviewing the diaries he'd kept during those years. Of the later entries, many included the word *God*.

The grim reality of war had drawn from him a spiritual response. Normally, he kept his religious feelings quiet, barely hinting at them. But war had roughly pushed those boundaries aside and revealed his hidden inner life.

March 1863, the White House. While composing a speech, President Lincoln found himself contemplating Providence. During his life, the Heavenly Father had not been a stranger to his thoughts; but the effects of war—with suffering and death on such a grand scale—had turned his mind more than ever in a spiritual direction.

Normally, he kept his religious impulses to himself. But now—when family members were sundered forever, when radical changes were occurring daily, when light and dark were so starkly contrasted that no one could guess what the future might bring—he mentioned God more and more often in his letters, conversations, and speeches.

* * * * *

Charles Lindbergh blinked as he soared over the tree-tops in a fighter plane.

It had all happened so quickly. He was bearing down on a man walking along the beach. According to the rules of

[1]From "Hush'd Be the Camps To-day."

war, the stranger was fair game and Lindbergh was going to shoot him.

And then the change came. One moment, he was about to pull the trigger and the next he refrained—a split-second decision caused by some instinct that told him he could not kill this man. The moment passed; he overshot the location and was off to his next target.

Lindbergh took stock of himself. He had been merciful to an enemy in war and it felt very good. He would never forget this incident and the fleeting but very real impression of unity with a man he should have considered his enemy.

President Lincoln smiled. He had just prevented the execution of two of Robert E. Lee's sons, and doing a good turn to an "enemy" brought a deep satisfaction.

* * * * *

World War II was over, and Lindbergh had been called to Europe to ferret out the Luftwaffe's secrets. Before long, he was driving across the German countryside. Turning his jeep off the main road, he passed through open gates. He was entering Camp Dora and about to witness the horrors of a Nazi concentration camp.

As he was being introduced to a survivor, he stared in disbelief. The man's muscle tissue had wasted away to nothing; even in baggy clothes, it was clear there was little left but skin and bone. How, Lindbergh asked himself, could anyone do such a thing to another human being? With growing revulsion he understood why so many despised Hitler.

And yet, before he could denounce the Nazis, Lindbergh instinctively did an about-face. He automatically thought of other brutal scenes: American soldiers killing unarmed Japanese prisoners, and the like.

He sighed. In war, both sides were almost always guilty of atrocities. And both sides had the potential for goodness as well. "Judge not," he murmured, "that ye be not judged."[2]

The quote struck Lindbergh as so apt that he wrote it that evening in his journal.

Abraham Lincoln closed his office door and sank into a chair.

He had just met with two survivors of Andersonville, a Confederate prison camp. When he'd first seen them, Lincoln could hardly believe his eyes. They might have stepped out of a coffin.

How, Lincoln asked himself, could people do such a thing, even in wartime? How could they let those men starve?

Earlier, when Lincoln had first heard how Union prisoners were cruelly mistreated, he began to denounce the South. But then, he remembered his duty.

He was president. It would be his job to welcome the Secessionists back into the Union after the war. He didn't have the luxury of judging them for even their most horrible mistakes. He had to maintain a broad objective view.

Lincoln was aware of the high death toll at the Union prison camps. Placed side by side, there really wasn't much difference. The people of the South were, generally speaking, good at heart, like their Northern brothers. War often brought out the worst in people.

"Judge not," he reminded himself, "that ye be not judged."

And Lincoln quoted Christ's words to Senator Charles Sumner when Sumner suggested that Jefferson Davis deserved

[2]Matt. 7:1.

punishment for the way the Confederates treated their prisoners. He would also include that Biblical phrase in his Second Inaugural Address.

* * * * *

Driving through Germany, Lindbergh witnessed the effects of destructive power unleashed. Later, while standing in Hitler's former headquarters, he pondered the legacy of dictators. He reflected on how one man could be the cause of a cataclysmic war that brought lasting repercussions, and how real people, with the fame that came with death, could become mythological symbols.

And then Lindbergh did something extraordinary: he put himself in Hitler's shoes. He projected himself into the place of a leader losing a war he had promoted, awaiting a tragic end while still in his seat of power.

Lindbergh meditated on how power could be used for so much good in the world, but how often the desire for power corrupted. In the ruins of Germany he had seen the horrible consequences of giving in to such temptations.

Abraham Lincoln was composing a speech to the Young Men's Lyceum of Springfield. His talk was a meditation on the perpetuation of the democratic system of government. At one point he reflected on the possibility of a dictator incarnating in America, and what it might take to stop "an Alexander, a Caesar, or a Napoleon."

Is it unreasonable to expect that some man possessed of the loftiest genius, coupled with ambition sufficient to push it to its utmost, will at some time spring up among us? . . .

Distinction will be his paramount object; and although

he would as willingly acquire it by doing good as harm; yet, that opportunity being past, he would set boldly to the task of pulling down.

* * * * *

While traveling through Germany, Lindbergh felt that the conquered Germans weren't so different from Americans. They, too, had their hopes and fears, their sorrows and joys. Now that the war was over, Lindbergh wanted to extend the hand of friendship to a vanquished foe.

As he observed the vindictive anger many American servicemen expressed toward the Germans, Lindbergh felt dismay. Certainly, if he were in charge of the reconstruction process, he would do things differently.

Ward Hill Lamon was setting down his recollections of Lincoln's hopes for America after the war.

"Mr. Lincoln ardently desired, on the return of peace, to exercise his functions as Chief Magistrate of a reunited country. This, with the reconstruction of the general government, was the darling aspiration of his heart."

Earlier, Lamon had written:

"Mr. Lincoln might have lived to prevent the follies and crimes of reconstruction, and to bless his country with an era of peace and good-will—thus preventing those long years of contention which followed the war's conclusion.

"What the great soldier might have done, if left to determine the proper course of action, can never be known."

February 1861. Abraham Lincoln was addressing a group of immigrants in Cincinnati: "In regard to the Germans and foreigners, it is not my nature, when I see a people borne down by tyranny, to make their lives more bitter by heaping on greater burdens. I would do all in my power to raise the yoke rather than add anything that would tend to crush them."

* * * * *

Brigadier General Charles A. Lindbergh glanced at the wings freshly pinned to his uniform. He had finally been welcomed back into the United States Air Force Reserve. President Eisenhower, former commander during World War II, had ordered the reinstatement.

It had been a hard thing for Lindbergh to resign his commission, a wrench to let go of something so deeply meaningful. Only an extreme sense of violated honor had brought him to do it. But now he was back. As he stood before the secretary of the air force, Lindbergh grinned.

"You might think," Lincoln told a friend, "that my political career has given me the most satisfaction. But nothing brought me greater pleasure than when I was elected captain of volunteers during the Black Hawk War, many years ago."

At heart, Lincoln was a military man.

CHAPTER NINETEEN

The Family Man

Anne Lindbergh stared at her typewriter. What with running the household, looking after the children, and keeping up with her correspondence, her plate was full. Yet Charles insisted that she write more. And she knew he would ask what she'd accomplished when he got home.

I have to keep working with her, Abraham Lincoln thought as he walked slowly from his law office to his Springfield home. Mary is intensely emotional, and it gets away from her sometimes. But if I continue to influence her with sweet reason, she is bound to improve.

* * * * *

Charles Lindbergh quietly opened the door and stuck his head in. Anne was seated at her desk, busily writing. Nodding with satisfaction, he eased the door shut and went down the steps two at a time until he reached his little office and his typewriter downstairs.

Abe Lincoln laid an item on the threshold of the Rutledge tavern and, moving swiftly, made his escape. He grinned as he walked back to the New Salem store where he worked. Ann would appreciate the book. It was a symbol of encouragement. He had lovingly inscribed the first page with the words,

"Ann Rutledge is now learning grammar."

* * * * *

Summer 1954. Anne Lindbergh was writing about the need for simplicity in these times of busyness and superficiality. While she dwelled on that thought, she pictured the lifestyle of a woman in the previous century. A log cabin, a wood stove, a wash basin, and a pair of knitting needles. The joy of meals made from common ingredients.

And she described and praised that lifestyle in *Gift from the Sea*.

Ann Rutledge radiated happiness and good will. She seemed to enjoy her father's tavern in New Salem, the quiet of the surrounding woods, and the simple texture of her days: the sewing and knitting, the cooking and cleaning, and the pleasure of relaxed conversation. Her lifestyle suited her philosophic nature.

* * * * *

Charles Lindbergh read the rough draft of *Gift from the Sea*. Anne was a deeply spiritual being, a beautiful soul, which Charles appreciated. He encouraged her in her metaphysical leanings. Her ethereal flights balanced his down-to-earth spirituality.

Abe Lincoln sat in a pew next to his wife and children. Although not inclined to join the church himself, Lincoln paid rent on the family pew. Mrs. Lincoln got a taste of paradise while attending church, and her husband wanted to encourage her in her spiritual leanings. He had his own inner life, but he could appreciate Mary's faith.

* * * * *

Anne Lindbergh flipped through the Christmas cards she'd saved. The cards all shared a common theme: angels. Renaissance and pre-Raphaelite heavenly messengers flew under her meditative gaze.

Anne loved angels; they represented something divine and pure. They seemed to encapsulate her soul's aspiration.

She drew out a winged art work by Sir Edward Burne-Jones. Her eyes lit up, and she smiled.

William Herndon had gathered first-hand descriptions of Lincoln's lost love, Ann Rutledge. Out of all these descriptions, one image summed up Ann Rutledge perfectly.

"She was as gentle and kind as an angel," Herndon quoted. "Her angelic nature was noted by everyone who met her."

* * * * *

Reeve Lindbergh and her mother were standing in an airport when Reeve noticed something odd. Anne had taken a luggage tag and was one-handedly creasing it into difficult shapes. The extraordinary thing was that she was accomplishing this magic with her mind miles away.

Reeve was amazed. She had no idea her mother was gifted with such manual dexterity. When she brought it to her mother's attention, however, Anne blushed. Hastily tossing the masterpiece into a nearby trashcan, she changed the subject.

In the midst of a conversation with Abe Lincoln, Ann Rutledge continued her embroidery. Since girlhood she had a pronounced ability to sew, knit, and crochet. Her fingers, flying over the pattern, instinctively followed the path that led to the most beautiful designs.

* * * * *

Anne Lindbergh gazed at her husband with rapture. There he was, surrounded by children, completely at ease. Charles was a natural parent, and children felt right at home with him. He had a gift that way.

President Lincoln squatted down and picked up Francis Carpenter's son. In moments, the boy was laughing. Lincoln had the ability to make youngsters he had never seen before feel so at ease that they accepted him as their nearest and dearest.

* * * * *

Charles Lindbergh boosted his daughter Reeve over his head. He grinned. He enjoyed giving piggyback rides at least as much as his daughter liked getting them. After she had gotten suitably scared from riding on her tall father, he deposited her on the couch.

For a few moments, Springfield was treated to the odd sight of a child's head bobbing over a seven-foot-high hedge. Then the participants in this mystery hove into view, and everything became clear. Mr. Lincoln was giving a neighbor girl a ride on his shoulders.

Lincoln was known for this pastime. It was fun for

the girl, given Lincoln's height, but it really seemed that he enjoyed the experience as much as she did.

* * * * *

Lindbergh stood in the dark behind his daughter Reeve. He turned to his son Jon. "Shhh," he whispered. "Keep still, now." The children obeyed.

They stood like statues as deer slowly made their way across the open space in the woods. The children were spellbound, their experience enhanced by the wonder shown by their father.

Little Willie Lincoln sat next to his father on the banks of a river, fishing. Willie liked to imitate his father—so he sat very quietly, without speaking, enjoying the wild, lush surroundings.

* * * * *

Anne Lindbergh walked into her house and saw that Charles and the children had rearranged the furniture. They had moved the chairs and sofa and had hung blankets over everything. Charles was maneuvering through the maze on his hands and knees with the children. The kids were loving it, and Charles was having a great time.

Abraham Lincoln crept surreptitiously into his home. He didn't want Mary to see the dirt on his knees.

He couldn't help join the fun when he saw the neighborhood children playing. Then it was that Abraham Lincoln, respected lawyer, got down on his hands and knees and gave the youths pointers on rolling marbles.

* * * * *

Charles Lindbergh walked the land surrounding his house, scanning for debris. He was determined that his children would be safe and to that end, made regular patrols of the woods, clearing everything that could possibly bring them harm.

Lindbergh had become a careful parent after the loss of his son.

President Lincoln was composing a telegram to his wife. Perhaps he was becoming a worrywart, but it was better to be safe than sorry. He was more cautious these days, after Willie's passing.

He wrote, "Think you had better put Tad's pistol away. I had an ugly dream about him last night."

* * * * *

The Lindbergh children were up early, feeding the guinea pig and mice. After breakfast, they inspected the turtle and snakes. Then they went outside, where they played with the family dogs.

Thanks to their father, the Lindbergh children were well acquainted with animals.

Sometimes Mary Lincoln felt like pulling her hair out. This morning she found her boys' pet turtle in the kitchen sink. Meanwhile, the talking crow was perched in the living room as if he owned the place.

Other times she'd discovered rats, cats, or frogs crawling on the carpet she worked so hard to clean. And that didn't take into account the numerous occasions she'd scooted the family dog off the furniture.

She told Abe and the boys time and again to keep the animals outside, but they never listened. Her husband had turned their home into a menagerie.

* * * * *

"Where's Daddy?"

This question, raised by the youngest of Anne Lindbergh's children, wasn't new to her. It had been voiced by all her offspring as soon as they could express their thoughts with clarity.

"He's away. Your father does a lot of traveling. But he'll be back."

As if speaking to herself, she repeated, faintly: "He always comes back."

"Where's Daddy?"

Mary Lincoln looked at young Tad and thought she would be happy if she never heard those words again. All her boys had asked that question, and it bothered her more than it did them.

"He's giving a speech today. But he'll be back. Don't you worry, Tadpole," she said as she scooped him up. "You know he always comes back."

* * * * *

Charles Lindbergh went over the lists of qualities he wanted his children to improve on—lists he intended to go over with them individually.

Lindbergh had a strong inclination toward control. He would have made a natural leader, but another, deeper impulse made him shy away from that role. Without a large organization to direct, he channeled these energies into his household, especially his children.

In addition, Lindbergh had things he very badly wanted to say to America. In a sense he should have been a politician, for he had grave concerns about the directions society was taking, and ideas for its improvement. But again, he steered away from politics. So he directed his need to caution and cajole toward his children.

To them he stressed the importance of balancing freedom with responsibility, and the like. He spoke so sternly to his children that it enabled him to avoid being consumed by the desire to alter the direction American society was taking.

Lindbergh's children bore the brunt of words intended for a nation.

* * * * *

Charles Lindbergh sat behind his desk, listening to Reeve argue. She wasn't keen on the spartan restrictions he had placed on her. It was a tense situation, and Lindbergh decided to defuse it with a little humor.

"This isn't a democracy," he informed his offspring, "it's a *non*benevolent dictatorship!"

And he chuckled, much to Reeve's chagrin. She knew the discussion was over as far as he was concerned.

A politician from South Carolina was at Lincoln's door. The man, elected by the secessionist government, was adamant that the president see him. It was a tense situation and Lincoln thought it called for some humor. It was his habit to defuse tensions with apt jokes.

"I'm sorry," he told the politician, "but I can't see you. I only have *constitutional* eyes."

* * * * *

Reeve Lindbergh was irritated. It was bad enough that her father saddled her with lists of habits to change, bad enough that he argued so forcefully. But when he insisted on making personal remarks while she was defending herself—remarks that surprised her so that she couldn't articulate her position clearly—well, that was just plain unfair!

Lincoln sat in a Sangamon County courthouse with an innocent look on his face. After practicing law in the prairielands for years, he had become familiar with the tricks of the trade. One involved the generous mixing of personal comments with the impersonal.

Standing, he pointed to opposing counsel and said in a forthright voice, "Mr. Logan may sound like he knows what he's talking about. But how much can we trust the word of a man who goes to work with his shirt on backwards?"

The courthouse erupted in laughter and Lincoln sat down, smiling. In a short time the jury found for Lincoln's client.

* * * * *

"Why don't you PAY ATTENTION **TO WHAT I SAY!?!**" Charles Lindbergh's voice crashed down on his son. He rarely lost his temper, but when he did you'd think the roof would fly off.

Abraham Lincoln was furious. He rarely felt this way and didn't like it. As he strode away from his Springfield home, he thought, What in the world is the *matter* with Mary? I do the best I can for her and the family, but it's never enough. And she never even *tries* to control her emotions. When is SHE GOING TO **GROW UP!?!**

Often Lincoln remained calm in the face of Mary's assaults, but sometimes he couldn't. As he mentally vented his ire, a gear in the machinery of the universe whirred into motion. The energy of Lincoln's judgment needed balancing. Sometime in the future *he* would have to experience what it was like not to keep a lid on his emotions, verbally.

* * * * *

Lindbergh could be domineering at home, but he suffered no guilt over it. He behaved as if it was something that was due him. He acted as if he had the right to do as he pleased and have his home life be just the way he wanted it. In the same way, he should be at liberty to fly around the world, go where he wished, and do whatever work he felt inclined to do. He had taken this approach since his youth and wasn't about to change it.

Since he was a boy, Abraham Lincoln knew that his life was dedicated to a higher cause. He had visions that mapped out his purpose, and their repetition only emphasized the selfless tenor of his existence. Later, as president, he did his duty. He saw the war to a successful conclusion, he freed the slaves, and did many other things besides. All of it had been necessary, and none of it had anything to do with selfish desire.

If Lincoln was a liberated saint who had fully merged his egoic desires into the will of God, then he left that carefully controlled life with no unfinished business. Otherwise, he died with unfulfilled yearnings. Many stifled impulses would have built up over the years, waiting for release.

Longings for a life of freedom: to go where he wished, do as he wanted, and say what he felt.

* * * * *

Charles Lindbergh walked out of a movie theater feeling disappointed. The films of his time were shallow and degrading. They did nothing to uplift the spirit or give a deeper understanding of humanity. He wondered why he bothered to go.

It was sad because he liked sitting in a dark, crowded theater being entertained. But something was missing.

President Lincoln applauded. He enjoyed stage performances in the dark and crowded Washington theaters. They took his mind off his problems. And there were times, like now, that he felt positively uplifted.

There was just something about Shakespeare. His works gave a deeper understanding of the human condition. Even his tragedies left one feeling cleansed. The man was a genius, and as duties allowed, Lincoln determined to see as many of Shakespeare's plays as possible.

* * * * *

Charles Lindbergh didn't like to hear that people thought he wouldn't allow anyone close to him. That wasn't so. Everyone was his friend. He was willing to do anything for someone in need. True, he didn't socialize much, but that didn't mean he didn't care or connect with people in his own way.

He just wasn't into small talk. When he called, it was to discuss important subjects, not indulge in meaningless chitchat. Just because he spent long periods between communications didn't mean he didn't consider people his friends.

"Abraham Lincoln didn't have friends."
William Herndon dropped this bombshell in a conversation with Jesse Weik.
"You don't mean that!"
"Oh, he socialized, to be sure. But he didn't have friends the way you or I do."
"How do you mean?"
"Lincoln didn't hobnob. Every connection he had was for a reason, even when he was joking. He couldn't care less about the things most people thought important."
"For example?"
"I mean he wasn't interested in who succeeded to the presidency of this or that society or railroad; who made the most money; who was going to Philadelphia and what were the costs of the trip; who was going to be married; who among his friends got this job or that. He couldn't be moved by them."
"So, he was *cold* to people?"
"Not at all. Don't get me wrong. He would give you the shirt off his back if you needed it. He was friendly to everyone. But it was only afterwards, when you looked back, that you realized . . ."
"Yes?"
"Well . . ." Herndon thought for a moment. "You know how, when you're weary, you stop and play with a little dog, and when recovery comes you push it aside?"
"Yeah. So?"
"Lincoln treated people the same way."

* * * * *

If Lindbergh had been Lincoln in a past life, he gave many people the experience of meeting a president and of staying at the White House. That karma would have returned to him . . .

Charles Lindbergh sat at a White House dinner with other guests. At one point Charles glanced at John F. Kennedy, who sat a few places down from him.

Lindbergh was not a stranger to chief executives. As a boy he had seen William Howard Taft and Theodore Roosevelt, and had met Woodrow Wilson. He'd had a fairly pleasant connection with Calvin Coolidge, the president who welcomed him back from Paris. He had also enjoyed the company of Herbert Hoover. And then there was all that fuss with FDR.

Lindbergh did not know it, but that evening he was introduced to a future president: Lyndon B. Johnson. Like Kennedy, Johnson was destined to host the Lindberghs at the White House. And finally, two years before Lindbergh passed on, he had his photograph taken with President Richard Nixon.

Lindbergh walked around a darkly appointed White House room, picking up objects from the tabletops and staring at the paintings.

It was easy to see why the Kennedys had offered him this room to stay in. The bed was certainly long enough for him. But his wife was feeling lonesome across the hall.

Lindbergh strode out of the Lincoln Bedroom, which had served as Lincoln's office during the Civil War. He entered the Queens' Bedroom, where Lincoln used to relax with his secretaries, Nicolay and Hay. In this comfortable salon with its gentle decor, Lindbergh spent the night.

* * * * *

Charles Lindbergh drove through the streets of Washington. Often in the past, he would glance at the historic sites he passed, but now he ignored them, his heart leaden.

He and Anne were passing through just after a riot had broken out, and the scenes of destruction taking place so close to the White House and Capitol building touched a nerve. Those images would haunt him for years to come.

* * * * *

In his future lives, Abraham Lincoln could expect to reap good karma from his kindness toward Africa and its people . . .

Lindbergh made several trips to Africa in the 1960s. Africa, the motherland whose children had been enslaved in America and eventually freed. Lindbergh treasured these breaks from the pressures of Western civilization, absorbing the African landscape and conversing amiably with Masai tribesmen. He felt a resonance with the native people. Immersing himself in the simple lifestyle and the wild natural beauty, his spirit was recharged. For Lindbergh, Africa was a spiritual oasis in the desert of the modern world.

In Africa, Lindbergh felt free.

* * * * *

Charles Lindbergh sat in his Land-Rover and watched as a nine-thousand-pound elephant rushed him. *Thud-um! Thud-um!* He felt the earth shake. A hundred yards away. Fifty yards. Thirty. He didn't flinch as impending doom drew near.

At fifty feet the elephant stopped in a cloud of dust. She snorted at Lindbergh, then stomped moodily away.

Lindbergh smiled. He had discovered that elephants would threaten, but not attack him in his vehicle.

President Lincoln stood calmly on a parapet at Fort Stevens and stared at the Confederate sharpshooters. Bullets whistled by, but he didn't care. There was serenity in facing one's fears.

Lincoln enjoyed the experience until the moment when, hearing a colonel's plea, he ducked out of the line of fire.

CHAPTER TWENTY

The Later Years

An important subject in the search for Lincoln connections is Lindbergh the writer . . .

Charles Lindbergh's forefingers were a blur as he typed the Acknowledgements page for *The Spirit of St. Louis.* According to his recollection, more than fifty people had contributed to his work, not to mention organizations and news services, and he was determined to mention every one of them.

President Lincoln proofread a letter he was writing. The Mississippi River was back in Union hands, and Lincoln wanted to ensure that everyone responsible was mentioned.

Lincoln nodded his head, satisfied. He had listed companies from the Northwest states, New England, New York, Pennsylvania, New Jersey, as well those from the Southern states. "Thanks," he had written, "to *all.*"

* * * * *

Anne Morrow Lindbergh was the celebrated author in the family, her literary work praised by the critics and public alike. Yet her husband, the airplane pilot, received the Pulitzer Prize for literature—and for a book that was a rehash of an earlier work. *The Spirit of St. Louis* retold the story of *We,* the book Lindbergh had written about his flight to France, but the later version was extremely well written. How did Lindbergh become such a great writer?

Here was a man whose education, from a literary viewpoint, left much to be desired. He had never really excelled in the classroom until he decided to become a pilot. In everything related to aviation he'd shown a touch of genius. But that had little to do with *writing*. Lindbergh should, if anything, have been an average writer. And yet, not only did he author books and win a Pulitzer, but he matter-of-factly edited the writings of his wife, whose literary education far outstripped his own.

It was a mystery.

With great concentration, Abraham Lincoln finished drafting the speech he was to give in Gettysburg, Pennsylvania.

Lincoln honed his writing skills on the whetstone of a brilliant mind. Early in life, he had begun to perfect his ability to express his deepest thoughts. That these efforts were successful was proved by his glittering literary legacy.

After Lincoln's death, he was lauded as one of history's great writers. His Gettysburg Address was acclaimed as a ten-sentence masterpiece of clarity and inspiration. Schoolchildren memorized it, and it served as the inspiration for several books. Lincoln's words roll easily off the lips, and a number of his phrases found wide usage.

* * * * *

Charles Lindbergh wrote slowly and carefully. He loved having the leisure to painstakingly compose his thoughts, and hated it when outside pressure forced him to rush. He wrote for awhile, stopped, and thought some more.

After he finished, he edited as often as it took until his words were just right. If it meant rewriting once, twice, even a dozen times, he did so without regret. The important thing was that he clearly expressed what he wanted to say.

A telegraph operator studied the president. While waiting for news from the battlefield, Lincoln had borrowed a desk, pulled a sheet of paper from his hat, and begun writing.

Lincoln wrote slowly and methodically, one sentence at a time. He formulated his words with extreme care and paused often to ponder his subject. Several times, he jotted a question mark next to a sentence he wished to reconsider. Then he went over the lines one by one, rewriting some until he was content.

* * * * *

Lindbergh was writing his final memoirs, later published as *Autobiography of Values*. Much of his pleasure came from relating his ancestors' stories of frontier times. He wrote enthusiastically about the log cabin they had lived in, the rough humor they had enjoyed, and their struggles to gain an education. He also enjoyed relating the details of his father's struggles as an up-and-coming lawyer and his rise in politics, culminating in an office in Washington.

* * * * *

Lindbergh wrote his final autobiography in segments. When it was finished, one could see that he had framed his work through the eyes of linear history: the beginning, his past in the setting of America's past; the middle, his middle years and experiences set in the broader context of the world;

the ending, thoughts of life after death and the future potential of humanity.

When Abraham Lincoln wrote his Gettysburg Address, he adopted a framework that set the events of Gettysburg and the war itself in the broader context of the unfolding history of America.

The president began with reflections about the past *("Four score and seven years ago,* our fathers brought forth a new nation"); described the present situation in context *("Now* we are engaged in a great Civil War"); and closed with a reference to the future ("that government of the people, by the people, for the people, *shall not perish from the earth"*).

* * * * *

As Lindbergh worked on his manuscript, he felt the urge to express certain thoughts to his fellow Americans. He had always felt a proprietary connection with his native land, and now, as he typed words of caution and encouragement, he prefaced them with phrases like "my America" and "our United States." At times, his writing had the tone of a presidential Fireside Chat. In spite of many painful experiences, Lindbergh always viewed America as his own. Put simply, he loved his country like few others in its history.

* * * * *

Charles Lindbergh scribbled on a sheet of paper while flying on an airliner. He was thinking about the potential backlash of racism, and he longed to get his ideas down on paper.

"Would other races," he wrote, "do to us as we had done to them?"

Abraham Lincoln was sitting at his bedroom desk, working on a speech, when a thought occurred to him. Looking through a pile of old notes, he pulled out a sheet. It was something he had written years ago: "If A. can prove that he may, of right, enslave B.—why may not B. snatch the same argument, and prove equally, that he may enslave A?"

* * * * *

Charles Lindbergh had the unusual ability of conjuring up distant recollections of people and events. These images glowed with new life, as if they lived anew through his memory.

Lindbergh described this odd pastime in his writings.

Abraham Lincoln was at home in Springfield, writing a poem related to a visit he had made a few years before to his old homestead in Indiana. The visit had brought up a slew of childhood memories. At present those recollections were so effervescent, so lifelike, that Lincoln was determined to set his experience down on paper.

He wrote:

O memory! thou mid-way world
  'Twixt Earth and Paradise,
Where things decayed, and loved ones lost
  In dreamy shadows rise.

And freed from all that's gross or vile,
  Seem hallowed, pure, and bright,

Like scenes in some enchanted isle,
All bathed in liquid light.[1]

* * * * *

Other images of Lincoln flickered in the pool of Lindbergh's later years . . .

Charles Lindbergh strode the long hallways of the Pentagon. He had been in this building many times lately. After the war, the military used him as a consultant on the development of nuclear missiles, and other matters.

Lindbergh had a keen interest in the safety and security of the United States against enemy powers, so he studied documents, attended group discussions, surveyed air bases, and produced lists of questions for himself and recommendations for those in charge. It was an honor and a duty to provide assistance. You never knew what lethal creations the other side would come up with. Best to be prepared.

President Lincoln grinned. He enjoyed reviewing new weapons designs. Besides, it was important for the Union to stay ahead of the South. One slip could mean the end. Hadn't they nearly lost everything when the ironclad *Monitor* barely arrived in time to hold off the *Merrimac?*

Lincoln examined the report. This new gunpowder seemed usable, but there were aspects he wasn't so sure about. Time to make a list of questions.

"Does this powder contain saltpetre or sulphur?" he wrote. "Do atmospheric changes, whether of moisture or heat, injure the powder? Will it explode with as little or less

[1] From "My Childhood-Home I See Again".

pressure than ordinary gunpowder?"

On and on the questions went. Lincoln prided himself on his lists.

* * * * *

Charles Lindbergh shaded his eyes as a Saturn rocket blasted off, carrying Apollo 11 astronauts to the moon. He was pleased that he had been invited to the launch.

Lindbergh had always been interested in furthering new modes of transportation. His flight to Paris was an example. It brought together the eastern and western shores of the Atlantic.

Afterward, he spearheaded commercial aviation through talks promoting it. In addition, he was instrumental in establishing one of the first airlines, and inaugurating the first transcontinental air route across America. He also flew pioneering flights, often with his wife, to find the best air routes around the world. It was largely through his efforts that aviation became so popular.

Lindbergh watched Apollo 11 vanish into the heavens. Even this space mission had his signature. He had helped pave the way for it by finding funding for Robert Goddard's early rocket experiments.

President Lincoln signed a paper with deep satisfaction. He had his space-and-time annihilator: the Transcontinental Railroad. Finally, there would be a quicker and easier way for people to see America. Gleaming rails, stretching across the land, would bring the East and West Coasts together.

Although its construction was controversial, coming in the middle of the Civil War, Lincoln had promoted the bill. He wouldn't let a national conflict deter him from a proposal of this sort. It was important to keep looking ahead.

But then, Lincoln had always felt this way. As a lawyer, he had happily represented the claims of steamship companies that, at the time, embodied the cutting edge of transportation. But when the railroads came along, he gradually switched his allegiances, even pleading cases against steamship concerns.

Lincoln had a vision that encompassed the future. With the signed bill in his hands, he ensured that that future would be set in iron.

* * * * *

Charles Lindbergh used his knee to hold down a box while he secured it with packing tape. He wrapped it up tight, then affixed an address label and postage.

Another box of correspondence, papers, notes, and extraneous items was ready to ship to the Lindbergh family vault in the Yale University Library.

The Lincolns were cleaning out their home—preparing to move to Washington—when Abraham pulled out a small folio.

"What's that, Mr. Lincoln?" asked Mariah Vance, a servant in the Lincoln home.

The president-elect chuckled.

"It's a collection of memorabilia from my early career," he said softly. "Pictures, newspaper clippings, buttons—that sort of thing. I call it my 'rogues' gallery.'"

He sat for a long time, examining and discussing the items with his wife and Mrs. Vance.

* * * * *

Historian Wayne S. Cole gazed at General Lindbergh with admiration. During the course of several lengthy interviews regarding Lindbergh's loss of face prior to World War II, the general candidly answered every question. Evasion was evidently no part of Lindbergh's personality, and Cole couldn't help but appreciate the general's honesty and directness.

Though elderly, Sarah Bush Johnston could still resurrect the past. She looked at William Herndon with her calm, clear eyes as she answered his questions.

"Yes. My stepson, God rest his soul, was the most truthful of men. I can tell you with absolute conviction that Abe never told me a lie in his life. But, more than that," and here she spoke with emphasis, "he never once evaded nor dodged nor turned a corner to avoid any chastisement or other responsibility."

CHAPTER TWENTY-ONE

The Infinite Blue

"I like this church, Anne. It's isolated and quiet."

The Lindberghs stood on the Maui coast, gazing solemnly at a chapel. It was a peaceful little place with a modest graveyard, and Charles was looking for such a spot to be buried in.

The church's only drawback was that it was old, built in the mid-1860s. It needed repairs to bring out its original luster, but Charles was willing to help make that happen.

April 8, 1865. The Lincolns were standing in a church burial ground outside Petersburg, Virginia, admiring its beauty and serenity.

"A nice quiet place like this one, Mary. That's where I'd like to be laid when my time comes. You know how I like peaceful, quiet places."

Later that year, Mrs. Lincoln made sure her husband got his nice, quiet place, at the Oak Ridge Cemetery in Springfield, Illinois.

* * * * *

Lindbergh lay on his deathbed with his eyes closed. He smiled as the sound of his wife's voice echoed through the room. He had asked Anne to sing some hymns so he might choose which ones would go with his funeral service, and she was complying.

Abe Lincoln sat in a chair and closed his eyes. Though ill, Ann Rutledge had insisted on singing one of Lincoln's favorite hymns. Her voice lilted with the words: "Vain man, thy fond pursuits forbear. . ."

* * * * *

Anne Lindbergh gazed at her husband while he slept. Theirs had been a long marriage with much to remember: the excitement of Charles's popularity, the stress of being celebrities, the loss of their son, the international goodwill trips, the war and its trials, the long periods of physical separation, and the mutual enjoyment of silence and nature.

They had passed a full life together, and it was sad to see it come to an end.

Ann Rutledge lay on her deathbed, aware of her impending departure, and of Abe at her side. She wanted to live, but she didn't have the strength to withstand her illness.

Abe had won her heart. She very much wanted to share his future—a great one, no doubt, full of wonderful experiences—but that was impossible now.

* * * * *

Lindbergh left a handwritten note by his deathbed, in which he contemplated an "infinity within."

As he lay on his bed, Charles Lindbergh gazed out the window at a vista of blue sky spreading over an ocean without end. Then, closing his eyes, he saw another ocean of blue within, also stretching out as far as he could see.

He had long been aware of the impending loss of his body, and he was unafraid. He watched the process with calm detachment, never letting physical pain or a bleak outlook affect his spirit. He maintained a positive attitude until the end.

Lindbergh made specific plans for his funeral service and burial, and discussed them with his family. There would be readings from a Hindu scripture and the Bible, and from the words of Eastern and Western saints. His attire and coffin were to be very simple, and the grave was to be reinforced with rocks that came from deep within the earth. It was important that everything be just so.

Yogananda said that Lincoln-Lindbergh had spent a past life in the Himalayas as a yogi. In Part Two of this book, we will look for links between these two American heroes and the philosophy and practice of yoga. The end of Lindbergh's life offers a preview.

Himalayan yogis often speak nonchalantly about their approaching death. Their detachment springs from a solid realization that the body is merely a temporary shell around their true essence. In that spirit, they may order the disposal of their remains. They also believe in the underlying unity of all religions. And because Hindu saints are usually buried rather than cremated, some may choose to have their bodies interred in the solid rock of their caves.

Lindbergh's attitudes and activities, prior to his passing, were perfectly in line with those of a Himalayan yogi.

* * * * *

Charles Lindbergh's consciousness began its final withdrawal from the senses. As a mystic, he had experienced withdrawal from the world many times,[1] so it was familiar to him. Now, as his wife and son Land sat at his bedside, he was already speeding to the Infinite.

Lindbergh's spirit passed into the deep spine. He felt himself confined, as if in a tight space. Then he moved swiftly up the long tunnel and out into the great light beyond; meanwhile, on earth, his body took its last breath and was still.

* * * * *

Even the aftermath of Lindbergh's life produced Lincolnian connections . . .

Anne Morrow Lindbergh sat in her house, looking out the window. She did a lot of that, nowadays, sitting and staring, her mind engrossed in things beyond this world.

After the death of Charles she had intended to do more writing, but somehow, with him gone there was less of a sense of urgency.

He had been a great man, and he had definitely left his mark on those close to him. Certainly, he had with Anne. After his passing, she had become less and less interested in the world.

Mary Todd Lincoln sat alone in the room next to her bedroom, with the lights down. She was counting the thick bolts of expensive cloth that she brought in large trunks wherever she went. She was anxious that nothing was missing, so she tallied the numbers daily.

Her family and friends thought her mad, but Mary needed something to ground her. Without it, she really would

[1]See Chapters Twenty-Eight and Thirty-Four.

go crazy. She would leave this earth entirely—first mentally, then physically. She had to keep busy.

Without distractions, her mind inevitably turned to her deceased husband. There was some guilt there. It was, after all, partly a result of her urging that he ended up in Washington, and died there, assassinated by that horrible man.

Mary shook her head. No, she had to think of something else—like Abraham's great soul, his wonderful spirit, his endless patience, his undying love.

Mary dropped her head, a tear rolling down her cheek. That was no good either. When she thought that way, she wanted to leave this world and join him. What was she to do?

Back to the bolts of cloth! She started counting again . . . What was this? Hadn't there been ten rolls of gold lame? There were only nine here! Someone had been at her things! Somebody was stealing from her! She would put a stop to it!

Stomping out of the room, she went to give that "someone" a piece of her mind.

And put off madness for another day.

* * * * *

Brendan Gill, biographer, looked over the information he had gathered. His subject, Charles Lindbergh, was an enigma in many ways, but there were qualities a good writer could hang his hat on. One was Lindbergh's penchant for tackling difficulties head on.

Musing aloud, Gill tried to put this idea into words: "One might say that a key principle of Lindbergh's life was, the harder the problem, the better it was to embrace it." He jotted a note to include that thought in his biography.

"Then, you aren't going to try to get out of it?" a

friend asked Lincoln, who was facing a personal tribulation.

"Nope," he replied. "There was a maxim my father taught me that I've always tried to live by: 'If you make a bad bargain, hug it all the tighter.'"

* * * * *

Anne Morrow Lindbergh was describing her departed husband. As his spirit of self-reliance came to mind, she said with great sincerity, "Nobody could ever tell Charles anything."

Mary Todd Lincoln glanced at William Herndon. They were discussing her deceased husband, and there was something she had to say.

She spoke. "None of us could rule him after he had made up his mind."

PART TWO

From Brahma to Abraham (Lincoln)

"[Lincoln's] eyes had an inexpressible sadness . . . with a far-away look, as if they were searching for something they had seen long, long years ago."
— Thomas Hicks

"I hoped someday to fly to India . . . and study mystical phenomena in the Himalayan mountains."
— Charles A. Lindbergh

CHAPTER TWENTY-TWO

Honest Abe

Think of all that you've learned in your life: insights about life and love; how to get by in the world; how to improve yourself. Is all of this hard-won understanding lost when we die? What a waste it would be!

In the second half of this book, I will show how the essence of what we learn in this life is carried into our future lives, and how, over time, our understanding is clarified into wisdom. I will also present evidence that a past-life immersion in the study and practice of the universal spiritual teachings of yoga produced one of history's greatest men—Abraham Lincoln. And that the wish of a dying yogi resulted in the Emancipation Proclamation.

Yogananda said that Abraham Lincoln—and, later, Charles Lindbergh—had been a Himalayan yogi in a past life. Is there any evidence that this is true? Are there hidden yogic qualities in their habits of thinking and behavior? their attitudes and aspirations? To verify such evidence, we need a guidebook.

When seeking evidence of a past-life familiarity with yoga, the best reference is the *Yoga Sutras* of the Hindu sage Patanjali, who lived around 200 B.C. The *Yoga Sutras* describe the "Eightfold Path," a quintessential expression of the yoga teachings. Any Himalayan yogi would be familiar with Patanjali's work, and engage in practices based on it.

The stages of Patanjali's Eightfold Path are:

1 & 2: Ten moral guidelines, consisting of five "don't's" and five "do's".
3: Physical posture
4: Energy control
5: Interiorization of the mind
6: Concentration
7: Absorption
8: Oneness

The first of the five "don't's" is non-violence. Mahatma Gandhi is famous for his practice of this teaching. Here is a brief explanation:

Non-violence is primarily an attitude of mind. Outwardly, one cannot avoid doing a certain amount of injury. The harm one does, however, by wishing harm to others hurts not only them, but oneself. Spiritually, a harmful attitude separates one from the harmony and oneness of life.

Non-injury, on the other hand, embraces that oneness, and is sustained by it. It is a powerful force for victory, for it enlists cooperation from the universe, whereas harmfulness incites endless opposition.

Are there any signs in the lives of Lincoln and Lindbergh of a past familiarity with this teaching? Let's take a look.

In Abraham Lincoln's writings and public talks, he often advocated non-violence. "Even though much provoked," he told one audience, "let us do nothing through passion and ill temper." The text of his famous Second Inaugural Address includes the words: "With malice toward none, with charity for all, let us achieve a lasting peace, among ourselves, and with all nations."

Lincoln had many non-violent traits. He disliked

leather gloves, because he hated to see animals hurt.[1] As a youth, he gave up hunting for that reason. And he refrained from spanking his children—something almost unheard of in his day. For these reasons and others, he thought it ironic that he was promoting the Northern involvement in the Civil War.

Lincoln counseled people taking up law to avoid litigation and be peacemakers. This may sound self-defeating, but Lincoln practiced what he preached. Many times, he defused strife by his words or actions, or simply by radiating calmness.

A study of Lindbergh's life yields similar findings. Like Lincoln, Lindbergh abandoned hunting big game, though he made this choice later in his life. And, even though both men could fight for a cause, they didn't believe in harming anyone unless given no other choice. Lindbergh, in fact, in one very awkward situation came up with an ingenious solution that allowed him to maintain his habitual harmlessness.

It was during a disastrous flood in China. Lindbergh and his wife were about to lift off in their small seaplane, when dozens of Chinese attempted to board. Lindbergh pulled a gun out of the cockpit, pointed it at a man on his right, then, lifting his arm in an arc, shot the gun into the air. By the time he leveled it on his left, the Chinese, convinced that he was a cold-blooded killer, retreated, thus allowing the plane to pull out safely.

Non-violence was so deeply a part of Lindbergh's personality that he wrestled with the question of why brutality and death had to be part of nature's way. In himself, he tried to strike a balance between kindness and strength.

Before the Japanese attack on Pearl Harbor, Lindbergh

[1]When Lincoln was a child, he wrote an argument against cruelty to animals.

spent months touring America, giving speeches in hopes of convincing people that diplomacy could eliminate the need for war with Germany. Yet like Lincoln, Lindbergh recognized that there were times when fighting was essential: not long after Pearl Harbor, he was shooting at Japanese planes. However, after the war ended, in his book, *Of Flight & Life,* he expressed his conviction "that the use of force is a sign of weakness on a higher plane."

It is worth noting that during the centuries when these men lived, non-violence was not a widespread concept in the West. It was a rare sentiment, even among religious people. But Lincoln and Lindbergh both practiced it. It was a habitual quality that they manifested from their earliest years. Although both men became angry at times, neither let their anger get out of control. And, in both cases, injustice set off their wrath.

* * * * *

Non-lying is the next "don't" in Patanjali's list:

Non-lying is a necessary attitude if we would overcome our false notions about life. Our path to God is entirely a matter of ridding ourselves of our delusions.

Truthfulness means to try always to see things as they are, to accept the possibility that one may be mistaken in his most cherished opinions, to entertain no likes or dislikes that might prejudice his perception of reality. In practice, it entails expressing the truth in speech, writing, thought, and action.

The connection here is easy to make. Who, after all, hasn't heard of Honest Abe Lincoln? The man who cautioned:

"You can fool all the people some of the time and some of the people all the time, but you cannot fool all the people all the time."

But there was a reason for Lincoln's nickname. He was about as steadfastly truthful as any man could be.

"I never encourage deceit," he wrote, "and falsehood, especially if you have a bad memory, is the worst enemy a fellow can have. Truth is your truest friend, no matter what the circumstances."

To Lincoln, it was absolute truthfulness, or nothing. His personal creed was that "he who makes an assertion without knowing whether it is true or false is guilty of falsehood, and the accidental truth of the assertion does not excuse him."

His law partner, William Herndon, wrote, "Ask Lincoln to sacrifice in the slightest degree his convictions of truth, and his soul would exclaim with indignant scorn, 'The world perish first!'"

One could see Lincoln's truthfulness shining through his face and eyes. A man once loaned him a substantial sum because he looked so honest. Known as a "straight-shooter" all his life, even Lincoln's political enemies had to acknowledge his personal integrity.

But there was a drawback. Because Lincoln was so honest, he assumed that others would treat him the same way. For example, after Lincoln and Stephen Douglas had both agreed to stop campaigning, Lincoln expected Douglas to abide by his word. When Douglas broke their agreement and gave a speech, Lincoln was shocked, and began to distrust him.

Lindbergh also had a hard time with dishonest people. He was outraged when an American newspaper, publishing what was supposed to be a personal account of his flight to Paris, related things that were untrue to his actual experience.

Lindbergh was the epitome of the old saying: "Honest as the day is long." He always kept his word. It was a wonder to people, on an aerial tour he made of America in 1927, how he consistently arrived on schedule, nearly to the minute. He only missed one landing, because of fog.

In Lindbergh's early years especially, truth was all-important to him. If something was true, he said so. If not, he pointed that out, too. He was incapable of falsehood, and had trouble understanding why anyone would lie.

Viewing it from another angle, both men faced their flaws without flinching and were honest to themselves. While in the White House, Lincoln said candidly, "I am sure that if I do not go away from here a wiser man, I shall go away a better man, for having learned what a very poor sort of man I am."

Some of his contemporaries claimed that they knew the will of God concerning the great issues of the time. Not Lincoln. During the Civil War, he admitted that God's will might well have been "something different from the purpose of either side." He also turned aside praise for his efforts during the war, insisting that the highest merit belongs to the soldier because he puts his life at stake.

Lincoln's self-honesty included an acknowledgment of his homeliness. When a photographer instructed him to look natural, he retorted, "That's what I'm trying to avoid!"

Lindbergh, too, put the truth ahead of showing himself in a good light. In his journal, he reported a fiasco of a hunting expedition that most people would have buried. While reflecting on fighting the Japanese, he freely pointed out the disparity between his superior armament and that of his opponents. And he never hesitated to state that he didn't deserve the lavish praise that came his way for crossing the Atlantic. He spoke glowingly of the brave souls who had developed aviation. The victory, he said, was theirs.

Like Lincoln, Lindbergh acknowledged his short-comings. He wrote plainly of his fear while descending in a parachute during a rainstorm, or of losing control of a bomber.

A study of truthfulness in the lives of Lincoln and Lindbergh brings to light another trait: both men were not only honest, but secretive—an odd combination. As you may recall from an earlier chapter, Lincoln's companions claimed that he was notorious for keeping his intentions to himself. And Charles Lindbergh led a dual life by siring at least one other family in Europe, the details of which did not surface until almost thirty years after his death.[2]

Patanjali wrote that there are powers that come to yogis who perfect a spiritual quality. For example, those who habitually tell the truth find that their thoughts or words become binding on the universe. Because of this, an advanced soul can heal others by simply saying, with deep concentration, "Be well!"

Both Lincoln and Lindbergh made predictions that came true. Lincoln once assured a general who was gravely ill that he could expect his wounds to heal. This happened. To some of his closest friends, he also repeatedly predicted his rise to power and subsequent death after achieving some great thing. After he was assassinated, they remembered his words and were startled at how close they came to the truth.[3]

[2]Of course, Lindbergh's double life was a deception, but when one looks at his life as a whole, and sees how scrupulously honest he was in every other way, it becomes clear that this was "the exception that proves the rule."

[3]On the last day of his life, Lincoln predicted again that he would be assassinated. Also, he said "good-bye" to his bodyguard, William H. Crook, instead of his usual "good night," indicating that he may have had a premonition that he would not last the night.

Similarly, Lindbergh once wrote Will Rogers and gently warned him against flying in small airplanes with no backup engine. One afternoon years later, while trying to rise above an Alaskan lagoon in a single-engine plane low on fuel, Rogers crashed into the frigid waters and perished.

CHAPTER TWENTY-THREE

Renunciation

Non-stealing, the third "don't" in Patanjali's list, means more than simply not taking another person's property. It also means not *coveting* his property. It means not desiring anything that is not yours by right. It means actually not even to desire that which *is* yours by right, in the realization that whatever is rightfully yours will come to you anyway, but that your happiness is not conditioned by whether you get it or not.

To take from another person in order to gain for oneself is merely to reshuffle the relationship of things. No overall gain is achieved, and therefore no gain to your *true* self.

Judge David Davis once conducted a mock trial of the wayward Abraham Lincoln, half-jokingly denouncing him.

"You are impoverishing this bar," Davis moaned, "by your picayune charges. Your fellow lawyers have every reason to complain. And if you don't make people pay more for your services, you will die as poor as Job's turkey!"

Lincoln answered the judge soberly. "Your honor, the high fee you are criticizing me for not charging would have come out of the pocket of a poor demented girl; and I would rather starve than swindle her."

This "trial" was not the first time Lincoln was called to task by his peers, who lamented that "his fees were not at all commensurate with the services he rendered." Ward Hill Lamon insisted that his fellow lawyer "acquired the name of 'Honest Abe' by a kind of honesty much higher than that which restrains a man from the appropriation of his neighbor's goods." Lincoln once instructed a potential client: "Yes, I can gain your suit. I can set a neighborhood at loggerheads. I can distress a widowed mother and six fatherless children, and get for you six hundred dollars to which, for all I can see, she has as good a right as you. But I will not do so. There are some legal rights which are moral wrongs."

Lincoln was aware of the subtle forms of thievery and opposed them. As president he once reprimanded a military officer for seeking a sort of retroactive promotion. Lincoln pointed out that to raise the man up meant demoting somebody else.

Lincoln worried that to free the slaves would be the equivalent of stealing from the South. At one point he proposed that the government buy slaves from their owners. This never happened. Yet, as president, Lincoln was pleased that, because he had issued the Emancipation Proclamation during wartime as a military necessity, no one could criticize that act as wrong. Anyone in his place, he said, would have had to do the same.

Although he worked hard to earn a living commensurate with public office, greed was foreign to Lincoln's nature. Not only did he not accept money to which he felt he had no right, but he also neglected to profit from financial opportunities presented to him. His tastes were very simple. "Wealth," according to Lincoln, was "simply a superfluity of things we don't need."

Lindbergh had a similar notion. During World War II, he told a potential employer that he intended to accept only $10,000 a year as a research developer, even though he was offered ten times as much. For another job, he received no salary at all. He thought it wrong to profit personally while his country was at war.[1] After his Paris flight, Lindbergh earned and was given more than enough for his family to live on—why build up an unnecessary fortune?

* * * * *

The next "don't" is non-sensuality or sense control.

When we overindulge the senses, we lose energy and become attached to the world with its neverending ups and downs. We feel a little pleasure for awhile, then become jaded and fatigued, moody and miserable. But when we control this leaking of energy, we experience joy and a rising energy that helps us to grow spiritually.

Patanjali's moral guideline of non-sensuality refers to control of all sensory indulgences, including overeating, alcohol and other stimulants, and any other means by which energy is wasted through the stimulation of sight, hearing, taste, smell, or touch.

If one were to list the activities that define worldly or sensual living, drinking, smoking, and swearing would almost certainly make the top ten. Both Lincoln and Lindbergh were well known for their abstinence from these habits.

Once, while Lincoln was riding in a stagecoach, a jovial stranger offered him a cigar. When Lincoln refused, the man tried to give him brandy. Learning that Lincoln never drank or smoked, the man said, "If there's one thing I've noticed

[1]Lincoln would have agreed with Lindbergh. Discussing the Wall Street bankers who were trying to get rich from the Civil War, he thundered, "I wish every one of them had his devilish head shot off!"

in life, it's that those who have no vices, by and large, have few virtues as well."

Lincoln remembered this conversation and repeated it many times over the years. But he continued to exercise self-control, just the same.

Lindbergh gently dissuaded those who wanted him to join them in a toast to his Paris flight. When this was impossible, he mastered the art of tilting a shot glass without sipping and of surreptitiously dumping the liquor into any handy container.

It is interesting that, although non-sensuality was the rule for both men, they both bent that rule at times. Lincoln once drank some beer to help him relax during a very tense moment in his life, and Lindbergh smoked a cigarette to demonstrate to America that he wasn't a paragon of virtue.

There is another, highly noticeable side to this teaching that is worth exploring here.

Although sense control is about mastering *all* of the senses, it is often referred to as a warning against excessive indulgence in sex. This makes sense, for the form of sensuality most obviously associated with a downward direction of energy is sexual enjoyment.

Many male yogis who live in the Himalayas are also celibate monks. They follow traditional rules of behavior designed to help them break the habits that might lead to intimate relations.

Whenever images of women arise in their minds, they try to banish them. They use mental clarity and will power to tame their passions. Sometimes they run cold baths to cool themselves off.

When in mixed company, a Hindu monk practices not looking at women, especially in the eyes. He avoids conversations with them. He tries to ignore them, as inoffensively as possible, in hopes that they will ignore him too. And this, he is glad to see, they often do.

If a monastic yogi feels attracted to a woman, he thinks of her physical defects, exaggerating them out of proportion. When at all possible, he avoids women altogether—even going out of his way to maintain a respectful distance. Sometimes, too, his brother monks will help by distracting any woman who shows too great an interest in him.

When combined with meditation, these habits bring Himalayan yogis inner freedom and joy. However, those same habits could cause problems if a yogi chose to leave his monkhood behind . . .

At a Springfield party, Abraham Lincoln decided that he'd had enough of bachelorhood. He was going to talk to a lady, by jing! Acting on that decision, he started walking toward an attractive woman when, the next thing he knew, he was in another room, surrounded by men. Some strange power seemed to prevent him from making contact with the opposite sex.

Walking home that night, Lincoln shook his head ruefully. He'd been shy ever since he was a boy. Back then he ignored girls and spent his time alone or with buddies. As he grew older, he had trouble courting. The idea of a relationship is to relate, but he did not grasp this essential point. He avoided women, often running away when they were nearby. On the occasions when he managed to stand still, he couldn't look at them. He found excuses not to talk to them. He was nervous in their presence.

"A woman," he admitted, "is the only thing I am afraid of that I know will not hurt me."

Unfortunately, when Lincoln did manage, hesitantly, to engage women in conversation, they didn't react well to him. "I have been spoken to by one woman since I've been in Springfield," he complained, "and should not have been by her, if she could have avoided it."

Like most men, Lincoln had a healthy sexual drive. Given his long bachelorhood, his saving grace was his ability to control his impulses. He reveled in his inner strength. He wrote, "Happy day when—all appetites controlled, all passions subdued, all matter subjected—mind, all-conquering mind, shall live and move, the monarch of the world. Glorious consummation! Hail, fall of fury! Reign of reason, all hail!"

Lincoln's virtue kept his interactions honorable. But problems arose when he broke through his shyness.

According to tradition, Ann Rutledge was the first woman Lincoln fell in love with. They shared a deep bond but, unfortunately, she was engaged to someone else. At one point, her fiance took a long, extended trip and the relationship seemed to be over. Although she then made a commitment to Lincoln, before anything serious could develop she became sick and died.

Lincoln passed through a time of intense pain, then tried again. He had met Mary Owens years earlier and had formed a good opinion of her. When her sister suggested that she come to Springfield with the thought of marrying Lincoln, he agreed. But he became ambivalent in attitude and action. Once, while fording a stream on horseback, Lincoln neglected to help her make the crossing as the other suitors had done. Mary was not amused.

Soon Mary returned to Kentucky. In his letters Lincoln continued to court her in his awkward way. He wrote, "I cannot see or think of you with indifference," but then stated,

"You can now dismiss your thoughts from me forever." He assured her, "Do not understand that I wish to cut your acquaintance," but quite confused her by saying, "I am willing to release you."

By the time Lincoln recognized he was in love, she had pulled away from him. He thought she wanted a deeper commitment, so he asked her to marry him. She refused, which surprised him. He tried again repeatedly, only to be rejected again. He thought, mistakenly, that she was being modest.

In this comedy of errors, Lincoln didn't know how to interpret the signs—perhaps didn't know they were there to interpret. He just plunged ahead. In fact, he did not relate *with* Mary as much as *at* her.

Afterward, he anguished over his failure. In a letter to a friend, he both exaggerated Mary's physical flaws and appreciated her good qualities. In the end he blamed himself and his pride.

Lincoln was depressed, but he had learned something. His next courtship was more successful.

Anne Morrow Lindbergh smiled. There was her Charles, utterly ignoring the lovely young damsels seated on either side of him. He was giving his attention instead to a man sitting opposite him. Charles liked to pretend that attractive women didn't exist, which endeared him to his wife.

On the other hand, he used to behave that way toward her when they first met. His callous behavior had hurt Anne's feelings. In her diary she complained of "being treated like a spoonful of medicine that's got to be taken!" Her lament was the universal reaction of women to Lindbergh, who from his earliest days had the habit of ignoring them.

While comparing biographies of Lincoln and Lindbergh, one sometimes sees phrases so similar that they seem almost like plagiarism. For example:

Abraham Lincoln's cousin John Hanks said, "I never could get him in company with women; he was not a timid man in this particular, but did not seek such company."

Charles Lindbergh's early roommate, A. J. Edwards, remarked, "He never seemed to care for the company of girls. . . . He didn't dislike women in any way, but girls seemed to have no place in his plans."

These similar descriptions highlight an aspect of reincarnation: our personalities don't change drastically from one life to the next.

Another point of corroboration stems from the fact that yogi monastics like to poke fun at the foibles of romance. Their laughter helps them maintain a light attitude while embracing the rigors of renunciation.

Lincoln, too, laughed at marriage as an institution. In his youth, he wrote a comic farce, *The Chronicles of Reuben,* about two brothers who were married on the same day. After the wedding celebrations, "the waiters took the two brides upstairs, placing one in a bed at the right hand of the stairs and the other on the left. Then the waiters of the bridegrooms took them upstairs but placed them in the wrong beds. The mother made enquiry and, learning the facts, took the light and sprang upstairs. She ran to one of the beds and exclaimed, 'O Lord, Reuben. You're in bed with the wrong wife!' The young men sprang out of bed and ran with such violence that they came near knocking each other down."

Abe shared this story with his friends. Some thought it strange that, virgin though he be, he still found amusement in sexual misadventures. And yet the fact remained that for all his life, Lincoln laughed hard at well-crafted lowbrow stories.

Similar situations existed in Lindbergh's life. As an air cadet, he entertained his mother with letters about the seamy side of barracks life. In spite of the subject matter, it was obvious he was unfamiliar with what he was describing.

It is no fluke that many Himalayan connections can be found in the beginning chapters of Lincoln and Lindbergh biographies. Studies have shown that past-life traits often appear at an early age, before a new environment affects the personality.

Other details also hint at a Hindu past life. For instance, there were some odd things that happened before Lincoln's wedding . . .

Lincoln met Mary Todd in Springfield and was strongly attracted. Courting her diligently, he beat out other suitors and, within a relatively short time, announced that they were to be married. Yet, his old habits of sabotaging relationships remained. Lincoln broke the engagement, telling his friends that he felt uneasy at the thought of being wed.[2]

Lincoln went through another difficult period. He wrote that if the pain he felt was divided among all the people in the world, he was certain there would not be one happy face.

Lincoln decided to approach Mary to confirm that they should go their separate ways. Instead, Mary persuaded Lincoln that he still loved her. Not long after, they renewed their betrothal and made preparations for their wedding.

Lincoln dreaded the thought of advertising their plans. It was as if he and Mary were involved in a clandestine operation. He insisted on privacy. They told virtually no one, fearing

[2]Herndon wrote that Lincoln didn't show up at a first attempt to marry Mary Todd. This assertion is debated by historians.

that people's interference might affect the outcome.

Even while preparing for the ceremony, Lincoln disparaged marriage. When asked where he was going all dressed up, Lincoln quipped, "To hell, I suppose." And he amused the wedding party by looking "as pale and trembling as if being driven to slaughter." Nonetheless, the ceremony went well, and Lincoln became a family man. Yet he kept the spirit of self-control alive and did not let the sexual urge control him.

Although Lincoln began his life feeling out of his depth with women, by the time he died, he no longer feared them. Probably, if he had to get married all over again, he would cruise through the process . . .

At twenty-six Charles Lindbergh concluded that he should choose a mate, but he was in no hurry to take the first suitable woman who said yes. To him, the whole business seemed quite simple. It would happen in its own time, and everything would go well.

After meeting Anne Morrow, Lindbergh wooed and wed her with impressive speed.[3]

So, from a life of monk-like renunciation spring habits that make starting a relationship difficult in the next life. Then, after suitable lessons, a relationship becomes easier to assume in the lifetime after that.

A comparison of the two men's families shows notable similarities: signs of a recurring karma. Lincoln had four boys, with one dying in infancy. Lindbergh also had four boys, with one boy dying in infancy, plus two girls.

---

[3]Lindbergh proposed to Ann Morrow after only a few dates. (See Chapter Thirteen.)

One might expect a former hermit to desire a small family, with one or two children. On the other hand, a monk living in a mountain cave might think often of what he was missing. If he were only partly successful in fighting off images of childraising, he might dive into parenthood in his next life. As I mentioned before, every desire is a commitment of energy that must be resolved through fulfillment or transcendence. One of the reasons for reincarnation is that we don't have the opportunities in any one lifetime to resolve all our heart's yearnings.

This notion of diving into parenthood certainly came into play in the life of Lindbergh, who started at least one other family while in his fifties. Perhaps the influence of a past-life practice of self-control faded toward the end of his life. Lindbergh's indulgence might be contrasted with the marital fidelity of Lincoln, who was, if Yogananda's words were true, feeling the full power of his past-life yogic practices.

As I wrote earlier, reincarnation is a system in which the ego gradually evolves from an animal-like state to an angelic one. Given this slow evolution, we might expect, in cases of reincarnation, a certain continuity of character. How, then, could Abraham Lincoln and a past-life celibate yogi become a bigamist in his next life?

The answer is that spiritual growth is a marathon run. It takes a long time for the soul to perfect every virtue. One may compare spiritual growth with an army advancing into enemy territory. Some sections of the army surge forward. Others fall behind. Although eventually the entire field will be won, even toward the end little skirmishes must be fought to their conclusion.

Abraham Lincoln was spiritually advanced, but there is no evidence that he had achieved the highest perfection.

He still had issues to work out and, if Yogananda's words are any guide, some of those issues surfaced in the life of Charles Lindbergh.

In Chapter Two, I likened a life like Lincoln's to a peak on a reincarnational graph. His soul had worked hard spiritually for many lifetimes before he could manifest that legendary life. It would not be surprising if, after several lives of intense self-control, he relaxed a few personal restrictions in his next lifetime or two. And although, as we have seen so far, Lindbergh matched Lincoln in many moral traits, he also demonstrated a few anomalies like this one.

While we're on this subject, it is interesting to note that there were past-life signs of marital infidelity in the lives of both men. Lincoln suffered greatly from his wife's jealousy: she nagged him whenever he spent time with other women. Some sources claim that Mary accused her husband of still being in love with the deceased Ann Rutledge, and that Mary actually loved Stephen Douglas and married Lincoln partly out of spite. For his part, Charles Lindbergh was cuckolded by his wife at least once; and Anne Lindbergh was romantically drawn to the French flyer Antoine de Saint-Exupery.

It is also worth reflecting on the words of William Herndon, who, after many years of studying his law partner's reactions to the fair sex, deduced that "Lincoln had terribly strong passions for women" and "could hardly keep his hands off them." In addition, Judge David Davis asserted that "Lincoln's honor saved many a woman."

Perhaps Lincoln's "honor" was a past-life practice of non-sensuality still holding firm.

There is a spiritual power that comes as one becomes adept at self-control:

Patanjali says that when non-sensuality becomes confirmed, mentally as well as physically, the yogi attains great vigor in body, and his mind becomes very powerful.

Some yogis find they can memorize long passages from the scriptures. Once something enters his mind it will remain there, to be drawn on at need.

Thomas Nelson was walking through a hotel lobby, when he felt a tap on his shoulder. Turning around, whom should he see but president-elect Abraham Lincoln! A dozen years before, Nelson and a friend had shared a stage coach with Lincoln, and they had discussed a comet that was making headlines. At the end of their conversation, Nelson had commented that he thought "the world would follow the darned thing off!"

Now, seeing him all these years later, the first thing Lincoln said was, "Hello, Nelson! Still think the world is going to 'follow the darned thing off'?"

Lincoln's recall was legendary. Joshua Speed said that "his mind was like a piece of steel—very hard to scratch anything on it, and almost impossible to rub it out." Herndon wrote that "no one had a more retentive memory. If he read or heard a good thing, it never escaped him." Lincoln had this ability at an early age, and he kept it throughout his life.

Lincoln memorized long passages from Shakespeare and the Bible and quoted them verbatim. He knew his favorite poem, a lengthy piece called "Mortality," by heart. He also memorized the speeches of Henry Clay. Furthermore, he had an endless capacity to remember people—who they were and how he met them—a priceless skill for an up-and-coming politician.

The chairman of the Minnesota Historical Society was reading a letter from Charles Lindbergh. The wealth of detail that Lindbergh recalled, relating to his childhood in Little Falls, was unbelievable.

How was Lindbergh able to summon those details sixty years later? Another astonishing point was that Lindbergh had written his letter while sitting in a hut in the Phillipines. He had no notes to consult. All the pertinent facts were stored in his brain, ready to access on a moment's reflection.

CHAPTER TWENTY-FOUR

Connecting the Dots

Non-attachment is the last of Patanjali's five "don't's":

There is a difference between non-stealing and non-attachment. Non-stealing means not to desire what is not rightfully one's own, while non-attachment means not to be attached to that which already *is* one's own, even your body. The yogi should realize that everything is God, and that attachment limits the mind to one body, obscuring the truth that the soul is, in essence, infinite and eternal.

A connection appears in the early chapters of a Lincoln biography . . .

Young Abe Lincoln was about to finish his maiden political speech. Now was the time to leave his audience with something that would imprint him, a political newcomer, in their minds as the best candidate.

"If elected," he said, "I shall be thankful; if not, it will be all the same."

His audience applauded half-heartedly.

He was not elected.

Lincoln's detachment (so odd for a politician—a calling defined by personal ambition) arose throughout his life. When he suffered a setback, he responded by saying, "Let it all go. I'll try and outlive it."

Lincoln's non-attachment manifested in other ways. He disliked any sort of pretentious display and requested that his wife not use the prefix Hon. on the envelopes of her letters to him. Being chief executive failed to swell his head. "I happen temporarily to occupy the White House," he told a group of soldiers, "I am living proof that any one of your children may end up here."

Lincoln felt detached toward himself, other people, and the world in general. He was much more attached to doing right. For the momentous decisions of his presidency, he sought to know the will of God. His inner drive, which his associates assumed was personal ambition, came from a sense of mission that transcended personal desire. He knew he had to put out great effort to accomplish his goal, and he did. But when the door to that destiny closed for a time, he lost interest and left politics. He returned only when the door creaked opened once more.

Lincoln also felt dispassionate toward his body. He neglected to protect himself, whether from Rebel soldiers or assassins. On the train ride to Washington to begin his presidency, Lincoln was in great personal danger. Yet, Lamon observed that, "at no time did he seem in the least degree alarmed." Lincoln was aware that men were out to kill him, but he calmly stated that if someone wanted him dead, he would probably succeed. Why worry about it?

In a speech, Lincoln declared, "I have said nothing but what I am willing to live by, and, in the pleasure of Almighty God, to die by."

Beyond this, the painter Francis Carpenter wrote of Lincoln, "there was no evidence to show that he ever thought of himself."

These words about Charles Lindbergh are recorded in

an early diary of Anne Morrow: "I don't believe he *ever* thinks about himself."

One would think he had good reason to. Proclaimed by the world as the hero of the age, he didn't consider himself important. He lacked self-consciousness. He never lost his head in the whirlwind of praise, never displayed pride or class-consciousness.

He really couldn't understand what the fuss was about. Lindbergh was dumbfounded by the lavish receptions in his honor, and gave away the many gifts showered on him. He continued to undertake little tasks that others in his position wouldn't have bothered with.

Lindbergh's detachment to his body manifested in his fearlessness. Wishing to experience life fully, he chose the risky career of aviation. And when the engine of his airplane suddenly stopped during a flight with his daughter Reeve, he discussed their predicament with a tranquility that set her fears at rest.

Lindbergh was also non-attached to the opinions of others. His wife cautioned against his habit of stepping into the line of fire with his public statements. But he responded, with a grin, "That's where I'd rather be."

And so, both men showed definite signs of a past-life immersion in the first step of Patanjali's Eightfold path.

Let us continue.

* * * * *

Cleanliness is the first of the five "do's":

The heart of man is impure when it longs for anything foreign to its nature. To long for the things of this world is a mark of impurity because the soul's true realm is the spiritual. Cleanliness, outwardly and inwardly, physically and mentally, is a necessary step towards freedom from physical imperatives.

Cleanliness also means to remain sequestered in one's own vibrational sphere. A sense of protection of the body from contact with others is important, for the vibrations of every man's consciousness are, in a sense, unique. The vibrations of other men, though not necessarily bad in themselves, may yet be subtly disturbing to your own particular line of inner development.

For the first time in a long while, Abraham Lincoln's shoulders relaxed. At the last minute, his duel with James Shields had been called off, and he was glad of it. It was all a big mistake. He had helped Mary and her friend with one of the letters the two women had published in a local paper, making fun of Shields, and Lincoln's involvement had resulted in Shields's challenge. Fortunately, Shields was induced to change his mind.

The experience left Lincoln with a bad taste. In future, he would be less likely to be drawn into dubious enterprises.

This mental adjustment helped solidify Lincoln's habit of remaining centered within. He already had the tendency, begun in childhood, to go off by himself and clear his mind of the opinions, thoughts, and feelings of others. His stepmother said, "Abe didn't care much for crowds of people; he chose his own company, which was always good."

In that spirit, Lincoln often left his house when his wife had a fit of temper. He also rode the circuit court, which allowed him to spend time alone. And he made a rule, while president, of not reading newspaper attacks against him.

In the press of the crowd, Charles Lindbergh spun around. Someone had pushed through the police lines and grabbed his arm. It infuriated him.

Why wouldn't they leave him alone? He didn't mind at first that people wanted to see or talk to him. But he had reached the point where the intense interest and physical crowding was making him feel unclean. After such an experience, he always felt the need for time alone to clear his aura and mind.[1]

Lindbergh liked to preserve a mental distance. During his preparations for the race to Paris, for example, he wasn't diverted by the opinions of others. While others opted for larger airplanes and multiple engines, Lindbergh stuck with his simple single-engine concept. He remained centered in himself, no matter what was happening around him.

* * * * *

Patanjali called contentment "the prince of virtues." If one can oppose with deliberate contentment the tendency of the heart to reach outside itself for its satisfactions, one feels inner joy unceasingly.

Affirm always in your heart, "Whatever comes of itself, let it come, but I am ever content in my inner heart." This practice, Patanjali said, leads ultimately to the realization of Divine Bliss.

"Every man is said to have his peculiar ambition," Lincoln declared in his first public letter announcing his candidacy for county representative, "and mine is that of being

---

[1]On one occasion, Lindbergh landed his plane in the Nevada desert to get away from people and enjoy some peace and seclusion.

truly esteemed of my fellow man, by rendering myself worthy of their esteem."

Lincoln's ambition had a tranquil quality. He didn't possess the nervous drive for power that often stems from a lack of self-esteem. He tended to look at his situation as if from a distance. Lincoln breathed contentment in his heart and maintained without complaint that, with him, "the race of ambition had been a failure."

Seated in an open car motoring down the main street of yet another crowded city, Charles Lindbergh wondered how he had ended up in such a fix.

Sure, he wanted to do something that had never been done before. The idea of flying the Atlantic had thrilled him. The project of creating an airplane that could make the crossing was a personal challenge, and he had enjoyed every minute of it. But he never wanted this endless series of parades and banquets and speeches. If he had anticipated the public's response to his Paris flight, he might not have gone through with it.

Lindbergh sighed and, turning in his seat, waved at the cheering multitudes.

* * * * *

The third "do" consists of heroic austerities, performed for spiritual ends: self-sacrifice that goes far beyond what most people consider reasonable. This is a great tradition among yogis, who sometimes compete to see who can perform the most amazing physical, mental, or spiritual feats.

Yogis make themselves hardy through practices like sitting in snowbanks or surrounded by bonfires. There are stories of yogis who stand on one leg, hold up one arm, or refuse to lie down at night, for years on end. Others go without sleep. These spiritual adventurers seek to go beyond body consciousness, to realize mind over matter. Those who succeed have a certain glow, demonstrating the joy to be found in harnessing their bodies to their will.

Patanjali said that from this redirection from external matter to the inner self, one develops certain subtle powers. Once these powers are gathered and directed one-pointedly by a consciousness in full command of itself, there is scarcely any feat of which one is not capable.

In the biographies, one reads of Lincoln's many austerities: wading through an icy river to rescue a dog . . . walking long miles to run an errand, fulfill a promise, or help someone in need . . . scything a large field to settle a debt . . . writing hundreds of letters and speeches . . . working and reworking his talks until they clearly captured what he wished to say . . . keeping his expenses to a minimum and his needs few after achieving success . . . riding the former, wider range of the circuit court after its perimeter had been reduced . . . tackling law cases for friends and strangers without charge . . . taking the humblest train accommodations while his political opponent rode the rails in style . . . keeping an open ear, all his life, to anyone in need . . . seeing hundreds of supplicants at the White House . . . staying up all night to contemplate deep thoughts, or wait for an important telegram.

Lincoln made many sacrifices. As for his counterpart . . .

Charles Lindbergh drove his car through the night. He had offered to donate his vehicle to the Henry Ford Museum in Greenfield Village, Michigan, and had set a deadline for himself. He was therefore not going to sleep.

Remaining awake was not a rare pastime for Lindbergh. Years earlier, he stayed up more than one night to get to Paris. And he challenged himself in other ways, too. He liked the self-mastery that came from transcending his boundaries, and he was savoring that feeling now.

CHAPTER TWENTY-FIVE

Heart and Soul

Patanjali's two remaining moral guidelines loom large in this study.

The fourth "do" is translated as *"self*-study." The proper study of man lies not in the gathering of intellectual information, but in the supreme adventure of self-discovery.

Not that one should give up reading. There are important insights to be gained through scriptural study. But each truth must be realized fully. As an aid to achieving such knowledge, a certain practice was taught by the seers of ancient India:

Repeat one passage at a time, slowly and out loud. Seek a deeper understanding with each perusal. Let your voice grow softer until it becomes a whisper. Finally, let your repetition be mental. Let your absorption take you beyond thought and into a soundless knowing. In that state, your realization will be pure and unruffled.

Many Himalayan yogis spend hours practicing techniques like this one . . .

Sarah Bush Johnston Lincoln gazed lovingly at the back of her stepson's head. Abe was studying once again, in his peculiar manner. From boyhood, he had a tendency of copying a phrase that struck him and reading it slowly to himself over and over until he understood it. It was as if he was trying to memorize it.

Abe had had little schooling, but when he found what he was interested in, he wanted to comprehend it fully. He had no use for fiction, but was drawn to "improving" books. And when he studied like he was doing now, he ignored the passage of time.

In later years, Sarah's stepson studied everything from law and government to the Bible. He demonstrated a grasp of the Constitution that historians would acclaim for generations. And he wove into his speeches quotes from the Scriptures that demonstrated a deep understanding of their meaning. Lincoln's appreciation of the Bible grew with age, and his exploration of the Good Book peaked during the Civil War.

There were parallels in the life of Charles Lindbergh . . .

Lindbergh sat with his nose buried in a book. Reading late into the night, he deeply absorbed his studies.

Lindbergh ignored novels but read scientific and technical writings with great interest. He also delved into spiritual texts, especially Eastern ones like the Tao Te Ching, which he sometimes quoted. Unlike most of his contemporaries, Lindbergh saw Eastern mystics as saints, and sought the means they used to achieve their exalted state. This search led him to the science of yoga.

At first, Lindbergh wasn't all that drawn to the Bible, but that changed as time wore on. When he left home to serve in World War II, the only book he brought with him was the New Testament. Around that time, he began to quote it in his writings.

Still focused on self-study, we read:

Patanjali said that when one becomes perfect in his practice of self-study, he attains the power to commune with beings on higher spheres of existence, and to receive their help.

Yogis, who practice techniques that open their awareness, and saints, who have developed such abilities in the past, receive waking visions of angels or other high souls who bring guidance, information, or warnings.

At first the conscious mind, hypnotized by the mirage of matter, may block such communications. When that happens, messages come only in the dream state. With continuing practice, however, the yogi finds he can communicate intuitively at will.

President Lincoln sat in his study, contemplating the dreams and visions written in the Bible. Many times he had pored over those pages and compared the experiences of the ancient prophets with his own.

When just a boy, he received the first of these messages. The image that arose spontaneously, like a lucid daydream, was of himself working hard for many years until he achieved a high position in life. From that high place he would accomplish something that would help many people. And, afterward, he would fall from that high place to his death. Throughout the years, Lincoln often reflected on that vision. Now that he was in the White House, he did so more than ever.

But there were other visions. Once, while lying in bed in Springfield, he saw a strange reflection in his looking glass. His face was divided, with one half showing a normal visage and the other cast with a pale, ghostly look. He thought the apparition meant that he would live through his first presidential term of office, but not his second. That vision, along with his interpretation, also remained with him.

Other signs and portents came. Some had come while he was awake, but most came through his dreams.

In one of these dreams, he spoke with his son Willie, who had died of typhoid. The experience was both wonderful and difficult, for he was aware, even while it was happening, that his boy wasn't alive. And yet, the conversations were so real that he felt they had to be true.

He also had a recurring dream that always seemed to precede a great event: it consisted of seeing a ship moving swiftly over the sea. And recently, he had another dream-vision, more powerful and disturbing than the rest. He was walking alone in a mysteriously empty White House. There were sobbing voices echoing through the halls. Following that sound, he arrived in the large East Room, where he saw a funeral bier and a body laid out as if for a wake. A large crowd was in attendance.

"Who is dead in the White House?" he asked. The answer came: "The president. Killed by an assassin!" And the sound of anguished weeping woke him.

The president stared at the Bible in his hands. After studying it, he wondered whether his dreams were a form of communication. Perhaps they were messages from the Almighty—warnings of soon-to-be momentous events.

The next century hosted an echo of Lincoln's metaphysics . . .

Charles Lindbergh lay in bed. Moments ago, while in the dream state, he was conversing with his father who had passed away many years earlier. In their conversation it was as if his beloved parent had never died. The two spoke of current events, got caught up on family news, and shared deep thoughts.

Lindbergh's experience, although strange, was not rare for him. Many times over the years, fallen aviators of his acquaintance had come from beyond the grave to chat. Often, Lindbergh had seen those disembodied souls immediately after their passing. In those moments, it really seemed as if they were more alive than they were in ordinary life.

So, Lincoln and Lindbergh had the otherworldly habit of speaking with the dead. An unusual trait, to say the least.

* * * * *

Devotion to the Supreme Lord is essential for spiritual progress. True devotion is not a slavish attitude, but rather an effort of the heart to lift itself up into that consciousness where Divine Love is felt and known.

Call to God as your nearest and dearest. Feel His presence in your heart. Awaken devotion through chanting and other practices. Deepen it through calmness. Don't let your feelings dissipate in restlessness, but offer them up on the altar of your soul.

The fifth and final "do" is nothing less than a call to religion. In biographies of Lincoln, we read of his first exposure to a worship service . . .

Eleven-year-old Abraham Lincoln sat in a Sunday meeting house near Gentryville, Indiana. The place was so noisy! They were supposed to be worshiping God, but the cabin was crowded, the congregation was restless, and it was clear that the pastor had had a little too much to drink before preaching "the Good Word."

I could do a better sermon than the pastor, Abe thought. In fact, I think I will!

When he got home, little Abe gathered his friends and repreached the sermon. And he rendered it with such feeling that they were moved to tears.

But there is more to religion than devotion. A religion is based on essential teachings and beliefs. And what are the teachings of yoga? Here is a brief summary.

Yogis believe that man was made in the image of God—that his soul is forever a part of God and that evil is a temporary phenomenon. They believe, too, that many great souls, not just the heads of religious organizations, serve as divine instruments, and that all true religions are one in essence. They believe further that salvation depends on a person's effort to attune himself with divine grace. They are also convinced that many revelations have come, over the centuries, through great souls in many lands, and that other revelations will come in the future, depending on the needs of the times.

To a yogi, miracles are performed by the workings of subtle laws—they are not inexplicable mysteries that man was never meant to understand. Yogis also believe in karma and reincarnation, and that each soul receives a just reward or punishment for good or evil actions, and that the final destiny of everyone (after much trial and error) is union with God.

A Himalayan yogi would have believed in and acted in harmony with all these precepts. Probably, by the end of his life, those yogic concepts were deeply imbedded in his brain.

And, probably, he carried them into his next lifetime . . .

Twenty-five-year-old Abe Lincoln sat in a dilapidated shop in New Salem, Illinois, watching the flames twist and curl the pages of the religious work he had written. He sighed. A friend had tossed the pages into the fire, saying it was for his own good. Lincoln had no idea that sharing his beliefs would upset people. His tenets made perfect sense—why couldn't others accept them, or at least discuss them reasonably?

After years of hearing the same religious dogmas repeated to him, parrot-like, by dozens of people, Lincoln's spirit had rebelled. He had written his pamphlet that he might, in his mind, put all to rights. He had pointed out the errors in many Christian tenets as those tenets had been explained to him. Included were the innate sinfulness of man, the supreme authority of the head of the church, the idea that Christ had atoned for everyone's sins (and that therefore their efforts were not necessary), the teaching that the Bible was the only revelation of God, the accepted explanation of miracles, the concept of eternal hellfire, and several other subjects taught in the churches.

Excitedly, Lincoln had read his booklet to his friends, expecting appreciation—or at least, intelligent discussion. Instead, he had been greeted by stony looks and whispers of blasphemy.

Lincoln gazed mournfully at the ashes. Maybe these people were not meant to understand, and he would carry his convictions to the grave.

"Well," he sighed, "so be it."

In future, he would be more circumspect in talking about his beliefs. He vowed to share a little here and there, only with those who understood, and in words they could accept. But he determined not to join any church that taught the precepts he couldn't abide. He would follow his own path and practice his own inner religion.

Let us compare Lindbergh's reactions to religion . . .

Charles Lindbergh shook his head. Having just finished a discussion with members of a Christian sect called the Oxford Group, he felt that, though their spirit was good, what they preached seemed wrong.

Lindbergh must have often felt this way while speaking with Western religionists, for he never joined a church. The only place he seemed to feel spiritually at home was in India, during his trip there in 1937. While absorbing lectures by Hindu swamis and teachers, he appeared to experience a deep contentment.

* * * * *

Biographers of Lincoln and Lindbergh used the same term to define their spiritual beliefs: they were "theists." In other words, both men believed in God, but refused to limit that belief by adopting any of the commonly accepted definitions. Both men were also tepid religionists at the beginning of their lives and more fervent in their devotion at the end. This initial rejection and later acceptance could be attributed to early exposures to a Western concept of religion that was foreign to their natures.

Lincoln and Lindbergh showed evidence of a past-life familiarity with all ten of Patanjali's "do's" and "don't's". What about the rest of the Eightfold Path?

CHAPTER TWENTY-SIX

Mind over Matter

The third stage of the Eightfold Path has to do with physical posture:

Patanjali refers to no particular set of postures, but only the ability to hold the body still as a prerequisite for deep meditation.

Yogis find that a seated posture is best for prolonged meditation. Furthermore, some poses seem elegantly designed to hold the body erect and relaxed for extended periods.

During meditation, energy rises in the center of the body. In order for there to be an unobstructed pathway, the back must remain straight.

The postures that many people practice belong to a side branch of the yogic tree known as *hatha yoga*. Hatha yoga enhances health, and those who practice it often look youthful even into advanced years. An accomplished hatha yogi can lie, sit, or stand using only the absolute minimum energy necessary, and then spring quickly into action with all bodily energy at his command. All of the postures confer spiritual and physical benefits: the inverted poses, for instance, send blood and energy to the brain. Many Himalayan yogis practice some hatha yoga in addition to Patanjali's seated meditation poses.

As you can imagine, there are no records of Abraham Lincoln sitting in the lotus posture or assuming the headstand. But there are other interesting facts . . .

In his office, Abraham Lincoln lay back in his chair with his feet up on the desktop. He liked to rest or read with his feet elevated. It was a habit he had assumed at an early age and never saw fit to change. He would rest like that for a long time, and then suddenly jump up and zoom out the door.

Although he liked to relax, Lincoln kept his spine erect—the only exception being a slight forward hunch to his upper back and shoulders.

Lincoln's stance, while giving speeches, was unusual. William Herndon said that while addressing an audience, Lincoln "always stood squarely, never putting one foot before the other, or leaning on anything. He made few changes in his position, and never walked back and forth." For large segments of his talk, Lincoln kept his body very still.

Lincoln remained thin all his life, partly because he didn't eat much. Yet his health was uncommonly good. And, except for facial wrinkles brought on by the strain of being president, he looked youthful until the end. His hair, for instance, had no gray streaks.

Lindbergh also showed signs of a past familiarity with hatha yoga . . .

Charles Lindbergh was a man surprised by illness. He found himself, at the end of his life, afflicted with cancer. Being sick was something he wasn't used to—his health was typically very good.

Although now in his seventies, it was not so long ago that he was traveling between tropical islands and corporate headquarters. And he'd always enjoyed great physical stamina. An aura of youthfulness suffused him even into old age.

But now his body had said "enough," and that was fine with him. He enjoyed studying new subjects; now he scrutinized his body as it fought with disease. With clinical detachment he withdrew his awareness from the external world and focused it on the changes happening within.

This is the attitude that hatha yogis adopt when they assume a yoga posture. Lindbergh did subconsciously what yogis do consciously.

In addition, the aviator seemed to have had an intuitive grasp of Patanjali's teaching on physical posture . . .

Lindbergh grimaced. His thigh muscles were cramping again. This always happened on long flights—and, no wonder: he was forced to sit in one position for many hours. Today, as usual, his body rebelled. "I need to move around and stretch!" it complained. But Lindbergh knew what to do. He continued to hold himself still. There was very little room in the cockpit of the *Spirit of St. Louis,* he told himself, and his body would have to deal with it.

Then, as always, after several hours his body accepted the upright, seated position. His muscles loosened their death grip, and the aches and pains vanished, allowing him to enjoy the flight. He smiled. He could sit in that position and fly forever—or at least until he ran out of gas.

During one's first attempts to sit still for a long meditation, the body fights hard. It takes effort, but eventually one masters the art of sitting motionless in one posture. Just like Lindbergh. The flier was a real yogi.

* * * * *

Patanjali's next step is energy control. This stage is important because, to attain soul-freedom, one's energy must be calmed, then directed inward from the senses to the brain.

It is also necessary to raise one's energy level. Patanjali wrote that those with high energy find greater success on the spiritual path. It is through lifting one's energy that enlightenment is achieved.

There are a number of practices that help a yogi master his bodily energies. Some of these include breathing exercises. Through calming the breath, the yogi can still his mind and attain expanded states of consciousness.

Awareness precedes control. Through various breathing practices, a yogi attains a heightened awareness of the energy in his body. Once a yogi has established that connection, he can harness those energies to the command of his will.

Some yogis are able to do amazing things, like lifting heavy objects and throwing them a great distance. These abilities are the results of energy control mastery.

But there are other, less obvious signs of energy control, such as plowing through mountains of work for a worthwhile goal, keeping one's spirits high no matter what the circumstances, and succeeding in any difficult endeavor.

Yoga means the union of soul with Spirit, but also, the union of body and mind. Energy links the two together. Mastery of his energy helps the yogi accomplish any goal—even the purpose of life itself: self-realization.

A fundamental principle of energy control is: "the greater the will, the greater the flow of energy."

With all the time Himalayan yogis have for practice, many achieve an advanced degree of energy control. Some yogis challenge themselves for entertainment. Living in the mountains gives ample scope for stretching physical limitations. Each victory brings the joy of energy mastery.

Yogis also learn to direct energy into the brain. This practice leads to intellectual brilliance . . .

The fifty-three-year-old Lincoln grunted. By gripping the end of its handle, he was trying to raise a heavy axe until it was level with his shoulder. He was sure he would succeed. He had done it many times in his younger days.

As a boy, Lincoln's body did what he asked. All youths test their physical limits, but Lincoln's tests went further than most. From a tender age, he was aware of untapped reservoirs at his command.

Secure in that knowledge, Lincoln imitated Superman in frontier America. He lifted and hauled a chicken coop weighing six hundred pounds. He scythed a large cornfield in two days. He beat local strong men in wrestling matches.[1] With the help of a few ropes, he hoisted a thousand-pound box of stones. He also lifted a large barrel of whiskey and took a sip. He tossed cannonballs and heavy mauls for great distances. And he excelled at running, jumping, and (of course) splitting wood.

When Lincoln gave his first public speech, he was interrupted by a hooligan. Lincoln calmly left the platform, grabbed the man by the shirtfront, and tossed him twelve feet. Then he resumed his talk.

[1]Out of many bouts, Lincoln lost only one.

Another time, while rebutting slander during a debate, Lincoln reached out and grasped the collar of the man seated next to him. Lifting and holding him in midair, Lincoln shook him, yelling, "This is Ficklin, who was at Congress with me, and he knows it's a lie!" Fearing for Ficklin's well-being, another man broke Lincoln's grip. Afterward, Ficklin told Lincoln, "You nearly shook all the Democracy out of me today!"

Once when William Herndon grabbed Lincoln's arm, he was amazed to find that Lincoln's sinews were hard as stone.

It is probable that Lincoln discovered what any master of yoga knows: that there comes a point in any physical exertion when the muscles have done all they can. If, at that point, one instinctively pulls on a deeper, nonphysical strength, one's body fills with power and joy. At those times, one feels that one could do literally anything.

As the years went by, Lincoln applied the principle of limitless energy to less-physical exertions: raising himself out of poverty, the study of law, and running for public office. He faced failure many times but eventually overcame all obstacles. His motto was, Don't say "if I can"; say "I will!" And he counseled, "Always bear in mind that your resolution to succeed is more important than anything else."

Whenever Lincoln needed energy, it was at his command. He was capable of working eighteen hours straight. He withstood the heavy burden of his presidency and held the Union together by the sheer power of his will.

Lincoln also had great reservoirs of mental energy. Herndon observed that his partner was "not only energetic, but industrious; not only industrious, but tireless; not only tireless, but indefatigable."

"There!" Lincoln exclaimed.

The head of the axe was level with his shoulder. His companions whistled and clapped while the president, still in control, lowered the axehead to the ground. Though others tried to duplicate the feat, they failed.

There was no evidence of outstanding physical prowess in Lindbergh's life. Perhaps that ability had diminished with the passage of time. Lindbergh's main connection with this teaching of Patanjali seemed to be his capacity to channel energy indefinitely through his form . . .

As he worked the control stick with his strong and capable hands, Charles Lindbergh banked the *Spirit of St. Louis.* He had made it. He had crossed the Atlantic Ocean and was now somewhere over Paris. The lighted ground below was probably Le Bourget Field, but he wasn't sure. He decided to swing around for another look.

Since childhood, Lindbergh had experienced a deep union between body and mind that left him free of fatigue. Later, he would expand this inwardly unified state to include any vehicles he was operating — motorcycles, automobiles, or airplanes. Lindbergh was always one with his machine, and while crossing the Atlantic, he believed he would get to Paris, as long as he deeply willed to do so.

Lindbergh enjoyed stretching the limits of what man could do in the air. In his mind, those boundaries were made to be broken. In time, his attitude would take him beyond physical flights and into the spiritual world.

But now he was coming back over the lights, and he saw that he had definitely arrived at Le Bourget. He prepared for his landing, but there seemed to be some movement on the ground. There was, in fact, a great mass of people trampling the field.

Charles Lindbergh had succeeded in doing the impossible, and the world was waiting to acclaim him.

In his early years, Abraham Lincoln instinctively adopted a meditative rhythm very much in harmony with a Himalayan yogi's. However, by the end of his life, and especially during the Civil War, he became used to putting out tremendous amounts of energy from morning until night.

Similarly, Charles Lindbergh at times was inward and contemplative, and at other times so energetic that his family found him hard to be around.

CHAPTER TWENTY-SEVEN

The Inner World

Yogananda said that Lincoln had been a Himalayan yogi in a past life. Since Lincoln was born in Illinois in 1809, the latest he could have lived as a yogi was the eighteenth century. If he dwelled in the Himalayas, he was probably born in northern India.

Given Lincoln's desire to bring about racial equality, it is possible that in his life as a yogi he suffered from racial prejudice. (Personal pain often teaches compassion.) Consider the Hindu caste system. Perhaps the yogi was born into a low-caste family like the *sudras,* or laborers. If so, he would have suffered from physical and psychological abuse similar to what the slaves of Lincoln's day experienced—an abuse that deeply troubled Lincoln.

Many Indian yogis find their calling at a young age, as this one may well have. Lincoln's spiritual maturity argues a long period of yogic study and practice. At some point this young man found a guru and was indoctrinated into the teachings of Patanjali. Eventually, he climbed from the Indian plains into the Himalayas, where yogis live like hermits in huts or caves.

Lindbergh and Lincoln both felt a pull toward spending time alone in nature. Most Himalayan yogis go into seclusion at some point. Similarly, this neophyte yogi would have retired to his cave in order to deepen his meditative practice and his understanding of the yogic teachings during a long period of solitude.

Given Lincoln's strong connections with the yogic quality of non-sensuality, it is probable that this Himalayan yogi had also been a *sadhu,* or monk. Perhaps he was even a member of the Swami order. Swamis take spiritual names, like Yogananda, which means "bliss through yoga."

As souls reincarnate, they often receive names similar to ones they have had before, as if they had begun to identify with the sounds of those names. We see, for instance, that Lincoln and Lindbergh are similar names; the first syllable is practically the same. (One might even consider Lindbergh an abridgement of the words Lincoln and Gettysburg—that Lincoln's soul was reborn into a family whose name combined his most recent life with the place where he had made his most famous speech.)

And so, this Himalayan yogi might have had a name like the one he was given in his next life. The closest Hindu name to Abraham is Brahma, which some etymologists believe to be the same word. Because nobody in India is named Brahma (which means "God the Creator"), this Hindu yogi could have adopted the fairly common monastic name of Brahmananda, "bliss through Brahma." The name is appropriate on another level, for the goal of the meditating yogi is "to become one with Brahma."

In a later chapter, we will consider how there could have been a Himalayan beginning for the names Lincoln and Lindbergh. But, for now, back to Patanjali and his Eightfold Path.

* * * * *

The fifth stage is interiorization of the mind.

Once the energy has been redirected, one must then interiorize one's consciousness, so that one's thoughts will not wander in restlessness and delusion, but will be focused one-pointedly on the deeper mysteries of the soul.

All great saints have manifested this quality. If you were to speak to them while they were praying or meditating, they would not hear you. They might not even know that you were there.

Successful people manifest some degree of sensory withdrawal while focusing on important tasks. Most people let their energies spill out into the world, but a yogi's energies flow within, feeding the joy in his heart. The experience of a deeply meditating yogi is blissful beyond any description.

A yogi is meditating. With patient effort, he goes so deep that he is not disturbed by flashing lights, tactile sensations, or sudden loud noises. In time he is able to maintain that state even when surrounded by people. Friends who approach him find that he no longer interrupts his meditations to greet them.

In the West, those who witness the raptures of saints often attribute them to mental illness or possession. We explain away unusual phenomena by defining them in familiar terms. Even the word *mysticism* signifies something mysterious. In India, by contrast, many words are used to describe spiritual ecstasies. None of those terms imply anything strange, but rather something admired and blessed.

While meditating, a yogi withdraws his life current into his inner core. Coming out of that state, his features may appear less animated, even when his being is on fire with joy . . .

Whack!

Abraham Lincoln was suddenly aware of his wife, shrilly berating him. "That's the last time I'm putting up with you ignoring me! I'm sick and tired of asking you the same questions over and over again!" Mary brandished the stick of firewood she had hit him with.

Mumbling apologies, Lincoln washed the blood off his nose. He understood her irritation. He did have a tendency to go off into deep silences.[1] And not only at home. Many people complained that they spoke to him without any response.

Some of Lincoln's friends were very concerned about him. They watched as he withdrew into silence—his gaze directed inward, his facial features losing their customary liveliness—and whispered about his unhealthy mental state. They wished they had the means to cure him of what was apparently a dark and habitual moodiness.[2]

There was only one recorded occasion in Lindbergh's life that seemed to mirror Lincoln's experiences . . .

Donald Keyhoe was visiting the Lindbergh home in New Jersey. All of a sudden, he put his hands to his ears. Lindbergh had turned on the radio so loud that the whole house shook. Keyhoe walked to the door of the den and saw Lindbergh deeply engrossed in a treatise on biochemistry. How the aviator could focus in spite of all that noise boggled the mind.

[1]Lincoln began experiencing these withdrawals at the age of eleven.

[2]Lincoln did suffer from melancholia during his life. (See Chapter Thirty-Four.) Yet the joy he shared with people, and the inspiration that flowed through his writings and actions suggest that some of his inwardness was upliftment mistaken for moodiness.

* * * * *

We come to the sixth stage of the Eightfold Path: concentration.

For true success in inner communion, the yogi must concentrate his mind, focusing it one-pointedly on a single thought or image. Since the goal is Spirit, the concept must serve as an antidote for worldliness.

With a strong lens the sun's rays, focused through it, can ignite wood. The practice of meditation, similarly, so concentrates the mind that the curtain of doubt and uncertainty is burned away, and the light of inner truth becomes manifest.

Concentration implies not only a focused mind, but the rippleless first stages of superconsciousness.

Many yogis focus on a mantra in meditation. Daily practice sharpens the mind and brings it to a state of one-pointed absorption.

Although most yogis practice their mantras mentally, they sometimes repeat other spiritual phrases aloud in a pattern of loud, whispered, and mental repetition. Similarly, mystically minded Hindus memorize and repeat long scriptural pieces in verse. Such repetition imbeds spiritual thoughts in one's consciousness . . .

Over and over Abraham Lincoln repeated the lines of William Knox's "Mortality," the poem he loved above all others—quoting the words until their meaning was etched in his brain:

Oh, why should the spirit of mortal be proud?
Like a swift-fleeting meteor, a fast-flying cloud,
A flash of the lightning, a break of the wave,
He passeth from life to his rest in the grave.

Lincoln had an extremely sharp mind. Herndon said that his powers of concentration were great. As a lawyer, Lincoln quickly cut to the heart of any matter. Judge David Davis recalled that Lincoln had the ability to "seize the strong points and present them with clearness and compactness," and that "his mind was direct, and did not indulge in extraneous discussion."

Lincoln's cherished poem was a meditation on the futility of worldly life, and the inevitability of death. Most people avoid thinking about death. The seeker, on the other hand, uses the awareness of his limited time on earth to stimulate himself to renewed spiritual effort.

So the multitude goes—like the flower or the weed
That withers away to let others succeed;
So the multitude comes—even those we behold,
To repeat every tale that has often been told.

Biographers supposed that "Mortality" infused Lincoln with a grim hopelessness, but in truth, it had the power to transport him. Musing on its lines, he could be lifted into a higher state of consciousness.

Lincoln revered "Mortality" in the same way that a saint reveres a scriptural passage. He memorized it, repeated it, and entered its rhythm into his being.

'Tis the wink of an eye— 'tis the draught of a breath—
From the blossom of health to the paleness of death,

From the gilded saloon to the bier and the shroud
Oh, why should the spirit of mortal be proud?

Hindus say: "That which is blackest night for the worldly man is bright day for the yogi." To remind themselves of the transitory nature of worldly goals, some yogis meditate in cremation grounds among the corpses and ashes. Similarly, Western monks of the Middle Ages used human skulls as drinking vessels. In a less spectacular way, Lincoln used a lengthy mantra to recall to mind the delusive nature of the world.

Although there was no evidence of mantras in the life of Charles Lindbergh, he had no problem concentrating . . .

Anne Morrow watched Charles Lindbergh while he flew an airplane. Charles sat perfectly upright and very still. He held the wheel with a calm, firm hand. It seemed as if Charles was deeply aware of everything and centered at his inner core at the same time.

His flight was a moving meditation.

CHAPTER TWENTY-EIGHT

The Yogi and Emancipation

The seventh step of Patanjali's Eightfold Path is absorption.

Absorption signifies that stage when the mind, calm and receptive, loses itself in the light of Spirit and finds its ego-consciousness dissolving in that light. The soul marvels in the realization: *"This* is what I am! Not a physical body."

Absorption is the true state of meditation. At this point the ego forgets its separate identity and becomes the soul.

Yogis learning to meditate are taught that, during a state of inner communion, their eyes might tilt gently upward with the eyelids relaxing and half-closing. To encourage this natural process, meditation teachers have their students practice with eyes half-shut.

Many paintings exist of Hindu deities whose eyes are depicted half-closed. Pictures of saints, East and West, often have a similar look. In many photographs of Yogananda meditating, one sees a fathomless calmness in his eyes . . .

Abraham Lincoln sat in a chair, waiting for the portrait-taking process to end. These sessions with photographers took a long time. Photography was in its infancy, and it was necessary that Lincoln remain as still as possible for at least forty seconds for the exposure to come out right. During this enforced stillness, he sometimes became bored, but usually he just turned inward. As he sat perfectly still, his mind became quieter, his breathing calmer, and his upper eyelids lowered until they were nearly half-shut.

This mystical look was not uncommon. Often, over the years, Lincoln's eyes assumed it, especially after long periods without moving. This habit of apparently doing nothing, with his eyes half-closed, gave him a semblance of laziness, which his early employers did not appreciate.

Lincoln was "in the world, but not of it," and his gaze, expressing that state, rested somewhere between here and infinity. It was an abstracted look, visible not only in photographs but also in paintings and sketches, when Lincoln had to sit still for much longer periods.

Lincoln was born with a slow, steady approach to things, a meditative rhythm. William Herndon wrote that Lincoln "could sit and think without rest or food longer than any man I ever saw."

Abraham Lincoln   The great yogi, Lahiri Mahasaya

Only one or two of Lindbergh's photographs show a hint of Lincoln's half-closed look. On the other hand, Lindbergh didn't have to sit perfectly still. Photography had come a long way. His images were more spontaneous, and his yogic look was less obvious, manifesting in another way.

Most people's eyes in their photographs reflect a wide range of emotional states. Lindbergh's didn't. A few of his pictures showed fatigue. Otherwise, even when he was in the midst of excited people, his eyes remained tranquil and deep. Gazing into them, one feels oneself growing still.

* * * * *

While juxtaposing pictures of Lincoln and Lindbergh, one can see the deep look the two men shared. Lincoln's photographs, and his long, abstracted silences, pointed to a past-life practice of meditation. Charles Lindbergh, for his part, regularly indulged in freestyle meditations during his long solo flights. In his *Autobiography of Values,* he wrote of his desire to access and remain in contact with what he called his inner core. This was so important to him that he adjusted his lifestyle to facilitate it.

* * * * *

Many Himalyan yogis have wondrous experiences in meditation: visions of saints and masters, or of a great light that fills every corner of their being. They hear the sound of Om: a celestial music that resonates in their hearts. They have deep realizations of truth.

One yogi among many—if he is fortunate, and if he meditates long and deeply—will have the most profound experience of all. After sitting for hours in a cross-legged pose, something opens up inside. To his astonishment, he can feel the atoms vibrating in his body. Next, his consciousness expands to embrace the air in his cave. As he watches, his awareness grows until it envelops the entire mountain. His being stretches to include other peaks, valleys, and mountain ranges. Without hesitation, his consciousness pours forth until it fills all of India, surrounding seas and distant lands, and the earth itself. Released from the boundaries of this world, it streams out to other planets, distant stars, and on into infinite space.

During this experience the yogi feels so much joy that he can barely contain it, and yet it keeps growing. He feels a love so exquisite that he longs to relieve the pains of humanity.

This experience is the final stage of Patanjali's Eightfold Path: oneness.

Once the grip of ego has broken, there is nothing to prevent the yogi from expanding his consciousness to infinity. The little wave of light, losing its delusion of separate existence, becomes the vast ocean.

Oneness is not a state of mind. It is cosmic consciousness, where the soul perceives itself as "center everywhere, circumference nowhere." In that state, no ripple on the sea of consciousness remains. Thoughts and feelings are completely stilled. The soul, in that emptiness, knows only that it exists. It is stripped to its ultimate, irreducible essence: the stark realization, "I AM."

There is no direct evidence of such an exalted state in Lincoln's life. However, it appears that Lincoln was in the habit of contemplating humanity's innate divinity, for he used phrases like "man was made for immortality" and "stamped with the Divine image and likeness." He also spoke with conviction of mankind's "ability to grasp the infinite."

"It is difficult to make a man miserable," he once wrote, "when he claims kinship with the great God who made him."

Speaking of himself, Lincoln asserted that he had "dreams of Elysium far exceeding all that any earthly thing can realize." And in response to someone who claimed that he believed "in God and Abraham Lincoln," Lincoln replied, "you're more than half right."

In his *Autobiography of Values,* Lindbergh described a sublime experience . . .

Slowly and ever so gently, Charles Lindbergh returned to mortal consciousness. He had been lying in a mountain pool on a South Pacific island, taking a breather from his work as unofficial aide to the U.S. Army's air forces during World War II. After immersing himself in the cool, refreshing water, Lindbergh became very peaceful. Then, his mind slipped into a deeper-than-conscious state and he was lost to the world.[1]

Years later, Lindbergh referred to this experience when he wrote of the inner spark of mankind's unity with God. Experiences like this one made Lindbergh question the reality of the world around him, and the ability of the physical sciences to chart the ultimate potentials of human existence.

* * * * *

Yoga means union, and the highest form of union is spiritual oneness. The oneness that Patanjali wrote about is deeply linked with freedom. A yogi knows that spiritual liberation is the only true freedom, compared with which all other forms of freedom—political, social, or personal—are merely symbols.

[1]On another occasion, while stargazing, Lindbergh had a meditative experience of expansion in space.

An essential yogic teaching says that freedom is a by-product of divine union. It comes after the fact, like the fruit that follows the blossom . . .

Abraham Lincoln was finishing his latest draft of the Emancipation Proclamation. He wanted the wording to be just so.

"That . . . all persons held as slaves within any State . . . shall be then, thenceforward, and forever free."

That should do it, he thought, laying his pen aside.

Freedom was a concept that inspired Lincoln. He was enamoured of liberty as expressed in the Constitution. And he hated slavery because of its injustice. It pained him to see men and women walking with their heads down, burdened with chains. To Lincoln, freedom was a universal right.

Unity was another ideal dear to Lincoln's heart. "I hold," he once wrote, "that in contemplation of universal law, the Union of these States is perpetual." Lincoln fought to preserve that union with a zeal that consumed him. Unity, he intuited, must be maintained at all costs. Without it, nothing else could be accomplished. That was why he quoted the biblical phrase "A house divided cannot stand," and why he placed union before freedom for the slaves.

* * * * *

If our past-life yogi had had a taste of oneness, it would have been something his soul would never forget. The memory of the inner light glimpsed in the Himalayas would remain permanently in his consciousness. And his soul would cherish the place where that experience came to him . . .

Charles Lindbergh stared at the Himalayan peaks in

frustration. He had flown to Calcutta for a conference of holy men, but his keenest desire was to meet a Himalayan yogi. He wanted to quiz him regarding his spiritual practices. And then a damaged airplane left him stranded just short of his goal.

Lindbergh had harbored this wish ever since he read books in a London library chronicling case studies performed by British physicians in India. The doctors had monitored unusual physiological changes manifesting in the bodies of yogis while they underwent ecstatic states. Lindbergh's interest grew as he read the findings.

Lindbergh himself had experienced exalted states. At least one of these came while flying,[2] and he wondered whether the rarified atmosphere had been instrumental.

While in England, Lindbergh had experimented on lab animals, exposing them to an air source similar to that of high elevations. He had watched as their breathing and pulse rates had slowed, then had stood in his makeshift laboratory, wishing that he could hook himself up to the diminutive instruments and see what would happen.

Years later, he found the opportunity to do just that. Part of his work during World War II was to test the mix of oxygen needed for a pilot to remain conscious at high altitudes. His interest was such that he didn't mind risking his life on those experiments.

But all that lay in the future. Right now, he was in India. Having flown a shortened route to the East, he had made the perilous move of crossing directly over the Swiss Alps, just so he could speak with a Himalayan yogi.

He had come so far! And he had so many questions. Of all the times for his engine to throw a rod.

[2]See Chapter Thirty-Four.

CHAPTER TWENTY-NINE

The Branch Paths of Yoga

So far, we have covered the central path of yoga: Patanjali's Eightfold Path, otherwise known as raja (or royal) yoga. But there are three branch paths that nearly all yogis practice.

Let us begin with *bhakti yoga,* the path of union with God through devotion . . .

During late summer, some Himalayan yogis journey south into the plains of India, where they attend celebrations of Krishna's birthday. They listen to devotees singing to Hari, the "stealer of hearts," and visualize Krishna playing his flute, whose strains represent God's call to the soul.

The devotional songs have words like these:

Your flute has called me to the fields,
Now I've no place to live;
Don't send me back rejected, Friend,
Whatever I call mine must end,
All that I am, I give.

I hear your flute in every tree,
In every flower and stream,
And sweetest melody of all—
A song that heaven's joy recalls—
Here, in my heart, you seem![1]

[1]From "Krishna's Flute" by Swami Kriyananda.

The sound of the plucked tamboura strings, combined with the singing, can transport the listeners to a place of beauty and light. Many in these gathering are moved to tears.

Through his meditative practices, a yogi's heart opens to the workings of divine love—to the point where he cannot hear a soul-stirring melody without being deeply moved. This experience is bhakti yoga.

In Washington, D.C., a group of former slaves was holding a worship service in an open field. Standing among them, President Lincoln listened while a man named Uncle Ben said a prayer. Afterward, the freed slaves sang with such feeling, with such a longing for the balm of God's presence, that Lincoln wept. Though he couldn't sing worth a darn, he blended his voice with those of his neighbors. There was comfort to be found in devotional song.[2]

Several of Lincoln's friends described his attraction to melancholy songs.[3] He used to ask Ward Hill Lamon to sing sad airs, which moved him to tears. It is interesting that many traditional Hindu devotional songs, similar to the one at the beginning of this chapter, have a melancholy tone.

Traces of bhakti yoga emerged also in Lindbergh's life . . .

Charles Lindbergh seated himself in the pew of a Connecticut convent church. As the Benedictine nuns began

[2]Lincoln also prayed at least once with devotion, during the battle of Gettysburg. Afterward, he was convinced that his prayer had been heard and would be answered. And it seems that he was right: the North won the battle.

[3]On one occasion, he asked a woman to write down the words to a plaintive song he had heard her sing while he was walking by her house.

their chant, he closed his eyes and smiled. He was glad that his wife had recommended this place for personal retreat. The monastic silence and devotional singing was opening his heart and spirit in a special way.

Perhaps it was this experience that encouraged him, years later, to request that religious songs be played at his funeral.

* * * * *

The next branch path is *karma yoga.* Many yogis embrace the attitude of a karma yogi, one who seeks to unite his soul with Spirit through selfless service, without desire for personal benefit. Yogis end their devotions with prayers for world peace and the enlightenment of humanity, in the hope that their meditations help others.

In August 1863, Abraham Lincoln was drafting a letter to James C. Conkling. He wrote: "I freely acknowledge myself the servant of the people, according to the bond of service—the United States constitution. . . ." He then went on to discuss the Emancipation Proclamation and the freeing of the slaves.

Lincoln's letter was similar to something he had written years before, concerning the struggle against slavery. In that paper, he had said, "I have never failed—do not now fail—to remember that in the republican cause there is a higher aim than that of mere office."

Selfless service and liberating the oppressed were linked in Lincoln's mind.

* * * * *

Some yogis embrace the spirit of karma yoga to such a degree that they are willing to perform the most menial tasks for anyone, providing it doesn't go against their conscience.

A representative of the World Wildlife Fund scanned the New York offices where an important meeting had just taken place, looking for his suitcase. He was about to ask if anyone had seen it, when he spotted his big, heavy suitcase being lugged by an old man. Charles Lindbergh, who had attended the meeting, had noticed the representative's frailty, and had taken on his burden without saying anything.

* * * * *

The secret to understanding karma yoga is not merely to act selflessly, but to rid oneself of the consciousness of self. During activity, a karma yogi tries to feel that it is not he who is acting. He acts, instead, with the thought that God is the Doer, and prays: "Lord, You are acting through me."

Abraham Lincoln was speaking with a visitor at the White House, and the conversation had turned to Lincoln's dependence on God.

"I should be the most presumptuous blockhead," Lincoln said, "if I for one day thought that I could discharge the duties which have come upon me since I came to this place without the aid and enlightenment of One who is stronger and wiser than all others.

"I hold myself in my present position as an instrument of Providence. I am conscious every moment that all I am and all I have is subject to the control of a Higher Power, and that that Power can use me or not in any manner, and at any time, as may be pleasing to Him.

"Whatever shall appear to be God's will, I will do," he concluded. "I have desired that all my works and acts may be according to His will, and that it might be so, I have sought His aid. If, after endeavoring to do my best in the light which He affords me, I find my efforts fail, I must believe that for some purpose unknown to me, He wills it otherwise."

* * * * *

Last is *gyana yoga,* the path of union with God through wisdom.

Wisdom comes first through the practice of discrimination, which means in all things to look for the kernel of reality—always penetrating to ever-deeper levels of insight. *Neti, neti,* the yogi says—"Not this, not that." By looking behind veil after veil that obscures the door to Truth, the gyana yogi comes at length to the Truth Itself, stripped of every superficial appearance . . .

William Herndon tried to describe his former law partner's nature.

"From a mental standpoint," he wrote, "Lincoln was one of the most energetic men of his day. He dwelt altogether in the land of thought. As Joshua Speed said, 'Intense thought with him was the rule and not, as with most of us, the exception.'

"His mental action was deliberate, and he was pitiless and persistent in pursuit of the truth. No error went undetected, no falsehood unexposed. He was thorough in his search, going not only to the root of the question, but digging up the root, and separating and analyzing every fiber of it. Lincoln dug down after ideas, and never stopped till the bottom facts were reached.

"Everything came to him in its precise shape and color. He saw all things through a perfect mental lens. He threw his mental light around the object, and, after a time, substance and quality stood apart, form and color took their appropriate places, and all was clear and exact."

Several writers, describing Charles Lindbergh, used the words *probing* or *penetrating* to describe the workings of his mind. Anyone who reads Lindbergh's works would have to agree that he possessed keen discrimination.

* * * * *

Gyana yogis tend to view God in impersonal terms. Charles Lindbergh saw God in that light, and Abraham Lincoln counseled his law partner to do the same.

CHAPTER THIRTY

The Teachings of India

Basic doctrines of Hinduism, such as dharma, reincarnation, and karma, are familiar to all yogis . . .

Dharma means doing the right thing generally, and fulfilling one's spiritual duty personally. Many Hindus repeat a phrase that can be translated as: "Where there is righteousness, there is victory." They learn from experience that doing the right thing fills them with inner strength.

It was evening in the Cooper Union building in Manhattan, and Abraham Lincoln was presenting the closing statement of his talk.

"Let us have faith," he declared, "that right makes might, and in that faith, let us to the end, dare to do our duty as we understand it."

The audience erupted in wild applause.

In "doing the right thing," Lincoln was inflexible. He once made the dramatic statement, "The world shall know that I will keep my faith to friends and enemies, come what will."

"You're kidding."

"No. I won't stand for it."

"But, Mr. Lindbergh, sir—they've kidnapped your son! These are not honorable people we're dealing with!"

"It doesn't matter. I said I wouldn't do it, and I'm going to stand by it."

Unscrupulous individuals had kidnapped Lindbergh's son, and the authorites wanted to send marked bills with the ransom money Lindbergh was to carry to the drop-off point. But he had promised the kidnappers he wouldn't try to catch them. He'd assured them that he only wanted his son back, and he was unwilling to break his word.

* * * * *

Hindus believe in reincarnation. It makes sense to them that a beneficent God, with infinite patience, would provide each soul with as many opportunities as it needs to "get things right."

Laboring over notes that would eventually be published as his final autobiography, Charles Lindbergh had an inspiration. He conceived of the human spirit as existing beyond its earthly demise and transmitting its essence via the gene pool. The idea was like reincarnation, only more scientific.

To underscore this thought, Lindbergh used variations of the word "reincarnation" while writing up this concept.

* * * * *

The average Hindu also believes in karma: that good actions are rewarded, and harmful deeds punished, in exact measure. He feels that there should be justice in the universe and laws under which everyone lives, and that those laws should guide one to right living and spiritual growth. In Hinduism, past and present actions determine one's future circumstances.

According to this teaching, we create our future through what we do now. Nothing can change the past; all we can do is control our reactions to present circumstances.

Abraham Lincoln was describing his philosophy to William Herndon.

"We are in the hands of an invisible, irresistable, and inevitable deaf power, an omnipotent force. Fate rules the world."

Herndon frowned.

"There are no accidents," Lincoln continued. "I believe in a universal and unvarying law in nature, governing both matter and mind, ruling everything, everywhere. Every effect has its cause. The past is the cause of the present, and the present will be the cause of the future. All these are links in an endless chain stretching from the finite to the infinite.

"People are the way they are—good or bad—because of conditions that made them that way. Conditions that have existed for perhaps a hundred thousand years. Everything was set in motion long ago. Man is compelled to feel, think, will, and act by virtue and force of these conditions; he is a mere child moved and governed by this vast world machine, forever working in grooves, and moving in deep-cut channels. Man does what is commanded.

"If a man does me a grievous wrong, he is a tool who obeys the powers. On the other hand, if he does me a great good, he still merely obeys orders. Everything, everywhere, is doomed to be what it is, for all time."

"Wait a minute! What about free will?" Herndon demanded.

"To me," Lincoln answered, "it's more a question of freedom of *mind*. At any rate, there is no absolute freedom in life. One always acts from some motive. And at the bottom of all motives is the self. Actions spring from desire; isn't that obvious?"

"Not to my mind," answered Herndon. "Your philosophy is too constrictive. I think we have more freedom than that. Children, for instance, often act without clear motives."

"The motives were there, whether they knew them or not." Lincoln smiled. "In fact, it is my belief that our motives were born before we were."

"What proof can you offer for your ideas? Where is the evidence for your concept in everyday life?"

"Why, don't you see that this is a world of compensations? Don't you agree that he who would *be* no slave must consent to *have* no slave? Or, more to that point, that those who deny freedom to others deserve it not for themselves?"

Charles Lindbergh was correcting his daughter Reeve.

"But, Daddy, what's so bad about being inattentive, sometimes?"

"The problem isn't just in doing it every so often. The problem is what happens to you when you repeatedly act unconsciously."

"I don't understand."

"How can I explain it?" Lindbergh thought for a moment. "Whenever you do something like that, you create a permanent record of it."

"A *permanent record?*"

"That's right," he went on, "and it can never be erased. Once it's done, it will always be there. And so, you see, you should always think before you act. Don't do things that you will wish later you hadn't done."

* * * * *

The average Hindu, with his belief in karma and past lives, tends to adopt a fatalistic attitude. But the proper view is that the law of karma gives control over future experiences. This attitude is more useful than dwelling on the thought that past karma will arise, regardless of anything one might do to prevent it.

"Don't you worry about what might happen to you in Washington?" Mary Todd Lincoln asked her husband while they were preparing to move.

"Not really," he replied. "That's beyond my control. As I often say, What is to be will be, and no prayers of ours can reverse the decree."

Anne Morrow Lindbergh was talking with her husband. She was expressing her concerns for the well-being of their friend Antoine de Saint-Exupery, who was on a war mission in Africa. Charles responded by stating, quite calmly, that his destiny was in the hands of fate and beyond their power to change.

Anne shook her head. She was incapable of adopting her husband's fatalism.

CHAPTER THIRTY-ONE

Caves and Clothes

Was America's greatest president a reincarnated yogi? What a revolutionary idea. But, on a spiritual level, how fitting. For great souls of every land and religion experience something similar to what Patanjali described in his *Yoga Sutras*. Perhaps there is a hidden reason why some consider Lincoln the equivalent of an American saint . . .

The president was dead. Across the nation, friends, acquaintances, and admirers of Abraham Lincoln sought to describe his noble character.

William Herndon wrote: "Through his originality and strength, his magnificent reason, understanding, conscience, tenderness, quick sympathy, and heart, he approximated as nearly as human nature would permit to an embodiment of the great moral principle, 'Do unto others as ye would they should do unto you.'" Lincoln was, according to Herndon, a "near perfect man."

Ward Hill Lamon recalled: "It may well be said that he is probably the only man, dead or living, whose true and faithful life could be written and leave the subject more ennobled by the minutiae of the record. His faults are but 'the shadows which his virtues cast.'" Lamon referred to Lincoln's "singular purity of heart."

Joshua Speed believed that "Lincoln had no vices, even as a young man." And John Hay called him "the greatest character since Christ."

The public showered similar praise on Lindbergh after his Paris flight . . .

Calvin Coolidge glanced over the lists of Charles Lindbergh's admirable qualities, written by Lindbergh's superior officers. Those military men weren't the only ones who had noticed Lindbergh's character. The American people, too, recognized his simplicity, graciousness, and calmness, his courage, truthfulness, and inner strength.

Lindbergh had an almost mystical aura. In speeches across the land, politicians affirmed that Lindbergh's name would remain unblemished. The mere thought of him had the power to inspire.

Without saying it in so many words, the America public canonized Charles Lindbergh.

* * * * *

Yogis are aware that an astral body of light suffuses the physical form, and that spiritual practice increases that light.

Saints are often depicted with an aura or halo, and a similar light surrounded Lincoln at times . . .

Mrs. Pickett gasped. The wife of the Confederate general whose men had made the fateful charge at Gettysburg was surprised to see President Lincoln standing at her Richmond door. And she was even more surprised when Mr. Lincoln asked to hold her baby. But her unease gave way to astonishment as she watched the president's face become transfigured, radiant with tenderness. It was the expression of a saint. Any discomfort she felt vanished in that instant.

The experience of the general's wife was not unique. Noah Brooks noted how Lincoln's features sometimes lit up like "a clouded alabaster vase, softly illumined by a light within." And William Herndon wrote that Lincoln's face shone so brightly at times that it seemed he had come "fresh from the presence of his Creator."

When placing their photographs side by side, Lincoln's radiance is often clearly visible,[1] and at times a similar light seems to shine through Lindbergh.

* * * * *

We have focused on the spiritual aspects of a possible Hindu past life, but there are other, more mundane details of such a life that may provide evidence.

For instance, caves are the residence of choice for many Himalayan yogis. Did either American hero have a connection with underground dwellings? . . .

Clickety clack.

Charles Lindbergh was typing in the small room he used for an office in his Connecticut home. He reached the bottom of a page and stopped to stretch. As he did so, one of his hands touched the stonework that made up one of the office walls. He smiled, and reached out to caress the stone surface for a moment. Then he returned his attention to his typing.

Lindbergh had a thing for cramped places, stone walls, and caves. When he was a boy, he used to work on projects in the stone basement of his family home in Little Falls, Minnesota.

[1]This is not a reference to apparent photographic "halos" caused by fading.

Later, after he had completed an ROTC training camp in Fort Knox, Kentucky, he went on a guided tour of Mammoth Cave. Then, while on a Pacific stint during World War II, he investigated some caverns that the Japanese had used as a staging ground for their operations. While in those caverns, he began to lose touch with his physical body, and to see himself as spirit.

On one occasion, Lindbergh and his wife visited the cave-enclosed White House Ruin of Arizona. While writing of that visit, Lindbergh measured how well the cave would serve as a dwelling. All the necessary requirements were on the tip of his mental tongue.

When Lindbergh was building his first family home in New Jersey, he specifically requested that the workers incorporate the rock cleared from the foundation into the walls. Years later, he bought a house on the French island of Illiec that was made of stone.

Some of Lindbergh's happiest moments came while flying the *Spirit of St. Louis*. When he was up there, completely alone, in a machine made of metals mined from deep within the earth, flying high above sea level, breathing in the thin, refined air in that frigid, confined space, with the cold wind whistling away outside—it was as if he was sitting in a portable mountain cave or hermit's cell.

* * * * *

A Himalayan yogi who takes vows as a swami wears a robe and perhaps a shawl made of cotton or, less often, silk. Also, many yogis sit on silk when they meditate.

The stovepipe hat that Abraham Lincoln used to wear was made of silk.

If a man wears silk next to his skin for decades, he gets used to the sensation. This is just the sort of little habit that shows up in future lives. The only silk item Lincoln wore was his stovepipe hat, and, oddly enough, it was the only item of his wardrobe that he was attached to.

* * * * *

A yogi who lives as a hermit doesn't worry much about his appearance. He usually has just one change of clothing. His garb is chosen for functionality rather than looks. Lacking anyone to please, his appearance tends to become ever more eccentric . . .

Mary Todd Lincoln counted slowly to ten. Her husband had shoved the beautiful kid gloves she had bought into his pockets again. Yesterday, she found half a dozen pairs secreted in his coat. The man was obstinate in his lack of fashion sense, and it took all her energy to keep him from turning himself into a buffoon.

She had heard how he had dressed when he first arrived in Springfield: shabby pants too short, no respectable frock coat, trousers hanging by one suspender, a worn cap, and everything out of date by who knew how long. Beyond that, he had neglected washing his shirts until they had permanent perspiration stains.

She had heard other women complain that their men were sloppy dressers, but her Abraham took the cake.

Even after she had succeeded in getting him nicely suited up, Mr. Lincoln didn't shine like he was supposed to. He looked uncomfortable, like an American Indian who had been forced to wear a Western suit.

She bit her lip. It was more than any woman should have to put up with.

On lunch break, a mechanic at an airfield nudged his companion. There was Lindbergh again. The way that hayseed dressed was a riot! His trousers were halfway up his calves, and his flying cap was too small. The two workers convulsed with laughter. Slim Lindbergh could fly, no doubt about it, but he sure could use help with his appearance.

* * * * *

Imagine the routine of a yogi living in the Himalayas. Waking up early. Meditating. Practicing yoga postures. Gathering kindling. Chopping wood . . .

Thunk!

Abe Lincoln straightened with a satisfied grin. He was done. He glanced around. The other men in the New Salem axe-wielding contest hadn't nearly finished their quota of rails. He was the winner again, by a long shot. No one could beat him at wood chopping.

In later years, he would be called "The Railsplitter."

Chock!

Anne Lindbergh looked out the window. There was her husband again, on the driveway chopping trunks into kindling. He liked to alternate writing with physical labor, and he always worked with gusto. And it seemed that he enjoyed sending his axe deep into the wood on the family's property.

* * * * *

After a yogi has cut and gathered his firewood, he builds a fire and enjoys its warmth. He sits for hours next to the crackling wood, meditating . . .

In the middle of the night, Lawrence Weldon heard a sound and woke. He turned over in bed and saw that his roommate and colleague on the circuit court was still up. Abraham Lincoln was seated in front of the fire, gazing into the flames with a distant look in his eyes.

Weldon rolled over and went back to sleep. He was used to Lincoln's odd habits.

* * * * *

Again, we picture a yogi in his mountain setting. Living alone, he becomes disorderly in his routines. With no one to influence his behavior, he develops ways of doing things that are practical yet eccentric. And he makes do with less than what most people think possible . . .

"My law partner, Abe Lincoln, was a great man," William Herndon said, holding court in downtown Springfield. "But he was mighty careless. He lacked orderliness in every particular. And he had some mighty strange ways of doing things: sticking letters in that stovepipe hat of his for storage, for example.

"But that wasn't his fault, mind you." Herndon waved a hand for emphasis. "He left home mighty early, and was on the road for years. In fact, he came into Springfield on a borrowed horse, and all he had back then were a couple of books and one change of clothing."

Herndon shook his head.

"I tell you, Lincoln was a true eccentric. You wouldn't find anyone who talked or thought like him, anywhere. Joshua Speed assured me that Lincoln was so one-of-a-kind, he couldn't think of anyone to compare him to. He kept to no fixed schedule: ate, drank, talked, read, slept as he wished, without paying any attention to the clock. And Mrs. Edwards—Mary Todd's sister—insisted that Lincoln went around in such an abstracted way, that she was convinced he thought there was no one alive on the planet."

CHAPTER THIRTY-TWO

Family Ties

An important aspect of the yogic path is translated as "fellowship with truth," and has to do with the atmosphere created whenever people come together to meditate on God. Most yogis break their seclusion at some point and reach out to those with whom they feel a connection . . .

Lincoln sat in his presidential office, smiling as he read a letter. It reminded him of the occasion a few years earlier when a group of Quakers had visited him. They wished, they'd said, to pray with Lincoln that he be guided by his Heavenly Father in the tremendous task before him. That was the only time he had had the opportunity to sit with a group of silent worshipers.[1]

He looked again at the letter, written by the Quaker woman who was their leader. Pulling out a sheet of paper, the president wrote his response:

[1]Lincoln knew another kind of fellowship with the two people with whom he spent the most time before being elected president. His law partner, William Herndon, was deeply interested in Transcendentalism (the nineteenth-century philosophical movement, expounded by Ralph Waldo Emerson and others, and based partly on the mystical teachings of India); some of Herndon's ideas were very yogic. Meanwhile, Lincoln's wife, Mary Todd, was a devout churchgoer who believed in life after death. Herndon's Transcendentalism and Mary's seances formed a natural complement to Lincoln's innate mysticism.

I have not forgotten—probably shall never forget—the very impressive occasion when you and your friends visited me on a Sabbath forenooon two years ago. Your purpose was to strengthen my reliance on God. I am much indebted to you.

Lindbergh also experienced a form of fellowship during his life . . .

Charles Lindbergh was a bit of a loner, but there were many people with whom he shared an atypical affinity.

First, there was Jim Newton, a deeply spiritual man who was also a good friend. Together, Charles and Jim had shared long periods of harmonious silence and had discussed the importance of dedicating one's life to a spiritual end.

And Alexis Carrel and his wife. Lindbergh had seldom felt happier than when he was with the doctor, listening to him propound one of his metaphysical theories.[2] Lindbergh's mind and spirit were stimulated by Carrel's company. Mrs. Carrel too was unforgettable, with her ability to read auras.

While in England, Lindbergh had enjoyed the company of Sir Francis Younghusband, the noted metaphysician. It was he who introduced Lindbergh to the teachings of yoga and invited him to a religious conference in India.

And then there was Antoine de Saint-Exupery. Lindbergh could recall an occasion when, during a conversation with St.-Exupery in the car, Lindbergh had become so absorbed in their discussion that he had run out of gas. St.-Exupery's words on an aviator's need for faith had utterly captivated him.

[2]Lindbergh wrote a preface to Carrel's book, *The Voyage to Lourdes,* in which he praised the doctor for his mystical, almost monastic, nature.

Lindbergh could also remember conversations he had enjoyed with Mr. Lin Yutang, an author of books on Eastern religion, and Teilhard de Chardin, the famous theologian and mystic.

Then, too, there was Igor Sikorsky, the helicopter designer. Both Sikorsky and his wife had a mystical side. Sikorsky was a devout Christian and had published a booklet on the Lord's Prayer.

Finally, there was Henry Ford, the automobile magnate. Lindbergh admired Ford's spirit. The eccentric industrialist was open to ideas like reincarnation and vegetarianism. Like Lindbergh, Ford had given up on looking for answers in the churches.

Lindbergh had many spiritual friends. Such friends were necessary for him and Anne; both were mystics at heart.

* * * * *

When a Himalayan yogi leaves seclusion, the first people he becomes acquainted with are those living nearby: mountain-dwellers like himself. The folk who live in that part of the world revere holy men, and are often simple and devout themselves.

Lincoln took his leave of the simple town folk with whom he had been speaking. Although it came as no surprise to him, he sometimes found wisdom in places where most of his friends did not guess it existed. Maybe it was his openness that drew these people to him. With "regular irregularity," he encountered deep spirituality in quiet townspeople of all backgrounds, including the Negroes.

Over time, Lincoln came to appreciate the innate wisdom of those whom he dubbed "the children of Nature."

Lindbergh, too, had an interest in "the children of Nature"...

As he studied the Tasaday natives squatting beside him, Charles Lindbergh relaxed in a way that he seldom did in modern society. For some reason, he identified with these Filipino cave-dwellers.

The Tasaday's primitive ways called to Lindbergh. A part of him wanted to answer that call and escape the world. Then he would live in a hut, alone in the silence that enveloped him whenever he immersed himself in nature.

* * * * *

Upon returning to civilization after a long seclusion, a yogi typically encounters certain problems. For one thing, silence has become a habit. Then, too, his voice suffers from lack of use. His first words come out as a croak—the harsh, high sound of vocal chords straining as they are put to work after a long intermission. It takes awhile for his natural voice to reassert itself. As time goes on it will improve, but it may never resume the smooth timbre he had enjoyed in his youth.

For a long time his conversations were mental. It may take years to regain the capacity to express freely and clearly what he wants to say. When he does, his verbal style is unique. In his talks, he will likely draw on ancient scriptures like the *Vedas* and the *Mahabharata* and give them new meaning.

Jesse Weik was quizzing William Herdon about his venerated law partner.

"Mr. Herndon, what exactly did Lincoln sound like when he gave a talk?"

"Oh, that was strange. It strikes me as funny, now that I think of it. When Lincoln started a speech, his voice was shrill. It wasn't until after he'd proceeded that his vocal organs altered, mellowing the tone."

"What sort of impression did he give his audience?"

"Well, he was awkward. His manner and looks worked against him, but only for a time. As he went along, he became more animated. His style, I would say, was clear and terse."

"Anything else?" Weik asked.

"Lincoln told me once that he didn't come to giving speeches naturally. He preferred to remain silent, and wasn't inclined to say anything unless he hoped to produce some good by it."

"So he didn't speak for the pleasure of hearing himself."

"Just the opposite."

"I see."

Herndon thought for a moment. "There's one other thing. Lincoln had a unique way of thinking. His individuality manifested in the peculiar way he presented his ideas. On the other hand, he sometimes used ancient works like the Bible to make his points. Some stories were a thousand years old, but he added just enough 'verbal varnish' to make them new and crisp."

* * * * *

Years of silent meditation can bless yogis with wisdom, and many people come to them for help. They clothe their lessons with images familiar to their listeners. Through their stories they persuade people to embrace truth.

A Himalayan yogi bends his thin frame forward as he addresses his students. He is something to see, with his wild hair, wrinkled ochre robe, and sun-battered complexion. But his eyes hold a warmth that suffuses the heart.

A circle of Springfield men surrounded a tall man who was the center of attention. Suddenly, the group convulsed with laughter.

Lincoln sat there—long, thin, and bony—leaning forward with his clothes at odd angles. The tales he spun were so strange and funny that his listeners' sides ached from laughter.

And then Lincoln changed his tone. He described a human foible in such a way that the men could see the importance of overcoming that fault in themselves.

But, it didn't really matter what Lincoln was talking about. While listening to him, the men forgot their cares. For a time, they felt good about themselves and the world. He exuded an aura of joy that permeated the group.

They listened to Lincoln's tales well into the wee hours. Many felt so drawn to him that they decided to return the following day. It was an excellent way to pass the time.

Anne Morrow Lindbergh grew reflective as she opened her diary. Being married to her famous husband, she wrote, was an adventure. During their travels around the world, they met many people who were as famous as Charles, but very few possessed her husband's gift of making people feel ennobled by a mere word or glance.

* * * * *

Yogis make deep connections with other people who are devoted to the spiritual search. Some are renunciates like themselves, others are peasants from surrounding areas. Advanced yogis become the nucleus of a small but growing group of disciples.

Male Himalayan yogis act as fathers to their followers, whom they engage in discussion as they gather around the firepit. These exchanges, which sometimes include sadhus of other lineages, often continue for hours.

"I would save you from a fatal error," Lincoln wrote to a friend. "You cannot fail in any laudable object unless you allow your mind to be improperly directed."

Although the advice in his letter was given unasked, Lincoln was the kind of person that people came to for help. It was obvious just by talking to him that he knew many things worth knowing. Holding court in Joshua Speed's Springfield store, he attracted many who came time and again to hear his words on religion, politics, or whatever was on people's minds. Other luminaries attended as well, but Lincoln was the center of the group. According to one witness, Lincoln and his friends resembled "Father Jupiter, surrounded by votaries."

Charles Lindbergh ran his household much as a traditional Hindu guru did.

In centuries past, Indian parents sent their youngsters to a sage's hermitage—called an "ashram"—for spiritual instruction. Included in the ashram experience were restrictions related to diet and the influences of popular society. The guru's word was law, and those in the ashram were to treat him with respect. At the same time, he was loving to those who came for instruction.

All of these practices were followed in the Lindbergh home.

Perhaps a subconscious projection, originating in Lindbergh's powerful mind, was responsible for turning his home into a twentieth-century equivalent of a traditional ashram. Whatever the cause, he pushed his children to a higher level of energy and awareness.

* * * * *

In time, a Himalayan yogi's influence can encompass a large area that may include surrounding towns. Many devout villagers feel the benefit of his presence. Through their appreciation they develop a soul connection, independent of physical proximity. Their relationship with the yogi brings them a growing sense of inner freedom.

Many great Hindu yogis do not divulge their names, but simply show up and begin their work of teaching and healing. Grateful students, wishing to claim these great souls as their own, name them after the places where they live.

Is there any place in the Himalayas that could have been connected in a similar fashion with Abraham Lincoln's past life as a yogi? Curiously enough, there is.

The village of Linkhim is located in Nepal, in a remote region of the eastern Himalayas. It is listed on trekking itineraries to the nearby peak of Kanchenjunga.

The people of Nepal are devout Hindus who take their religion seriously. More than 2,700 temples and shrines are located near the capital city of Kathmandu, and many sadhus, yogis, and villagers frequent them.

If the Himalayan yogi Yogananda referred to as Lincoln's former incarnation had settled in this area and reached a high spiritual state, he may well have been given a name like "Linkhim Baba," or the "Master of Linkhim" . . .

The former slave wept. Like most of his brethren he had none of the white folks' learning. But he had a strong sense of intuition, and that sense told him that something had gone terribly wrong with he whom his wider family called "Massa Linkum."

These grateful people were in touch with Lincoln on a deep level. Through their openness they beheld him as an instrument of God's liberating power.

* * * * *

Some yogis are cautious about sharing too much of their backgrounds. They allow their disciples to write only very brief biographies of them. One yogi-author, Rama-krishna's disciple Master Mahasaya, shortened his name to an impersonal letter: "M" . . .

Abraham Lincoln was creating his autobiography, to be used for the presidential campaign. It took him awhile, but when he finished, he only had a few pages. And, instead of his name, he had written "A." and "Mr. L."

Charles Lindbergh was toying with titles for his final autobiographical work, searching for the right words.

In regard to book titles, the aviator tended toward the impersonal and self-effacing. His first memoir, published soon after his Paris flight, was called *We* — which stood either for Lindbergh and his airplane, or he and the group that financed the venture.

Later, he went even further in that direction. He rewrote that first story and titled it *The Spirit of St. Louis*. (Apparently, at that point the airplane had flown itself across the Atlantic.)

Now he was near the end of his life. This was his last chance to share himself with the world. What title would he choose?

Lindbergh leaned forward and wrote: *Autobiography of Values*. Then he sat back, stared at the words, and smiled. Yes, he thought, that has just the right ring to it.

CHAPTER THIRTY-THREE

The Wandering Monk

Constant movement is a tradition of Indian sadhus. By never remaining very long in one place, they affirm that nothing belongs to them. They expand their sense of identification until they see the whole world as their home.

Staying in his cave for months or years can leave a hermit-yogi with an incurable wanderlust. Taking up the life of a wandering sadhu, he then goes on pilgrimage in the fall and returns to his cave in the spring. Initially, to increase his stamina, he walks to town regularly. After that, he explores the region where he lives. In time, he gets used to walking even great distances without being bothered . . .

Abraham Lincoln sat in the Executive Mansion, thinking of his early days, when he could pack up and leave on a whim. He had done a lot of traveling in his life. In his youth, he had walked many miles to stretch his long legs. Later, he expanded his means of transportation to include horses, carriages, and trains.

The open road was the life for him. The best scenario was roughing it, with as little baggage as possible, and even as president he made sure he could get around whenever he felt the urge. He was the first chief executive to have a presidential yacht. During his administration, he traveled to Pennsylvania, Maryland, and Virginia. He visited battlefields and military hospitals. Even while at home, he often stretched his legs to see the sights of Washington.

And he planned, when he turned over the White House to its next occupant, to travel farther than he had before.

An elderly Charles Lindbergh sat in his Connecticut home with his hands clasped behind his head. As a youth, he had longed to travel, but he had now fed that need to the point of indigestion. It was hard to think of many places he hadn't visited by automobile, boat, train, or on foot. And especially by air.

In this respect, Lindbergh's life had been one extended vacation. He had roamed at will, taking little with him and roughing it. His fame had furnished him with an open passport. And he had found jobs that stipulated constant travel.

* * * * *

Himalayan yogis hike on dusty trails past fragrant cedars. In the evenings, they gather dung to burn. If they see other pilgrims, they eat with them—often bread with butter or yogurt.

Even in those high mountains, market bazaars are popular at villages and crossroads. People barter for food, clothing, and other goods. Historically, many nationalities gather at these spots. Because of this, Himalayan yogis learn to become comfortable with exotic ideas and cultures. And, as practitioners of karma yoga, they serve the people they meet in any way they can.

Alone at night, Abraham Lincoln trotted his horse along a muddy road. He was riding the circuit court—traveling through the townships of central Illinois and filling the people's legal needs. He was one of a group of lawyers serving the counties northeast of Springfield, but his colleagues had retired for the weekend. He was the only one who continued after the mandatory five days had ended.

Lincoln loved being on the road. He enjoyed meeting new people, serving them, and relaxing with friends or strangers afterward at a local inn. Traveling in the country-side was medicine for his soul. So he spent more time on the road than at home, rode a wider circuit than his colleagues, and charged less for his services.

* * * * *

Yogis often make pilgrimages to Hindu temples and Buddhist monasteries. Their journeys expose them to Jainism, Sikhism, Taoism, Confucianism, Islam, and Christianity. India has always been a melting pot of religions, and yogis taste that blend to the full. Each belief system holds something of interest, and yogis try to absorb the truth in every teaching, as their schooling encourages them to do.

A pair of pastors, representing different Christian denominations, laughed and joked as they exited the White House. Their interviews with President Lincoln had left them with a feeling of brotherly affection. He had conversed with each of them affably, showing a respect for their individual beliefs that made each pastor feel at home.

Lincoln was sitting in his room in Springfield, Illinois, working on a speech he was to give to the Wisconsin State Agricultural Society. At one point, he wanted to express the ephemeral nature of the world, and an oriental story came to mind. It was about a king who had offered his wise men riches if only they would tell him how to be always at peace.

The wisest counselor replied that there was only one formula that guaranteed peace of mind: "And that is, Sire, in all things to say, 'This, too, shall pass away.'"

Lincoln nodded and wrote the story to end his speech. He was willing to quote teachings from any source, East or West, when applicable. It didn't matter where the story came from, so long as it was true. He would just as readily recite a Bible passage as the oriental legend he planned to tell.

Charles Lindbergh thumbed through his well-worn copy of Lao Tsu's *Tao Te Ching*. He appreciated the Chinese teacher's peaceful philosophy. There were aspects of the Tao that reminded him of Christianity, Buddhism, and yoga. They all expressed in different ways the same profound truths.

* * * * *

Through his travels, a wandering sadhu sees the broad picture of humanity. He observes that even though people follow different customs, they have similar needs. They might call God Krishna, Allah, or Jesus, but they all pray with devotion to the same Omnipotent Being who created them.

President Lincoln, while drafting a speech, was trying to emphasize the underlying unity between the people of the Northern states and those of the South. How could he express it in the clearest possible way?

"Well," he reflected aloud, "as human beings we're all brothers and sisters, for God is our Father. No matter our differences, each of us prays to the same God."

Now there's a thought to keep, he decided. And he carefully added it to his speech.

* * * * *

Many wandering yogis enjoy hiking in the Himalayas and reveling in the beauties of nature. If a yogi is of a gyanic (wisdom) bent, his analytical mind may became engaged. How were these majestic mountains formed? he might ask himself. When did those unusual boulders arrive at their location, and what caused them to look so different from other rock formations?

Abraham Lincoln stood with his hair blown back, watching the roar of Niagara descending above him. It was fantastic: a place of rushing, natural force. He felt Niagara's power as he stood in silent awe.

Then his mind clicked in. How did this spectacle come into being, and how long had it been there? His imagination turned back time, seeing Niagara flowing continuously throughout the great events of history. He witnessed the cycles of weather and water that resulted in the falls, and he marveled at the great elemental shifts that had brought it about.

Later that evening, he put his reflections on paper.

Charles Lindbergh stood at the brink of a precipice and sighed. Nature and its pristine wildness: he had seen more than his share. But he had also seen it vanishing, little by little.

Decades before, when he had first flown over much of the world's surface, he had reveled in its scenic glory. And yet, over time, he had seen unblemished acres transformed into housing developments, factories, and parking lots.

Lindbergh felt a deep urge to preserve the natural environment. Following this impulse, he became a conservationist.

* * * * *

Sadhus often make pilgrimages to holy places like Mount Kailash, sacred to Lord Shiva, the "King of Yogis." This is a serious Himalayan trek which, if done on foot, can last for several months.

The path is arduous for the traveling yogi, but the terrain becomes more hospitable as he nears the mountain. The farther he travels, the more pilgrims he sees. Soon, he may become part of a group of Hindus and Buddhists, chanting and meditating as they go.

Arriving at the mountain, he sets up camp, then joins the pilgrims. The sight of the holy peak fills him with exaltation. It is easy to practice his techniques in the uplifting atmosphere. A yogi's meditative practices make him sensitive to spiritual currents, and at Mount Kailash, subtle energies are intensely present.

There are other natural shrines in India, including one at Tarakeswar, where Hindus bow before a sacred stone. At this site, many visitors are healed of their infirmities.

Abraham Lincoln had brought his son Robert to Terre Haute, Indiana, on a pilgrimage of sorts to see a healing rock called the mad-stone. Robert had been bitten by a rabid dog, and Lincoln had heard of the strange object that could cure most ills. He hoped the stories of its powers were true.

It had been a long trip, but Lincoln considered the strain worthwhile. He had faith that subtle healing energies emanate from certain special stones.

Charles Lindbergh sat on a rock on the isle of Saint-Gildas, off the coast of Brittany. Every time he walked on this island, he felt close to the spirit world, and a subtle energy coursed through his limbs. The sensation was pleasant and uplifting, and he decided to enjoy it at his leisure.

Lindbergh felt similar energies in other places: in nearby Mont-Saint-Michel, for example, and in a Greek temple in Sicily. It refreshed his spirit to bathe in the invisible rays present at these places of power.

CHAPTER THIRTY-FOUR

Whispers from the Past

Written and verbal reports tell of the extraordinary abilities that some yogis possess as a result of their meditative practices. A number of these powers, familiar to Himalayan yogis, were accessed by Lindbergh during his historic trans-atlantic flight[1] . . .

Charles Lindbergh was in trouble. The youthful pilot was almost halfway across the ocean and highly unlikely to reach landfall in Ireland, let alone his goal of Paris. He was exhausted. With virtually no sleep for two days before the flight, he was about to face yet another sleepless night in the cockpit.

Craning his neck out the side window, he saw a thick, murky fog that opened occasionally to reveal the crests of waves below and another thick cloud bank beyond. And now the sun was sinking again. It was almost more than he could do to keep his eyes open.

"It would be so wonderful to nap," his subconscious whispered. "Why don't you close your eyes, just for a little while." His head sank toward the instrument panel.

---

[1] Lindbergh thought his metaphysical experiences on this flight so significant that he wrote about them three times in his *Autobiography of Values.*

"No!" Lindbergh jerked his head upright as his conscious mind reasserted itself. "If I fall asleep, I'll die! *Stay awake!*"

Midnight came and went. The darkness outside was dreadfully thick. The only roadmaps to his destination were compass and altimeter. Meanwhile, the hum of the engine and the endless whirr of the propeller blades sang a lullaby to Lindbergh's tortured mind and spirit.

Again and again, Lindbergh's head sank. And again and again, he forcibly brought it upright.

Finally, the struggle was too much. He sighed aloud, like a prayer.

"I must rest somehow."

A calm voice spoke within his mind. "And rest you shall."

Immediately, his conscious mind was on alert.

"But I can't! It's impossible! If I drop my guard, I'll die!"

But the still voice answered, "No, you won't die. And you won't fall asleep, either. Don't worry. Everything will be just fine. You will rest more fully than you ever have, but you will not fall asleep."

Too tired to argue the fine points of this odd proposal, Lindbergh gave in.

He sat upright, in a state of deep rest but with his eyes open. He felt a profound peace such as he had not touched before, a rest that was deeper than sleep; yet he was awake, and perhaps more aware than he had ever been. As his body, directed by a deeper part of his mind, steered the airplane, his spirit was recharged.

After Lindbergh had enjoyed this peaceful state for a timeless period, he noticed several things simultaneously.

One was that his consciousness had expanded beyond his physical body into a world of energy. "Lucky Lindy" was now "flying" two planes at once: the *Spirit of St. Louis,* and the astral plane.

Lindbergh's instrument of seeing had also changed. Instead of the two-eyed linear sight he was accustomed to, the spiritual eye[2] midway between the eyebrows had opened, giving him the ability to see all around himself at once.

Coinciding with these extraordinary events, yet another unusual thing occurred. In touch with the astral world and seeing the subtle "blueprint" of his airplane there, Lindbergh watched as the space in that astral cockpit began to fill. Non-corporeal beings appeared—one moment, the space was empty, the next, there they were.

As Lindbergh gazed at these beings, something about them seemed familiar. He could not place this odd familiarity, but it was enough that it was so.[3]

After floating with Lindbergh for a few moments, the spirits spoke to him with thoughts, images, and feelings. They communicated mind to mind, spirit to spirit. They explained profound truths.

Lindbergh was enthralled. And the next thing he knew, his spirit was moving up and out of his physical body and into open space beyond.

He was flying! Yes, flying, but not like he had flown before. He felt a greater freedom than he had ever known in his airplanes.

Then Lindbergh felt a pull back to his body. He needed to return to his airplane. He had a work to do, a goal to accom-

[2]The spiritual eye, or Christ Center, is the seat of spiritual vision in the body.
[3]In *The Spirit of St. Louis,* Lindbergh wondered whether these astral beings were the spirits of past-life friends.

plish. His karma drew him back.

Lindbergh sat in the cockpit and stared at the altimeter and compass. It was nearly dawn. He was worried that during his experience he'd had no control over his steering. Yet, when he sighted land and checked his map, he was exactly on course.

* * * * *

In India there is an ancient tradition where, every twelve years, thousands of holy men, yogis, and pilgrims gather at the city of Allahabad for the greatest of Hindu spiritual festivals, the Kumbha Mela.

On these occasions, Allahabad teems with vast crowds. Top-knotted mahatmas rub shoulders with ash-smeared sadhus. Brahma bulls meander through the busy streets. Dogs and children run loose amid the dust and babble. Yet, a spiritual atmosphere lies hidden beneath the chaos.

At the moment that the local astrologers determine to be most auspicious, thousands of sadhus enter the confluence of the Yamuna and Ganges Rivers. Immersing themselves in the flowing waters, many feel a profound peace. Afterward, multitudes of pilgrims take their turn and wade in.

At these festivals, one may meet fraudulent mystics who perform tricks like snake charming but have no divine realization. A clever yogi, using his common sense, can see through their fakery. Yet a few wonder workers who attend the Kumbha Mela display real powers like levitation or mind-reading.

Abraham Lincoln smiled. The medium he had invited to the Executive Mansion was good—better than the trickster who had filled the room with supernatural sounds by using a device hidden up his sleeve.

During seances, Lincoln sometimes suspected the machinations of counterfeit mystics. On the other hand, he also experienced marvels he was unable to explain scientifically, and these enigmas fascinated him.

The current spiritualist had created a very convincing atmosphere. Entering a trance state, she began to speak in a dramatic masculine voice. Lincoln listened as the voice delineated in clear and concise words information regarding a dire situation related to the Union cause—information that the president had just discussed with his cabinet a few minutes before.

Lincoln looked around the room. How could the medium have heard this news? It was impossible for her to have received this intelligence by human means. Was there such a thing as telepathic communication?

Charles Lindbergh watched the man called Romano as he performed a card trick. Lindbergh liked to investigate wonder-workers, and he was pleased when he heard that a magician planned to attend the party. He thought mystics were intriguing and was curious about their metaphysical feats.

Tonight, Romano had already sent a cool stream of air through his hand (possibly via a tube up his sleeve, Lindbergh thought) and made his pulse stop (which Lindbergh later learned he achieved through the simple technique of putting pressure on his inner arm near the shoulder). Everything the self-styled yogi did Lindbergh thought he could explain scientifically. It seemed as if the man were nothing but a trickster.

And then Romano asked Anne to participate in an experiment. Displaying the faces of a deck of playing cards, he asked her to pick one without saying which. He then took the cards and looked at them. Placing one of the cards face down, he asked Anne which card she had chosen. After she said which card, he then turned the card over to reveal the same card she had picked.

Lindbergh was amazed. If Romano had done this with another person, he could have imagined a setup. But, as it was . . .

Perhaps it was telepathy, he thought.

* * * * *

Astrologers and fortune-tellers also frequent the Kumbha Mela. Hindu astrology is an ancient esoteric art, and many a yogi has sat and listened as an astrologer read his chart and divined his past, present, and future.

Abraham Lincoln had journeyed down the Mississippi and was wandering around New Orleans with his friends, when he spotted a stall with a sign that said: Fortune Telling, Your Future Seen!

Asking his companions to wait outside, Lincoln entered. The men looked at each other and shrugged. They'd had no idea that Lincoln went in for this sort of thing.

* * * * *

Standing in the midst of a Kumbha Mela throng, a yogi might smell incense, dung, curry, and sweat, all mixed in one indescribable odor. He might hear beggars pleading, pilgrims reciting mantras, musicians chanting, and conches blowing. The sensory overload one often encounters in urban India can deplete a yogi's reservoir of peace.

Without frequent meditation, an introspective mind easily becomes prey to moods. Fortunately, a Himalayan yogi has techniques for raising his inner energy. Finding a secluded corner, he assumes the lotus pose. Within minutes he is gazing into the inner light, and the nectar of his joy makes sense pleasures seem like sour milk.

Joshua Speed came upon Abraham Lincoln seated on a curb, holding his head. It was clear that Abe was suffering from another attack of the "hypo," and it tore Speed's heart to see his old friend down.

When Lincoln was caught in a mood, his whole being proclaimed it. His back slumped, his hunch was more pronounced, and his face mirrored his dejection.

Normally, Lincoln enjoyed being alone. It was a pleasure to allow his mind to roam where it wished. In deep thought, he often found inspiration and enlightenment.

But occasionally his thoughts led him into melancholy, and then his mind became his enemy. When he entered that maze, it was hard to escape.

He knew of few ways to break the spell. Activity helped; sometimes the company of people brought relief. But the joy of socializing was temporary. When the laughter ceased, he found himself alone again, saddled with his mental world.

Lindbergh didn't seem to share Lincoln's painful melancholy. Perhaps a lifetime of selfless acts had freed him from that karma . . .

Charles Lindbergh was flying in his beloved *Spirit of St. Louis,* on his way from New York to St. Louis. He had been airborne for several hours, and as he sat upright and still in his chair, he found his consciousness receding from the world around him, from the instrument panel and the view out of the window.

Lindbergh's mind passed from the realm of ideas and into scenes of past experiences. He recalled bygone days with crystal clarity. And then, delving deeper within, he entered a sphere of silent, blissful awareness. He sat in his airplane, enjoying that state for a long time.

In years to come, Lindbergh would repeatedly experience these freestyle meditations during long solo flights. He worked hard to simplify his life in order to hold on to the feeling those meditations gave him. And when he reached old age and those flights were no longer possible, he wrote wistfully of those silent hours and the joy he had felt while accessing the innermost core of his being.

CHAPTER THIRTY-FIVE

The Obsession

As I wrote earlier, one of the determining factors in a case of reincarnation is the persistence of a deeply held thought. Ideas that have captured a person's attention will almost certainly manifest in the mind of his or her next incarnation.

For Lincoln and Lindbergh, a shared obsession could have originated in northern India . . .

The Himalayan region has beautiful vistas, but perils as well. Death wears many guises for those who dare to brave the high altitudes. A traveler may run the risk of sunstroke, frostbite, altitude sickness, or of being caught in rivers swollen with melted snows. There are rockslides, avalanches, and rickety bridges over deep chasms.

Spotted leopards hunt from tree perches, and Bengal tigers camouflage themselves in woods. There are wolf packs, crocodiles, and cobras.

It takes courage to visit the Himalayas, and more to make them one's home. Even an accomplished yogi may find himself facing his mortality.

A lifetime of Himalyan pilgrimages can increase a yogi's awareness of the possibility of death at any time. Many yogis have experienced more than once the shock of a companion's sudden passing, and the grief it brings.

Such experiences may cause a yogi to meditate long and deeply on the mortal condition, and to conclude that until one achieves union with God, one lives under the tyranny, the torment, the shadow of death's dominion.

Abraham Lincoln was sitting in the White House, brooding on death. To his mind, death was always near.

His favorite poem, "Mortality," was based on that idea. But Lincoln also wrote a rhyme that featured death. Entitled "My Childhood-Home I See Again," it included the words,

> I hear the loved survivors tell
> How naught from death could save,
> Till every sound appears a knell,
> And every spot a grave.

> I range the fields with pensive tread,
> And pace the hollow rooms;
> And feel (companions of the dead)
> I'm living in the tombs.

The carnage of the Civil War and the death of Willie, his favorite son, only added to Lincoln's obsession. Then, too, he had dreamt about his approaching early demise.

Death was very much a part of Lincoln's life. He had lost his mother, two sons, and his father—and many friends during the Civil War. It was almost as if, before he was born, Lincoln had purposely chosen a life of immersion in the cold cessation.

Death's finality and capacity to cause pain occupied Lincoln's mind to a profound degree; all his life he pondered it, seeking solutions.

Sometimes a great man has a nemesis that spurs him to the heights. Lincoln's spur was Death itself. Death sobered Lincoln, toughened him, transmuted him.

And when they finally met on the morning of April 15, 1865, Lincoln and Death were well acquainted.

Six-year-old Charles Lindbergh was lying on his bed, thinking about what he had seen that day—a chicken carried upside down from its pen, laid with its neck on the block, and slaughtered. Charles shuddered. He was remembering, to his horror, the feathered body jerking. And he was recalling everything he had been told about God.

Why, he wondered, did God invent such a horrible thing as death, that all creatures—animals and people—have to experience?

It didn't add up. Death was gruesome and final. Yet God was supposed to be loving.

Something was very wrong here.

An elderly Charles Lindbergh sat at his desk, working on his memoirs. As he did so, he considered how his understanding of death had changed.

As a boy he had hated death with a surprising passion, and it continued to bother him for his first decades. This was partly because he'd had many experiences of it. His father, who was very close to him, had died while Charles was a young man. The kidnapping-death of his first son, Charles Jr., was another trial for his spirit. His sister-in-law, Elisabeth Morrow, came down with rheumatic fever and perished. And then he became immersed in World War II.

And yet, as time wore on, Lindbergh came to accept that death and life were two sides of the same coin. He also began to consider the possibility of life after death.

Just as in his youth, thoughts of death and God still danced in his mind. But now he judged God less harshly. His meditations had brought a deeper understanding, bringing hints of what had been his true goal all along: the realization of deathless immortality.

* * * * *

Here is the purpose of reincarnation, played out in microcosm. Through one soul's interest in the meaning of life and death, we can see how our souls learn over long spans of time.

At some point, we grow curious: We have an experience, or hear words that compel us to know more. Perhaps in that lifetime we have no opportunity to delve further into the matter. Never mind; for in our next life, our interest draws us forward into deeper knowledge. Slowly our understanding develops. As lifetime follows lifetime, our curiosity evolves into study, doubts into certainty, pedestrian knowledge into personal illumination, until we reach the height of understanding: the end result of the curiosity we first felt centuries earlier.

In the meantime, our souls attract experiences that bring us closer to the knowledge we seek . . .

Shaken, a Himalayan yogi stares at death. A moment before, he was walking on a high mountain path, enjoying the view, but then his foot slipped and he was falling, sliding, slamming into rocks until he came to an abrupt halt at the base of a tree on the edge of a sheer drop.

Abraham Lincoln opened his eyes to see a group of people gazing down at him with concern. He lifted his head and winced at the pain that movement brought. What had happened? He was in his bed. His shirt smelled of cornmeal . . .

Oh, yes. Now it all came back.

Lincoln had brought his mare to the local mill to grind corn. Everything was going smoothly until she balked at pulling the wheel around. The last thing Lincoln remembered was bringing his lash down on her back and the mare bunching her thigh muscles for a kick. Then he blacked out.

Lincoln sat up and his relatives clustered round and patted him on the back. It had been a near thing. He had been out for so long that they feared he might not return.

This episode made Lincoln think. He wondered what exactly had happened to his mind during the time when he was out cold.

Suspended from a parachute, Charles Lindbergh watched calmly as his airmail plane spun toward him, then angled away. Thinking his aircraft had run out of gas, he had bailed out. But its engine stubbornly kept going, and now it was making passes at him as it augured its way to the ground.

Lindbergh watched the lethal propeller blades spinning nearer. And then, just as before, the deadly airplane curved aside.

Lindbergh had been curious about death since his early days when he was almost flattened by a plow blade. He had always challenged himself to face his fears. Years before, timid of heights, he had made himself climb a water tower until vertigo ceased to disturb him.

Not very long ago, Lindbergh had almost been killed in a situation similar to this. An airplane he had ditched came very close to killing him as he parachuted to the ground. He had tensed his body on that occasion, waiting for the collision. Now, as his plane rushed toward him, his impulse was to see how detached he could be.

But it turned aside once more, then crashed a short distance away. Lindbergh landed without mortal injury. He had faced peril with courage, but wondered what was on the other side of death's door. Perhaps it was only through repeated brushes with mortality that he would learn what death really was.

* * * * *

True understanding arises from experience. No one who merely imagines doing something has the same comprehension of someone who has actually done it. And traumatic experiences often serve as catalysts for growth . . .

A Himalayan yogi's near-fatal fall spurs him to make a vow. He will not be hampered by fear, but rather will force himself to brave the Himalayan heights again. Death will not find him unprepared. He will uncover its secret and overcome its mastery.

Closing his eyes, he repeats aloud from the *Bhagavad Gita:*

"Never the spirit was born;
        the spirit shall cease to be never;
    Never was time it was not;
        End and Beginning are dreams!
Birthless and deathless and changeless
        remaineth the spirit forever;
    Death hath not touched it at all,
        dead though the house of it seems!"

President Lincoln shivered as if a bucket of cold water had been thrown over him. In the past few weeks, his grief over the death of his son Willie had exhausted his spirit. But now, Lincoln felt transformed. The words of a compassionate preacher had entered some deep marrow of his being, sparking a realization into flame.

"Your son," the preacher told him, "is alive in Paradise. Remember: 'God is not the God of the dead, for all live unto Him.'"

In that instant Lincoln recognized a hidden truth. With tears in his eyes, he embraced the man who had kindled his resurrection.

Charles Lindbergh sat in the laboratory of his friend, Dr. Alexis Carrel, handling a piece of Pyrex. Lindbergh's sister-in-law Elisabeth had rheumatic fever. She needed an operation, and Lindbergh hoped that his invention, a new type of perfusion pump, might help her. The thought of Elisabeth leaving her body at a young age saddened him, and he wanted to do everything in his power to help her.

As he turned over the tubular glass, Lindbergh meditated on the limitations of human existence. Was it possible to prolong a lifespan? This was something he often thought about. The idea of one's mind and spirit existing perpetually, minus the bodily limitations, fascinated him, and his experiments in Dr. Carrel's laboratory had heightened his interest.

* * * * *

Himalayan yogis believe that the human spirit lives forever, and that, through reincarnation, it puts on bodies and discards them like clothing, undergoing many cycles of birth and death. But they also know that it isn't enough just to believe this teaching. They have to realize it.

Yet, that realization does not come easily. The fear of death turns many away from its secrets. Past-life memories of mortal diseases, injuries, and sorrows confront the seeker.

One has to overcome those obstacles before he can know for a certainty that no one ever truly dies.

* * * * *

Here we end our comparison of the beliefs and experiences of Himalayan yogis with those of Lincoln and Lindbergh.

What can we learn from these comparisons?

If Yogananda's words are true—and the connections described in this book offer strong evidence that they are—then Lincoln's greatness was the outcome of a past life dedicated to spiritual growth.

If that is so, then it follows that you or I can also become great by following the same spiritual principles.

What noble desires lie hidden in our hearts that we give up on, thinking we could never achieve them: a wish to help humanity, to fix the world, to make a great scientific discovery, to cure cancer, to end war, to bring peace on earth.

What seeds of greatness are buried in us, waiting for the right conditions to sprout and bless humanity?

If you have felt the urge to imitate Lincoln or any other great person, be assured that you can do so, and here is how. Dedicate yourself to spiritual growth and self-discipline. If you fully embrace the univeral teachings and practices of yoga, or any other true spiritual path, sooner or later, you will become just as great as they were.

It's only a matter of time.

CHAPTER THIRTY-SIX

Meditations

We tend to encapsulate noteworthy lifetimes in convenient, easy-to-remember packages. By this token, Abraham Lincoln was born in a log cabin, became a lawyer and politician, debated Stephen Douglas, was elected the sixteenth president, led America through the Civil War, issued the Emancipation Proclamation, gave the Gettysburg Address, and was assassinated by John Wilkes Booth.

Similarly, Charles Lindbergh made the first solo transatlantic crossing by air, became an American hero, married Anne Morrow, grieved when his first son was kidnapped and killed, fought American involvement in World War II, secretly fathered a second family in Europe, became a conservationist, and was buried in Hawaii.

Comparing these statements, one struggles to see any relation between the two men. But digging deeper, as we have in this study, one finds extraordinary connections.

One might expect to find *some* connections in a comparison of *any* two people. And some intriguing studies have been done: the eerie similarities between the assassinations of Presidents Lincoln and Kennedy, for example. From these, one might make a case for reincarnation. However, such arguments are weak when they are founded on a narrow basis of comparison, a mere handful of similarities, or on circumstantial links.

By contrast, the connections between Lincoln and Lindbergh are widespread, manifold, and for the most part, habitual ways of thinking and behaving. These habits comprise the foundation of personality; they are the very definition of individuality.

The Lincoln-Lindbergh connections encompass every aspect of the human condition: from the physical to the mental, emotional, spiritual, and interpersonal. Their depth and number make one think that if Lindbergh weren't Lincoln reborn, he *should* have been. When we add in the curious circumstantial links, they offer a firm foundation for Yogananda's statement of a past-life tie.

Some writers have observed that Lindbergh's values and attitudes were more in tune with an earlier era—the nineteenth rather than the twentieth century. Certainly, in the realm of mores and cultural preferences, Lindbergh was out of step all his life. Which raises the question: How would Abraham Lincoln have handled the challenges of Lindbergh's era, or our own?

Historians have pointed out that Lincoln was in harmony with his times to such a degree that his life epitomized them. In many ways, Lindbergh's personality was nearly the same as Lincoln's. So, it is conceivable that Lincoln would have been as out of step with modern society as Lindbergh was.

No one can say that Charles Lindbergh matched Abraham Lincoln's greatness. Lindbergh doesn't loom as large, morally or historically. Yet, a lifetime like Lincoln's is a tough act to follow. When looking for signs of a reincarnation of someone so great, it is enough, aside from the other significant connections, that the individual in the second life manifest a comparable *energy* to that of the first; and this, it is clear, Lindbergh did.

Lincoln filled his life with good deeds, and this study suggests that Lindbergh reaped some of the benefits of those actions. When a soul spends a lifetime reaping good karma, it is difficult to maintain spiritual progress. Think of people on vacation. They like to relax and not be so hard on themselves. Lindbergh's life, to a large degree, was a working vacation. He did what he wanted from an early age. It isn't surprising, then, that he relaxed a few of the controls that Lincoln had held so tight—and, who knows how Lincoln's unblemished legend might have changed had he lived into old age. His early death came at the end of his great work, leaving his life perfect in the eyes of history.

One of the lessons one can glean from the diminishment that came in the transition from Lincoln to Lindbergh is that a soul needs concentrated effort to keep moving forward spiritually. Neither man engaged in regular spiritual practices, beyond spontaneous meditations and occasional prayer. Lindbergh exhibited an interest in mystical spirituality that grew over time, yet he never took on the discipline of any specific inner path. And it seems that some of the momentum of spiritual and moral force gained from years of Himalayan meditations waned a bit in Lindbergh's life.

Regarding the statement that launched this book, it is worth reflecting that Yogananda didn't scour libraries or research hundreds of lives until he found two people with enough similarities to make the claim of a past-life connection. Actually, many of the corroborative facts enclosed in this volume were unrecorded in Yogananda's day. Yogananda simply sensed Lincoln and Lindbergh's soul unity and intuited that Lincoln was a reborn Himalayan yogi. Imagine such a consciousness.

Notes

The interpretations of Patanjali's *Yoga Sutras* are based primarily on Kriyananda's *The Art and Science of Raja Yoga,* which is founded on Yogananda's teachings; I also borrowed from Kriyananda's *Affirmations for Self-Healing* and *Superconsciousness: a Guide to Meditation.* The *Bhagavad Gita* excerpt in Chapter Thirty-Five is from *The Song Celestial* by Sir Edwin Arnold.

Visits to Lincoln's Boyhood Home on Knob Creek, near Hodgenville, Kentucky; the Lincoln Home, the Lincoln-Herndon Law Offices, and the Lincoln Tomb in Springfield, Illinois; Lincoln's New Salem in Illinois; the Gettysburg National Military Park in Pennsylvania; the Mall and Ford's Theater in Washington, D.C.; and the Charles A. Lindbergh House in Little Falls, Minnesota, provided atmosphere for the Lincoln/Lindbergh stories.

It would take too long to list the numerous materials from which I constructed the Lincoln and Lindbergh anecdotes. What follows is a grateful nod to primary sources.

For the Lincoln excerpts, I borrowed heavily from his own writings, the best source of which is *The Collected Works of Abraham Lincoln,* edited by Roy P. Basler. For a quick tour through Lincoln's words, I highly recommend *Of The People, By The People, For The People* by Gabor S. Boritt.

Other Lincoln sources, in the order of the author's name:
The Life of Abraham Lincoln by Isaac N. Arnold
Lincoln in the Telegraph Office by David Homer Bates
The Inner Life of Abraham Lincoln by F.B. Carpenter
The Lincoln Nobody Knows by Richard N. Current
Life of Lincoln by William H. Herndon and Jesse W. Weik
The Hidden Lincoln and *Lincoln Talks* by Emanuel Hertz
Twenty Days by Dorothy Meserve Kunhardt and Philip B.

Kunhardt, Jr.
Lincoln: An Illustrated Biography by Philip B. Kunhardt, Jr., Philip B. Kunhardt III, and Peter W. Kunhardt.
Recollections of Abraham Lincoln by Ward Hill Lamon
Lincoln: His Life In Photographs and *Lincoln: A Picture Story of His Life* by Stefan Lorant
The Face of Lincoln, compiled and edited by James Mellon
With Malice Toward None by Stephen B. Oates
Lincoln's Unknown Private Life edited by Lloyd Ostendorf and Walter Oleksy
Abraham Lincoln: The Prairie Years and *Abraham Lincoln: The War Years* by Carl Sandburg
Conversations with Lincoln by Charles M. Segal
Abraham Lincoln Returns by Harriet M. Shelton
Abraham Lincoln: A Spiritual Biography by Elton Trueblood

For the Lindbergh anecdotes, I found Lindbergh's autobiographical writings essential: *"We"; The Spirit of St. Louis; Of Flight & Life; The Wartime Journals of Charles A. Lindbergh; Boyhood on the Upper Mississippi;* and *Autobiography of Values.* I was also helped by the diaries and writings of Anne Morrow Lindbergh, including *Bring Me a Unicorn; Hour of Gold, Hour of Lead; Locked Rooms and Open Doors; The Flower and the Nettle; War Within and Without;* and *Gift from the Sea.* The Reeve Lindbergh stories were inspired by passages found in her heartfelt memoir, *Under a Wing.* Of the many Lindbergh biographies, I found *Lindbergh Alone* by Brendan Gill the best for capturing his spirit. Other sources include: *Lindbergh: Triumph and Tragedy* by Richard Bak; *Lindbergh* by A. Scott Berg; *Charles A. Lindbergh and the Battle Against American Intervention in World War II* by Wayne S. Cole; *Lindbergh: His Story in Pictures* by Francis Trevelyan Miller; *Loss of Eden* by Joyce Milton; and *Charles A. Lindbergh: A Photographic Album* by Joshua Stoff.

The source for Lindbergh's visit to Springfield, Illinois, in August 1927, was the *Illinois State Journal.* The Walt Whitman poetry was excerpted from *Leaves of Grass.*

Order Form

Fax orders: 408-456-0444. Send this form.
Phone orders: 866-763-4922 (toll free)
email orders: orders@CrystarPress.com
Postal orders: Crystar Press
P.O. Box 640965-812
San Jose, CA 95164-0965

Please send ___ copies of *Soul Journey.*

Please send FREE information on:

☐ Other books   ☐ Audiotapes   ☐ Seminars

Name: _____
Address: ___
City: _____
Telephone: _____   Email address: _____

Sales tax: Please add 8.25% for orders shipped to California addresses.

Shipping by air:
U.S.: $4.00 for first book and $2 for each additional book.
International: $9.00 for first book; $5.00 for each additional book.

Payment: ☐ check   ☐ credit card
☐ Visa   ☐ MasterCard   ☐ Discover   ☐ AMEX

Card number: _____
Name on card: _____ Exp. date: _____